Prosperity

Lakshmi, the Hindu goddess of wealth, health, fortune, and prosperity. The root of the word is lakṣ (लक्ष्) and lakṣa (लक्ष), which respectively mean to perceive, observe, know, and goal, aim, objective. Together they signify 'know and understand your purpose'.

Prosperity

Better Business Makes the Greater Good

Colin Mayer

OXFORD
UNIVERSITY PRESS

OXFORD
UNIVERSITY PRESS

Great Clarendon Street, Oxford, OX2 6DP,
United Kingdom

Oxford University Press is a department of the University of Oxford.
It furthers the University's objective of excellence in research, scholarship,
and education by publishing worldwide. Oxford is a registered trade mark of
Oxford University Press in the UK and in certain other countries

First Edition published in 2018
Impression: 4

Published in the United States of America by Oxford University Press
198 Madison Avenue, New York, NY 10016, United States of America

British Library Cataloguing in Publication Data
Data available

Library of Congress Control Number: 2018933535

ISBN 978–0–19–882400–8

Printed and bound in Great Britain by
Clays Ltd, Elcograf S.p.A.

To Hannah and Ruth
If children don't get it,
Who does?

Praise for the book

'Our world does not have long for business to escape its 40 year-long capture by the Chicago school. This book is a historic milestone in economic theory because it marks the final nail in Milton Friedman's intellectual coffin. It does this by illuminating a pragmatic pathway for business and policy makers to follow, to escape an anachronistic orthodoxy that is killing our beautiful planet and our precious communities. They must study it closely and then move fast, so that we all—and those who come after us—might avoid calamity and, instead, prosper.'

James Perry,
Chairman of Cook.

'Here is the case for reinventing the corporation so that it serves human well-being. Colin Mayer shows both why an exclusive focus on shareholder value is damaging, and how purposeful changes could support trustworthy corporations that combine social and business benefits.'

Baroness Onora O'Neill of Bengarve,
Emeritus Professor of Philosophy,
University of Cambridge.

'In his humane and readable book *Prosperity*, Colin Mayer makes a compelling case for a new concept of the corporation, and the need to treat corporate purpose as far more than shareholder value. In showing how restoring trust is key to a true future prosperity, this book will reframe much of our thinking on this central subject.'

The Hon. Mr Justice William Blair,
High Court Judge of England and Wales.

'A wonderful manifesto for change and essential reading for any who remain to be convinced that business can—and should—be a force for a societal good. One of the most insightful and comprehensive accounts yet of how and why the corporation needs to change if it is to meet the needs and expectations of a new era. Thoughtful and well-argued, Mayer has done the cause of enlightened capitalism great service.'

Paul Polman,
CEO, Unilever.

'One of the most pressing questions facing the world today is "What is the role of the corporation in society?". Thanks to Professor Colin Mayer we now have a definitive answer: the corporation's role is to fulfil its purpose. This wonderful book could have been titled "From Profit to Purpose"; in the recent past we have confounded the two. They are separate and purpose comes first. When purpose is achieved, profits will follow. In an intellectual and very readable *tour-de-force* Professor Mayer brings to bear an astonishing range of academic disciplines to present a very practical framework for how companies need to be managed today. For their own sake and the sake of us all.'

Robert Eccles,
Founding Chairman of the Sustainability Accounting
Standards Board and Professor of Management Practice,
University of Oxford.

'The financial crisis and its aftermath called for answers—questions were raised instead. Our corporate and political environments have been severely shaken for more than a decade. We have to find new approaches and look for better answers to bring our social market economies into balance. Colin Mayer relentlessly challenges conventional wisdom, combining diverse academic fields and bringing business to meet academia. *Prosperity* is building on a wealth of research looking at the broader picture and its many corners to seek appropriate answers to the challenges of our world. Is "purpose first, prosperity follows" the answer?'

Daniela Weber-Rey,
non-executive director of HSBC Trinkaus &
Burkhardt and Fnac-Darty.

'Rarely in the history of economics and law does a person observe the current state of the world, recognize its deficiencies, and put forth a policy and paradigm that is destined to change the world. John Maynard Keynes in the twenties and thirties and now Colin Mayer are prime examples. In *Prosperity* Mayer builds on two decades of essays and articles and his 2013 book *Firm Commitment* to make the case for radical change in the way business corporations are perceived and operate. Mayer sees the corporation not as a vehicle primarily for creating shareholder wealth, but as having a purpose to enhance the wellbeing of all stakeholders. *Prosperity* envisages employees, customers, suppliers, communities, the environment, and the economy as equal participants with shareholders in corporations that operate to better them and mankind, now and in the future. This book is destined to be the "bible" of the

Mayer-Paradigm of corporate governance, and the template for the policy changes that are necessary to implement it.'

Martin Lipton,
Senior Partner, Wachtell, Lipton, Rosen & Katz.

'Businesses have a duty to do well by stakeholders as well as shareholders. How did too many corporations lose their sense of purpose? What is the right path to build responsible and sustainable relationships with society? This insight-rich book offers a comprehensive guide for restoring trust between companies, consumers, and communities. Professor Mayer makes a compelling argument that the purpose and values of modern corporations have been diluted and it will take the work of executives, legislators, regulators, bankers, investors, and even shareholders to fix them.'

Dominic Barton,
Global Managing Partner Emeritus, McKinsey & Company.

'Colin Mayer has elevated the conversation about business and society. Bold enough to reimagine an economic system, specific enough to drive action, *Prosperity* introduces the higher-order thinking necessary to build a more inclusive capitalism.'

Lynn Forester de Rothschild,
CEO of E.L. Rothschild and the Coalition
for Inclusive Capitalism.

'With characteristic courage and purposeful passion, Mayer challenges the status quo as to who corporations serve and benefit. *Prosperity* presents a paradigm shift revealing tomorrow's corporation today. It marks the start of a new age of enlightenment, which will stimulate the sensibilities of all who care about the role of business in society.'

Guy Jubb,
former Global Head of Governance and
Stewardship, Standard Life Investments.

'This is a timely and highly insightful treatise on the urgent need to revisit today's misguided and simplistic views on the purpose of the corporation. It is a significant contribution addressing the growing economic and social challenges confronting us today.'

Cyrus Ardelan, Chairman,
Citigroup Global Markets Ltd.

'*Prosperity* makes a limpidly clear and convincing case for an urgent rethink of the role of business in society. The fifty years since Friedman gave the doctrine of "shareholder value" totemic significance have seen the interests of proprietors, governments, and communities diverge. This has produced unacceptable inequalities in outcomes and shocking destruction of the environment. The arguments Colin makes for radical reform of the role of the corporation in society are compelling, and rooted in common sense and fairness. I hope that many others involved in defining the purpose of their businesses learn as much from *Prosperity* as I have.'

Peter Norris,
Chairman of Virgin Group.

Preamble

In 2013 I produced the book *Firm Commitment: Why the Corporation Is Failing Us and How to Restore Trust in It*. That book identified a problem with the corporation and a need to identify ways of reforming it. This book attempts to provide solutions to the questions posed by *Firm Commitment*.

In so doing, it draws on the considerable number of research programmes in which I have been engaged with several people since 2013. I would like to thank Bruno Roche and Jay Jakub of Mars Catalyst, Mars Incorporated's think tank, with whom I have been involved over the past four years in a voyage of discovery about the mutuality of Mars' business, and all the many people in Oxford and Mars Catalyst with whom I have worked on the project, in particular Kate Roll, Alastair Colin-Jones, Richard Barker, Marc Thompson, Marc Ventresca, and Ruth Yeoman.

I have been fortunate to direct a programme of research on European corporate financing entitled 'Restarting European Long-Term Investment Finance'[1] for the Centre for Economic Policy Research in London. Thanks to the support of Stefano Micossi, the programme was associated with Assonime and funded by Emittenti Titoli. I would in particular like to thank the steering group for the project, namely Brunella Bruno, Alexandra D'Onofrio, Immacolata Marino, Marco Onado, Marco Pagano, and Andrea Polo.

I have been a member of the Steering Group of the Big Innovation Centre project on the Purposeful Company. This has produced an interim report surveying the relevant literature and a policy report of recommendations for reform in the UK.[2] I have benefited immensely from working with other members of the Steering Group—Clare Chapman, Will Hutton, Birgitte Andersen, Alex Edmans, Tom Gosling, Andy Haldane, and Philippe Schneider.

I participated in the writing of a text on the Principles of Financial Regulation[3] based on a course of the same title on the Masters in Law and Finance at the University of Oxford with five members of the Law Faculty at Oxford and one at Columbia Law School. I am very grateful to my co-authors—John Armour, Dan Awrey, Paul Davies, Luca Enriques, Jeffrey Gordon, and Jennifer Payne—for stimulating discussions about financial regulation.

I have been involved in a programme of research at the Balliol Inter-disciplinary Institute at Balliol College in Oxford on The Evolution of Business Ecosystems. This programme is examining the interface between biology, economics, and management studies and I am grateful to Yunhee Lee, Denis Noble, and David Vines for providing fundamental insights into the relevance of biology and the Korean economy to theories of business.

I have undertaken research with Paul Collier on infrastructure investment in developing countries and with Dieter Helm on infrastructure in developed countries. I have continued a programme of research on the evolution of ownership and control of corporations around the world with Julian Franks at the London Business School and Hideaki Miyajima at Waseda University in Japan. The programme has focused in particular on recent developments in corporate finance and ownership in Japan.

Over the past year, I have been the academic lead of the British Academy programme on the Future of the Corporation. This is a major cross-disciplinary programme of research into how the corporation will need to adapt over the coming decades to address the economic, political, social, and technological challenges and opportunities it confronts. I would like to thank the members of the Steering Group with whom I have been working, Mohamed Amersi, Marco Becht, Bill Blair, Victor Blank, Alun Evans, Luke Fletcher, Onora O'Neill, Lucy Parker, Paula Woodman, and Mike Wright, the members of the Corporate Advisory Group, and the staff of the British Academy, in particular Jo Hopkins, Jennifer Hawton, Henry Richards, Kate Rosser Frost, and Michelle Waterman.

I am engaged in a Ford Foundation programme of research on Purposeful Ownership at the Said Business School in Oxford University examining the role of families and institutional investors in promoting purposeful ownership. A previous study assessed how more than forty non-governmental organizations are seeking to promote inclusive business and economies.[4] I would like to thank the co-director of the programme Peter Tufano, the Dean of the Said Business School, and the researchers Clarissa Hauptmann, Mary Johnstone-Louis, and Bridget Kustin.

I have also continued to work with many of the people and organizations that I acknowledged in *Firm Commitment*, so I will not repeat them here. I will, though, add that I have been involved in several activities since then on which I have drawn in writing this book, in particular in conducting board reviews of major listed UK corporations, being a member of the UK Natural Capital Committee, being part of the International Advisory Board of the Securities and Exchange Board of India, helping to establish Aurora Energy Research, being a Trustee of the Oxford Playhouse, and sitting on competition and regulatory hearings at the Competition Appeal Tribunal. I appreciate the support that I have received from the many people with whom I have worked in these organizations.

I have had immensely helpful discussions and received comments on the book from numerous people. In particular, I am very grateful to Anat Admati, Nathalie Baudry D'Asson, Mohsin Alam Bhat, Amar Bhide, Peter Block, Clare Chapman, Paul Collier, Bob Eccles, Julian Franks, Gay Haskins, Thomas Hellmann, John Hicklin, Will Hutton, Marty Lipton, Annette Mayer, Hannah Mayer, Ruth Mayer, Stephanie Mooij, Denis Noble, Avner Offer, Gita Piramal, Andrea Polo, Bruno Roche, Ira Unell, David Vines, and Yishay Yafeh for very helpful suggestions.

I would like to thank Adam Swallow and Phil Henderson, who, as in the case of *Firm Commitment,* have been wonderful editors at Oxford University Press with whom to work on this book, and Katie Bishop and Kate Farquhar-Thomson, who have been immensely helpful in the preparation and promotion of the book.

Of course, the greatest burden of writing a book is borne by one's family and I would like to thank Annette for the love, support, and consideration she has shown during its production. As Benjamin Franklin is reputed to have claimed, 'early to bed, early to rise makes a man healthy, wealthy and wise', but it comes at a cost.

Colin Mayer

1 January 2018

Contents

Preface

The Challenge

The law is to justice, as medicine is to health, as business is to ... How would you complete this sentence?

I am afraid that you do not get many points for giving the title of this book—'prosperity'—as your answer. This is what we would like to believe. But it is not the answer most people would give, or if they did then they would mean it in a negative sense: the prosperity of the few—shareholders and executives—at the expense of the many—employees, customers, and communities—and the unborn—future generations.

The corporation is the creator of wealth, the source of employment, the deliverer of new technologies, the provider of our needs, the satisfier of our desires, and the means to our ends. It clothes, feeds, and houses us. It employs us and invests our savings. It is the source of economic prosperity and the growth of nations around the world.

At the same time, it is the source of inequality, deprivation, and environmental degradation, and the problems are getting worse. They are getting worse because the corporation is getting bigger to a point where in some cases it is larger than nation states. And as nations find themselves unable to service their debt obligations, they turn to corporations to supply the goods and services that they provided in the past. But is the corporation capable of bearing the responsibilities that are being placed on its shoulders?

The evidence is not encouraging. Over the last few years there has been a steady erosion of trust in business. At first we associated this with just banks and financial institutions after the financial crisis of 2008, but we are increasingly recognizing that it afflicts everything from automobiles to energy, from food to pharmaceuticals.

At the same time, technological advances offer greater opportunities today than at any time in the past for business to transform our lives for the better, in everything from automobiles to energy, from food to pharmaceuticals. How can we ensure that we harness business as a source of societal benefits and avoid its detriments? How do we make it the creator of prosperity of the many not just the few, and of the future not just the past?

These are the questions to which this book seeks answers. They are very different from the ones that most business books try to address. Their starting point is not the lofty ambition of this book but the following: 'there is one and only one social responsibility of business—to use its resources and engage in activities designed to increase its profits so long as it stays within the rules of the game, which is to say, engages in open and free competition without deception or fraud'[1]—the Friedman doctrine, so named after its author, Milton Friedman.

While the name of Milton Friedman is closely associated with the economic paradigm of monetarism, his most enduring legacy arguably lies elsewhere. It is more than fifty years since he first presented what has now come to be known as the 'Friedman doctrine' in his book *Capitalism and Freedom*.[2] It has been a powerful concept that has defined business practice and government policies around the world for half a century. It has been the basis of business education that has moulded generations of business leaders. Indeed virtually every MBA course begins from the premise that the purpose of business is to maximize shareholder value, and everything, and the rest of the course, follows from that. It reflects the power of ideas to influence behaviour to a point where many people now believe that the Friedman doctrine is a law of nature from which we are unable to escape.

The message of this book is that the Friedman doctrine is not a law of nature. On the contrary, it is unnatural; nature abhors it, if only because it has been the seed of nature's destruction. If it ever deserved to have its time, the Friedman doctrine has had it. It is not the business paradigm of the twenty-first century, and as long as we continue to believe it to be so, the greater will be the damage it inflicts on our societies, the natural environment, and ourselves. Few social science theories are both so significant and misconceived as to threaten our existence but that is precisely what the Friedman doctrine is doing in the twenty-first century.

The Cause

At the end of Chapter 8 of *Capitalism and Freedom*, Milton Friedman provides an explanation for his views: 'A major complaint made frequently against modern business is that it involves the separation of ownership and control—that the corporation has become a social institution that is a law unto itself, with irresponsible executives who do not serve the interests of their stockholders. This charge is not true. But the direction in which policy is now moving . . . is a step in the direction of creating a true divorce between ownership and control and of undermining the basic nature and character of our society. It is a step away from an individualistic society and toward the corporate state.'

In other words, corporations are the instruments of individuals, their shareholders, and ' "business" as such cannot have responsibilities . . . only people can have responsibilities.'[3] And the responsibilities of those running business are clear. 'In a free-enterprise, private-property system, a corporate executive is an employee of the owners of the business. He has direct responsibility to his employers. That responsibility is to conduct the business in accordance with their desires, which generally will be to make as much money as possible while conforming to the basic rules of the society, both those embodied in law and those embodied in ethical custom.'[4]

This is unequivocal—the purpose of business is exclusively to make money for the owners of the business, while sticking to the letter of the law and the spirit of social conventions. The executives are the owners' hired hands who have no right to deflect from furthering their owners' interests for one moment. Executives' own preferences and interests are irrelevant and must be subsumed to the greater good of their owners.

This is simple, clear, and uncompromising. It derives from what is described as 'a property view' of the firm—shareholders are owners of the firm in the same way as they possess a home or a washing machine. They have purchased it and in the process acquired the right to require it to act in their own interest and to direct it to do so.

An Alternative

In fact, the analogy with home or washing-machine ownership is a poor one. It does not work for the simple reason that in the case of the home or washing machine, you and you alone are affected by what you do with them, provided of course that in the process of using them you do not harm or inconvenience others. That is clearly not the case with a business. It does not even apply to small local firms. A decision of the grocery at the end of my street to shut up shop can deeply affect my well-being. This takes on multiple orders of greater significance in relation to whether General Electric (GE) decides to shut up shop.

GE's actions affect not just its shareholders but also its millions of customers, employees, and local communities around the world.

The assets of the firm have been accumulated on the back of the investments of virtually every segment of society—employees, suppliers, communities, nations, and nature—on the basis of extensive privileges and protections deriving from incorporation and limited liability. Shareholders do not and should not have rights to do with their companies what they please, even while staying within the law and social norms. They have roles and responsibilities as well as rights and rewards deriving from their dependence on and obligations to the societies in which they operate. Equally customers, employees, and communities do not 'own' cooperatives, mutuals, or public enterprises any more than shareholders own companies. Their responsibilities are as great and rights as restricted as those of shareholders.

Instead, the corporation should be recognized for what it is—a rich mosaic of different purposes and values. It exists to do what it sets out to do, to fulfil its purpose—its rationale for its existence. Everyone else—shareholders, executives, employees, and suppliers—are there to help it do that. The corporation is an employer, investor, consumer, producer, and supplier all rolled into one. It uses capital, labour, land, materials, and nature in varying proportions to produce a dazzling array of things that clothe, feed, house, entertain, and finally bury us. In other words it is a user of a range of inputs to produce an even greater number of outputs.

The corporation is an extraordinary institution and we should recognize its potential to create remarkable benefits. It can contract and be contracted, employ and be employed, and sue and be sued—just like us. But it can achieve much more than we are capable of as individuals. It can provide degrees of commitment to which we can only aspire, and in the process it can overcome the deficiencies and failures to which we are prone. It can do this on account of the separation of ownership and control—the very thing that Friedman saw as a deficiency of the corporation is an attribute allowing it to balance the degree of commitment it offers to different parties with the control that it exercises over them.

So not only does the corporation have the potential to determine an almost boundless set of purposes and objectives but, through its ownership and governance, it also has the means to ensure that it delivers on them. It is a vehicle for committing to the fulfilment of its stated purposes, and once freed from the shackles of particular interest groups, be they shareholders, employees, or governments, the corporation is capable of delivering substantial benefits to its customers and communities.

This repositioning of corporations, capitalism, and control has as fundamental implications for business, economics, and public policy as the Copernican Revolution had for astronomy. Corporations, business, and public policy do not and should not revolve around their shareholders any more than the planets revolve around the earth. There is a multiplicity of corporate systems with their own foci, and just as the planetary system is the richer for this diversity, so too is our world for the corporate diversity that it has created.

In particular, this repositioning of corporations, their capital, and control has implications for the way in which businesses are owned, governed, and run, how academia analyses and models them, and how governments formulate economic and business policies towards them. It is central to the successful performance of business, to the competitive advantage of nations, and to the achievement of the goals of government. It determines not only economic efficiency but also the distribution of income and wealth, and it lies at the heart of growing disparities in developed economies.

These assertions will be established using an extensive array of ideas, evidence, and case studies. Part 1 of the book will look at the intellectual underpinnings of these ideas through the lens of the history of economic thought, moral philosophy, and biology. Part 2 will turn to business history and international comparative analysis of the development of the corporation. Part 3 will address the challenge posed to corporations of realizing their potential through the lens of business, management, and accounting practices.

Part 4 describes how legal theory legitimizes and lays the foundations for the rich array of corporate forms that have existed over time and locations. But this is not an innate right; it has to be earned as part of the corporation's public responsibilities. The state in turn performs those functions and activities that cannot be expected of the private sector alone; Part 5 draws on economics to describe how it does so by aligning public and private interests through a combination of finance, taxation, infrastructure, and investment.

The Vision

Why do companies exist? The question is so fundamental that it is barely ever asked or, when it is, the Friedman Doctrine is cited as the answer: to make money for shareholders. That is how virtually every business school course begins. The purpose of business is to make money for shareholders and everything—accounting, finance, marketing, operations management, and strategy—follows from that. In fact, the answer is much more straightforward—the reason why companies exist is to fulfil their purpose. That is self-evident because the definition of purpose is the reason that something is created, exists, and is done, and what it aspires to become. So the purpose of the corporation is its reason for existing.

Tautological though this may seem, it is actually of fundamental significance. It establishes purpose as an ultimate goal, not an intermediary objective in the attainment of something else. Our purpose is our purpose. Corporations exist to fulfil their purposes. We do not pursue purpose just to achieve happiness, and they do not pursue purpose solely to promote profits. On the contrary, our happiness and their profits may both be inputs into the achievement of both of our purposes, not vice versa.

The importance of this stems from the fact that while the significance of purpose in the promotion of corporate success is increasingly being recognized, it is in the context of creating success as conventionally defined—namely profits. So long as purpose contributes to greater profits, it is unequivocally desirable—'win–win', to use the oft-repeated phrase of losers. 'Doing well by doing good' describes the process of making money (doing well) through benefiting others (doing good). Who could possibly quarrel with that?

In fact, there are at least two reasons for objecting to it. First, it constrains company purposes to doing good, when in fact many at best do not purport to save the world and at worst positively damage it, and in most cases do a mixture of the two. Car companies allow us to travel comfortably (good), but pollute the environment and kill us (bad). Confectionary companies feed us and give us pleasure (good), but make us fat and cause diabetes (bad). Teaching in Oxford University, I am instructing young and bright minds (good), but also advancing a privileged and exclusive elite (bad).

Second, if purpose is constrained to enhancing corporate profits, it is just another input or hidden ingredient in the promotion of the Friedman Doctrine. This prevents purposes that diminish profits from being pursued and it requires those that are no longer enhancing profits to be discarded. In other words purpose is not intrinsic in its own right but instrumental in the attainment of profit. It thereby lacks authenticity and justifiably should be regarded cynically by those dependent on it as self- rather than selflessly interested. Companies are not charities; they need to be able to finance their functions but they do not function to fund their financiers either.

'Doing well by doing good' is a dangerous concept because it suggests that philanthropy is only valuable where it is profitable, and it converts charity into profit-generating entities in the way in which we have transformed utilities and other public services into shareholder-value-maximizing organizations. We have turned our models of businesses on their heads and lost sight of what they and we are trying to do. We are all here to fulfil our purposes, not necessarily as a means to either a greater or a richer end. We should not moralize our goodness or maximize our greediness but instead recognize our humanness and humaneness.

Put simply, the traditional view that the structure of companies drives their conduct, which in turn determines their performance as measured by their profits and share prices, is wrong. It is the purposes of companies that determine both their structure and conduct which in turn determine their performance measured in relation to their purposes. It is only once one has defined a company's purposes that one can ascertain either its appropriate structure and conduct or its performance. Until one knows what the corporation set out to do, one has nothing to say about how well it has done.

Is it practical? Can businesses survive in a world of intense and intensifying competition? Will they be able to earn a sufficient return on capital in the brutal product, labour, and financial markets in which they compete if they do not prioritize profits and shareholder interests above all else? There is one answer to all three questions: yes. If they focus on their purposes, companies are more likely to succeed in achieving them than if they do not. It is a failure to prioritize purpose that is the source of their failure to flourish financially and fundamentally. There is nothing to stop companies emphasizing shareholder interests where it contributes to the fulfilment of their purposes, and the book will describe the circumstances and types of companies to which this applies, but there is nothing to suggest that it always does. On the contrary, a persistent preoccupation with shareholder interests is a serious constraint and divergence from the business of business.

This is of relevance not only to business but also to academia and government. It means that twenty years of research on the relation between purpose and performance has focused on the wrong outcome ('dependent variable' to use the econometrician's terminology). The measure of performance that has been used to date has been financial performance, for example the stock-market value of a company. This presumes that the purpose is to maximize financial returns. If instead the purpose of the company is its objective then it is its success in the achievement of that purpose which is its measure of its performance. A successful company is one that delivers on its purpose and in the process may or may not make much money and therefore may be more or less profitable than others.

The significance of this conception of the firm for government is that it too like a corporation has a purpose, to promote the public interest and to provide the goods and services that society needs. Private corporations are part of the attainment of that public purpose, and government establishes laws, regulations, taxation, and partnerships that align the private purposes of companies with the public well-being of societies. Through law it enables corporations to promote their private purposes, through regulation it restricts them, through taxation it incentivizes them, and through partnerships and public ownership it participates in them. It is therefore neither indifferent to nor presumptive about the validity and value of different corporate purposes but instead guides the corporate sector to the attainment of the greater good.

This concept is very different from the conventional one that on one side sees governments, lawmakers, and regulators setting the boundaries—the 'rules of the game'—within which, on the other side, companies play hard and fast in the pursuit of their profit-led financial interests. It is a simple, clear framework within which everyone knows what is expected and permitted of them.

The conventional view is powerful not only because it offers a laser-sharp view of the purpose of business but also because it precisely defines the role of other parties as well. Governments, regulators, and the judiciary set the rules of the game; business plays by them and makes profits. Other institutions, such as charities, religious and non-governmental organizations (NGOs), and civil society provide charity, and moral and social guidance. Economics adds a combination of contracts and competitive markets that together convert the self-interested pursuit of profits into the social benefits of the invisible hand.

The world is neatly compartmentalized; confusion and obfuscation are avoided. It is analytically elegant and practically powerful. And nearly all policy in the post-WW2 period has been directed towards enhancing it: competition policy, monopoly regulation, investor protection, corporate governance, and corporate law all take this as their fundamental premise. After more than fifty years since the Friedman doctrine first appeared, we should therefore be nearing a state of nirvana. Instead, on the contrary, trust in business, government, and regulation has never been lower.

The vision of the firm, law, and government in this book is the antithesis of this conventional view. It is cooperative not confrontational, permissive not restrictive, realistic not idealistic. It recognizes that the current paradigm does not work, has failed society, has undermined business and is not how any business, government, or regulation function or succeed in practice.

The problem with the Friedman view is that it is hopelessly naïve. It is based on a conception of the world that produces simple elegant economic models that simply do not hold in practice. It fails to understand what motivates people, what makes for good business, and what regulation is capable of achieving. I say this not as an anthropologist or sociologist but as an economist—and a financial economist at that—who has spent his academic career working on and producing such models. But I also speak as someone who has created and worked in business, government, law, and regulation and seen what motivates people at the bottom and top of organizations, and how law and regulation operate in practice. And the answer is that it most certainly is not the Friedman view of the world or its attendant global economic consensus.

Of course money and profits are important. But they are not the main motivator of people or the primary source of success of companies. Of course regulation and laws are needed but stop believing that they can constrain anything or anyone who is given a sufficiently strong incentive to violate them. Where the current view of business and economics goes wrong is in suggesting that more profits (or increasing profits as Friedman put it) are better. This leads automatically to the economic statement that the function of business is to maximize profits subject to the constraint of regulation. It is this that has promoted the emergence of financial markets, takeover markets, financial institutions, and hedge-fund activists that seek more and more profits to a point that, unless directors of companies devote every waking (or preferably delete 'waking') hour of the day to producing them then their jobs and futures are at stake. And it is this that leads to ever more stringent regulation to restrain them from doing that and to ameliorate its disastrous consequences.

This simply does not work, has never worked, and will never work. And everyone—business leaders, institutional investors, regulators, governments, and law enforcers—knows it but no one knows what to do about it and many are highly conflicted in benefiting immensely from maintenance of it and the pretence that everything is just fine.

Profit is not a purpose any more than the pursuit of happiness is a purpose of mankind. Indeed profit maximization is as unlikely to create wealth as hedonism is to achieve happiness. Profits and happiness are the products of a successful commercial venture and a fulfilling life, and the outcome of the attainment of success and fulfilment.

That confusion between purpose and product is a natural consequence of an economic paradigm in which companies and individuals trade goods and services at given prices and the invisible hand guides them in the direction of attaining their goals of value and utility maximization. But in a world of creation rather than consumption where companies and individuals are innovating not just implementing then this mechanistic view of institutions and individuals as automatons guided by unobservable forces cannot apply. Elegant and precise paradigms of economics descend into a babble of amateur biology and psychology, captured by such concepts as 'animal spirits' and 'creative destruction', when confronted with matters of innovation. Once economics strays from the confines of markets and contracts then it has little to say about processes that involve the creation of products and processes, which previously had not even been contemplated.

Innovation and invention involve the binding together of many different types of capital in a way in which financial capital on its own cannot capture. For one thing, financial capital is a small component of the total capital of the world. According to the 2014 UNESCO *Inclusive Wealth Report*,[5] just 32 per cent of the world's wealth is attributable to produced capital. Fifty-five per cent of it is accountable by human capital and 13 per cent by natural capital. At the very least then focusing on financial capital misses a vast segment of the world's capital.

But there is a more fundamental reason why the traditional concept of the corporation, capital, and control are wrong. It cannot capture how the world evolves. Placing financial capital at the epicentre of business and economic systems is to elevate it to a position of importance that it cannot possibly command in the innovations that drive radical change. It is not just the mind of the financier that lies behind the most important innovations and inventions that have occurred, and it is not the pursuit of money alone that drives the minds of those who innovate and invent. To put financial capital at the heart of capitalism is to make the heart of man the master of his mind rather than just one of a complex system of interacting organs.

Once one understands the failure of business studies and economics to explain adaptation and change then their broader deficiencies in relation to economic performance, distribution of income and wealth, and social well-being become evident. In particular, the intensifying tensions that have emerged in economies and societies around the world and the cynicism that pervades popular perceptions of business and politics are inevitable consequences.

They reflect a failure to appreciate that the motivation of man is not, as traditional economics would lead us to believe, the pursuit of happiness or utility but the creation and building of worthwhile endeavours. As a holocaust survivor of Auschwitz and someone who lost his family in concentration camps, Victor Frankl drew on the extremity of human suffering and man's inhumanity to man to identify the source of man's humanity.[6] It is in such extreme circumstances that the importance of Frankl's phrase, 'It is not what you expect of life but what life expects of you', becomes clear. What the holocaust demonstrated to him was the significance of hope and love in circumstances where there appeared to be no hope: the one tree that the dying woman saw as symbolizing eternity of life; the fact that there was someone somewhere to whom everybody's thoughts could go; the realization that there was an incomplete piece of scholarship and unresolved scientific enquiry.

This explained what every human, animal, and insect seeks to achieve—some contribution, some project, something that will allow them to have left a lasting legacy however small in the world from which they can then depart in contentment. Frankl observed that it was those who lost sight of this, who felt no purpose or reason to go on living, for whom there was real misery in conditions of misery. For the others they rode above this as 'angels lost in perpetual contemplation of an infinite glory'.

In reversing the question from what should one expect of life to what should life expect of us, Victor Frankl identifies what one should be looking to achieve. It is not simply pleasure but the pleasure one derives from a fulfilling existence and the contribution that one makes to a bigger endeavour. To see one's existence within oneself is therefore destined to fail because it has no meaning. To see one's existence within the context of the communities of which one is a part and the attainment of a common goal is the source of happiness.

Economics errs in drawing an incomplete set of prescriptions of what enhances people's well-being. It focuses on individualism when the purpose of life derives from community. It suggests that the purpose of work is to earn and survive when it is also to participate and contribute. It suggests that consumption is desirable when production is sought. It suggests that the accumulation of wealth is a primary objective when its production and disposal are of greater significance.

We derive well-being from a sense of purpose, achievement, and contribution not just profit, income, and consumption. We seek to fulfil larger goals and the importance of the corporation is in its ability to assist us in this. We once constructed temples, pyramids, and shrines to satisfy the gods, but we now make washing machines, cell phones, and movies that contribute to our material more than our spiritual well-being.

This is not a theory of socialism, or mutualism, or stakeholder capitalism. It is not about the sharing of benefits to different parties in organizations. It is not about the adoption of religious principles or moral dogma. It is about creation, development, and innovation—how we as individuals and societies can together build a better world for the benefit of all both today and in the future—and the purpose of business as producing profitable solutions to problems of people and planet. We all want to contribute to that endeavour, and the corporation is a vital component in our ability to do so.

The Book

This book will take you across history, around the world, through philosophy and biology to business, law, economics, and finance to arrive at an understanding of where we have gone wrong, why, how we can put it right, and what specifically we need to do about it. It will provide you with an understanding of why our businesses and corporations are such powerful instruments for advancing human well-being and how their incorrect depiction has had such devastating consequences for our societies, politics, and environment. There are no tables or regressions, just words and a few illuminating photos, because, while pictures may be worth a thousand words, what cannot be said in words is not worth saying.

Part 1

Part 1 begins with principles. Chapter 1 sets out the case for reinventing the corporation. This centres round a reconsideration of the values and purpose of the corporation and the ownership and governance that are required to achieve them. Chapter 1 will argue that the rise of the 'mindful corporation'—an all-intangible no-tangible entity—is the most recent in the six ages of the corporation. Each age has been the source of profound development in economic and social conditions. They have all emerged in response to fundamental shifts in the nature of the corporation from public to private, to family, to stock-market listed, to international organization.

The conceptualization of the corporation as a shareholder-motivated entity is a serious impediment to that innovation. It shackles the corporation to one particular manifestation, and it is at variance with its intellectual origins in the Age of Enlightenment as a balance between ethics and economic efficiency. It is more than a century and a half later that we find the company's conceptual foundations in economic efficiency emerging as an antecedent to a focus on shareholder interests and an emphasis on corporate governance and control as ways of aligning its interests with those of its owners.

The notion of the firm in this book, as a multi-faceted organization that the law empowers and encourages to evolve in whatever way it sees fit, liberates it to adopt the many different forms that we have observed it taking over time and around the world, and allows it to meet the changing needs and opportunities available to society. Our conceptualization of the corporation should promote not impede its metamorphosis to produce profitable solutions to problems of people and planet.

Chapter 2 lays the philosophical foundation of this on the basis of the corporation as a conscious entity that can engage in a reflexive assessment of the consequences of its actions for the well-being of others. The chapter starts with biology not philosophy. It observes the remarkable parallels that exist between the evolution of the corporation and the evolution of life. Both involve the creation of entities consisting of, but distinct from, their constituent parts. The example that is used from biology is the endosymbiotic relationship between foraminifera and algae. The symbiosis creates an entity that is distinct from its constituent components. Likewise, a corporation involves the creation of a common pool of equity that comprises but is distinct from the individual contributions.

But the corporation is more than just an evolving living entity. It is one that has developed a consciousness of the environment within which it operates, allowing it to establish general principles of conduct that promote its economic efficiency and commercial performance. More significantly, it embraces a normative as well as positive consideration of the value it should attach to its activities and how it should aggregate together the interests and preferences of different individuals. As we move from a world of automation to artificial intelligence in which not only products and services but the minds and management of corporations will also be machine rather than man made, these normative considerations take on a particular urgency.

They point to the corporation as an organization with purposes and values that are distinct from both those who own and run it. It can either debase our own high moral principles or accentuate them beyond anything that we as individuals are capable of achieving. Over the last few years we have seen more of the former than the latter as corporations have pursued shareholder-value agendas with increasing intensity and in the process grown cultures that have converted the most upright into the most downright dishonest. The values transformation function of businesses is what we conventionally term their 'corporate cultures' which have powers to be forces for good or ill in equal measure—what will be described in the chapter as 'saintegrity' and 'sintegrity'. The separation of the mind of the corporation from those of any individuals who comprise it confers an ability on it to demonstrate a quite different level of integrity from the individuals who comprise it.

As Chapter 2 describes, philosophers have an ambivalent attitude towards concepts of integrity reflecting their failure to identify the values that are associated with them. However, in a corporate context it is easier to define and measure the values with which an organization is associated (as developed in Chapter 6) and for a corporation to put in place the structures, processes, and culture that ensure it abides by those values. In other words, corporations can elucidate both their principles and practices in their culture with a clarity that it is difficult for individuals to do with conviction. The chapter illustrates this with the example of the promotion of corporate cultures of kindness through leading by example.

Part 2

Part 2 looks at the corporation through the lens of history and its comparative evolution around the world. Chapter 3 steps back to document the 2000-year history of how the corporation was invented. Understanding the stages through which the corporation has evolved from the public institution of the Roman Empire to the emergent business organization of the seventeenth century is important in determining what was originally intended of it.

The chapter records the remarkable evolution in purpose of the corporation over its 2000-year history and how innovations in its legal form, governance, and regulation were required to allow it to adapt in this way. It describes how the corporation was created with a public purpose to provide public services and how this extended to embrace the administration of municipalities, university education, and religion. Under canon law in the Catholic Church during the twelfth century, it established an existence that was distinct from the public bodies that had previously created and controlled it, and, for the first time, it recognized the rights of its members as well as its senior representatives to determine its actions. In other words, it conferred freedom to incorporate and self-determination on a group of people in pursuit of a common purpose.

Meanwhile there was a parallel development elsewhere in the world of another organization, the partnership, which had a more commercial orientation. It was with the subsequent fusion of these two organizations into an entity that combined administration with financial capital that the foundations of the modern corporation were laid. There were remarkable innovations in the form of perpetual existence, fixed capital, and transferable shares that allowed it to evolve into the trading companies that built empires and ruled the world. Combined with the introduction of financial innovations of banking and stock markets, the corporation was then able to move into its third age of the private corporation and manufacturing.

However we do not have to go back 2,000 years to appreciate what the corporation is capable of achieving. The last hundred years provide us with an even finer tapestry of its multifarious forms and evolution into its final three ages as a service, multinational, and ultimately mindful corporation. In particular, contrasting the evolution of the corporation in Germany, Japan, the United Kingdom, and the United States in the first half of the twentieth century, Chapter 4 demonstrates how one organization has adopted many different guises of varying properties and performances.

Why? Why has one institution adopted such different forms? One answer is that it is capable of it. Just as human genetics spawns a plethora of individual types, so too corporations reproduce in varying ways. But it is not simply that it is possible. It is also desirable. Human evolution has benefited from a combination of randomness and natural selection. So too has corporate evolution. There is no single best corporate form, and corporations like humans need to adapt to their environment and social context. The study of corporate evolution is as fascinating and important as its anthropological equivalent.

Chapter 4 records the consistent contribution of trust and trustworthy institutions to the flourishing of financial markets around the world. It documents how institutions of trust promoted the growth of stock markets and the participation of large numbers of individual investors who otherwise enjoyed little or no protection from regulation at the beginning of the twentieth century. Indeed, when investor protection was finally introduced, often around the middle of the twentieth century, far from enhancing the trustworthiness of institutions, it undermined it. Regulation substituted for rather than complemented trust and prevented institutions of trust that were commonplace at the beginning of the century from surviving to the end. The country where this was not the case and investor protection remained weak throughout the twentieth century, namely Germany, was the one where family ownership proved extraordinarily resilient to periods of unprecedented political turmoil.

But Chapter 4 also documents where corporate evolution went wrong. It is only over the last fifty of its 2000-year existence that we have witnessed the retreat of the multi-purposed, publicly oriented corporation into a single-focused, self-interested entity. The innovation of liquid, divisible, transferable equity capital was a remarkable one. It allowed the development of stock markets that culminated in the rapid dispersion of equity ownership in the twentieth century to occur. It was the basis of the financing and growth of firms through the century and their merging into the entities that became the transnational corporations of the fifth age of the firm. However, it was also the cause of the steady erosion of ownership by founding families, at least in certain parts of the world. Where it occurred, it left a vacuum in ownership that was filled by a process of 'financialization' prioritizing shareholder interests over everyone else's. Dispersed shareholdings without anchor owners were devastating for both financial development and corporate governance.

This does not always occur; on the contrary, as Chapter 4 records, it is the exception rather than the rule, and, while the afflictions of stock-market economies are now all too evident and increasingly pervasive, they do not by any means prevail everywhere. We are therefore able to learn a great deal from the diversity of ownership that exists across the world as well as across time, and in so doing we can appreciate that what are conventionally regarded as superior forms of ownership are often defective in many critical respects. In particular, what emerges is the need for a combination of long-term, concentrated ownership and dispersed, liquid stock markets to give companies the stability and financing they require to realize their purposes. Chapter 4 documents how the largest and most successful companies in the world have had access to both.

Part 3

Part 3 turns from principles to practice—business practice. Most business-school courses are organized in such a way as to suggest that there is a best way of doing business—learn from cases of currently or recently successful businesses about finance, leadership, marketing, operations management, organizational practice, and strategy and your success as an entrepreneur, manager, or business leader is assured. Nothing could be further from the truth. Yesterday's successful business practices are destined to be tomorrow's business graveyards. Every business book should come with the health warning that the past is no guide to the future.

The reasons are obvious. First, everyone does the same, adopts similar business practices, and drives down their profitability through normal competitive processes. Second, technologies, consumer needs, and societies change, requiring different practices. Third, and most significantly, the source of corporate success is business innovation not replication. The history of business in Chapter 3 documents the repeated reinvention of the corporation. The cross-country evolution of corporate sectors in Chapter 4 reveals how countries as well as companies have derived competitive advantage from business innovation.

Chapter 5 describes one of the most exciting forms of innovation that is currently in progress—innovations to address the plight of the worst off or nearly worst off members of the world's population—what are sometimes described as the 'bottom of the pyramid' or 'middle of the diamond'. These have been the neglected members of the global economic community because they lack buying power. They do not have the means to pay for the goods and services that those in the developed world routinely purchase, and, because demand is absent, the costs of employing them cannot be justified either. They are locked in a vicious cycle of deficient demand and employability.

What some companies are beginning to appreciate is that this conventional description of economic deprivation is not irresolvable. Turn the story on its head and start from the position that in the absence of employment opportunities, the cost of employing people at the bottom of the pyramid or the middle of the diamond is very low, and what looks like an impediment is actually an opportunity. However, to create an opportunity for the recipients as well as the providers it has to be more than a story of employing people at subsistence incomes to perform menial tasks. It has to incorporate an element of being able to break out of poverty through income growth and meaningful employment—giving people a purpose to life.

This is where corporations can play a key role because they can provide not only employment but also education and training. In other words they can offer investment in the human capital that is required to escape from poverty. They can do so through entrepreneurship as well as employment by providing the under- and unemployed with the skills needed to develop their own commercial activities.

This does not have to be either philanthropy or corporate social responsibility. It should not be an add-on or nice to have for business, jettisoned as soon as business conditions deteriorate and the nice to have becomes the nasty to retain. It has to be core to the delivery of the corporation's purposes and mutually beneficial to it, as the provider of business opportunities and training, as well as the recipients. In other words, it should be a commercial as well as social necessity. Chapter 5 describes the sleight of hand required to perform this conjuring trick.

One of the tricks of the trade is the establishment of relations—partnerships with a variety of different parties, many of which in the past business would have shunned and not have deigned to go near with a barge pole—partners such as governments, NGOs, and academics. One of the reasons for these partnerships is to help corporations identify potential entrepreneurs. This depends on trust—trust that the recipients of the good are good for their word. Operating in some of the toughest markets in the world with which they are unfamiliar, corporations are not well placed to separate fish from foul. They need the assistance of organizations they can trust to establish relations with those living and working in the slums and rural communities of developing economies. In essence, the business innovation is to build pyramids of relations that allow corporations to create an ecosystem of new commercial opportunities.

New relations of trust are the backbone of nearly every innovation. Sole entrepreneurs working in isolation may be able to invent, but to convert their inventions into commercial innovations they need to come out of their garden sheds and converse with others. This is where so many entrepreneurial activities fail and where ecosystems such as Silicon Valley are so successful at providing the mentoring and networking that are critical to corporate flourishing. The new social networking organizations with which the book begins in Chapter 1 are as much dependent on unconventional partnerships as the corporations working in the slums of the world in Chapter 5.

Caution is required in interpreting these developments as inherently beneficial for the poorest in the world. They can all too easily degenerate into exactly the opposite—contracting-out of activities to the cheapest sources of labour employed in unsafe and unsanitary conditions at below subsistence wages. Whether this is enlightened entrepreneurship or extortionate exploitation depends on the trustworthiness of companies—whether they are true to the good that they profess to produce. It is the ownership, governance, and leadership of firms that together establish the commitment of corporations to their purpose and their capacity to create the greater good.

The profound changes in the nature of the corporation described in the first chapter have significant implications for the governance of companies. Whereas financial capital was scarce during the nineteenth- and twentieth-century age of manufacturing firms, it is becoming increasingly abundant. While shareholder control could previously be viewed as a response to a need to allocate a scarce resource efficiently, this is no longer the case. Scarcity has moved elsewhere to human, natural, and social capitals. Chapter 5 describes a set of principles of corporate governance by which control of corporations is allocated to those capitals that are scarce and prioritize their own over other parties' values.

These principles imply that as the sources of scarcity shift from financial to other capitals so too do the required governance and measures of corporate performance. They identify the fundamental defect of the Friedman doctrine as being the unrelenting pursuit of profits to maximize shareholder value at all times, intensified by the fear instilled in corporate boards by hostile takeovers and short-term institutional activism. They demonstrate that authenticity and trustworthiness in pursuing corporate purposes may require the sacrifice of profit. They emphasize the importance of balancing the interests of different parties to the firm, enhancing the welfare of all not just the wealth of a few, and recognizing that doing good does not always do well.

The implications for corporate governance are profound. Corporate governance is currently viewed as serving one function: addressing the 'agency problem' of aligning the interests of the management of companies with their owners—the shareholders. Recommendations regarding board composition, separation of chairmen and chief executives, remuneration, auditing, risk management, reporting, and investor relations are all designed to ensure that companies are run for the benefit of their investors. Since the Cadbury Commission first reported in 1992,[7] countries around the world have progressively adopted corporate governance codes with this end in mind.

It is fundamentally misconceived. The purpose of corporate governance is not and should not be predominantly to promote shareholder interests; it is to promote the interests of the firm as a whole and, in particular, to assist it with achieving its corporate purposes. A company's governance is indeterminate so long as its purposes are undefined, and once they are then its governance is determined by its purposes, not the interests of any one party. Shareholders are one but only one component in the delivery of purpose, and corporate governance should reflect the balancing of theirs as against other parties' interests in the promotion of purpose. All of board composition, chairmanship, leadership, remuneration, auditing, and reporting should be focused on what the company exists to do and the relations that it needs to form with all of its stakeholders, including shareholders but not excluding others.

This leads to the question of how gains to trade should be shared between the different parties to the firm—the rich owner and the impoverished farmer—and how they are measured. Practice is conditioned by measurement because the capability to manage depends on a capacity to measure. At present measurement is a unidimensional record of financial performance. Business seeks profits so it measures profits. However, if the values of corporations are more than those of their shareholders, it is necessary to measure those values. And if the attainment of profits does not come from their pursuit but is the product of some other purpose then the achievement of that purpose requires the measurement of other forms of capital, such as human and social as well as financial capital.

This has significance not just for corporate profits but also for the way in which we measure our national income. Currently we are misstating both corporate profits and national income and this is having damaging consequences for the allocation of resources in our businesses and economies. While Chapter 5 referred to human and social capital, Chapter 6 will illustrate this with perhaps the most serious omission and mismeasurement and that is in regard to natural capital.

At present neither corporate profits nor national income take account of our utilization of natural capital—air, forest, lakes, wildlife, ecosystems, and environment. That was not a problem until comparatively recently because consumption of natural capital was sufficiently modest that nature was able to renew itself and preserve the stock of natural capital. But over the last few decades, destruction of natural capital has been on such a scale as to overwhelm nature's restorative properties and cause irreversible declines. The mismeasurement of corporate profits and national income is now having a devastating effect on the destruction of our natural capital.

Chapter 6 sets out a way in which we can redefine existing corporate accounts to incorporate other values and forms of capital. It leads naturally to a definition of profits that accounts for the cost of avoiding the deterioration or exploitation of other capitals—'fair' profits not the conventionally reported 'fake' ones that fail to account for the cost to companies of remedying the damage of their activities. It thereby establishes whether the new types of business described in Chapter 5 are indeed enlightened or exploitative. It yields what might be termed genuinely sustainable levels of profits, not just in an environmental sense but also in relation to human and social as well as natural capital.

The costs of maintaining human, social, and natural as well as material capital provide a good benchmark for distinguishing fair from fake profits. They establish that companies and economies are at least able to remedy detriments of their activities, as against where profits are fake and insufficient to remedy the detriments. In other words, whether profits are fair or fake is the determinant of whether businesses and economic activities more generally are generating net social benefits that protect the interests of all parties and yield what are described in economic terms as 'Pareto improving' outcomes.

Fair profits can be used to establish whether companies are fulfilling their purposes by making the benchmark for fair profits not just capital maintenance but also the realization of corporate purposes. So if, for example, the purpose is to enhance the well-being of customers in relation to their health or leisure then a company will be reporting fake profits if it fails to deliver on its promises, and if the true profits are actually losses then they are cheating their customers to a point that they cannot fulfil their promises profitably. Fixing financial reporting of profits to be fair rather than fake therefore promotes purpose from being a persuasive principle to a powerful practice.

Underpinning the accounts are balance sheets that report a company's assets and liabilities. At present, these record stocks of physical assets, such as buildings, inventories, and machinery, and financial assets, such as bank deposits, bonds, and equities. However, their coverage of other assets—intangibles (brands and patents), human, natural, and social capital—is very limited. In particular, investments designed to enhance the quality of human, natural, and social capital are not in general separately identified.

As a consequence, rates of return on companies' assets are exaggerated by, first, overstating profits in not giving due consideration to the costs of maintaining human, natural, and social capital and, second, understating assets employed in excluding most human, natural, and social capital. Companies are, as a result, encouraged to devote too many resources to activities that are detrimental to society and the environment, and too few to those that enhance them.

The monopolization of modern accounting by financial and material capital is a reflection of the scarcity of these forms of capital and the relative abundance of human and natural capital in the third age of the manufacturing corporation. However, with emergence of service, transnational, and mindful corporations in subsequent ages, financial and tangible assets are having to recognize the significance of consumption of human, natural, and social capital in statements of profits, and relinquish their dominance of balance sheets in favour of the new forms of predominantly intangible capital scarcity.

Accounting deficiencies are even more acute in public-sector and national accounting where balance sheets are less well developed than in the corporate sector and fail to reflect fully investment in physical as well as intangible, human, natural, and social capital. As Chapter 10 records, this has been one of the main causes of underinvestment in national infrastructure in all its guises—physical as well as intangible, human, natural, and social assets—around the world.

Part 4

Having established the centrality of corporate purpose in Chapter 1 and the relevance of values, ownership, governance, and measurement to its achievement in the subsequent chapters, Part 4 then turns from practice to policy and describes how the transformation of corporations can be translated from a visionary ideal to a practical reality through an embarrassingly simple policy.

The existence of corporations and the form that they take is a product of law. Laws legitimize corporations and determine the nature of their existence. Some aspects of laws are enabling in providing the basis on which corporations can determine their purposes and relations with the rest of society through contracting with their investors, employees, customers, and societies. Others are restrictive in limiting the purposes and activities in which corporations can legitimately engage.

Chapter 7 describes the framework provided by corporate law and public regulation. They establish the instruments for enabling, empowering, and enforcing—enabling different forms of corporate activities; empowering different parties to produce them; and enforcing the outcomes that were intended. Understanding how the law enables, empowers, and enforces is key to the promotion of diversity in corporations.

The law has a particular role to play in enabling companies to commit to as well as control different parties. It does this through facilitating the adoption of ownership, governance, and measurement systems that lend credibility to the promises that it makes to other parties. It is the basis on which the corporation can establish its trustworthiness in justifying the trust that others place in it. Without legal foundations, commitments lack conviction; with them they are powerful vehicles to sustain values. In particular, the law should enable corporations to adopt public as well as private purposes, accountability to parties other than shareholders, and forms of custodianship as trustees and foundations as well as agents of investors.

Where the purposes and functions of corporations conflict with the wider interests of society then they have to be constrained. Alongside the permissive legislation that legitimizes the corporation, there is a need for prescriptive legislation that requires the corporation to abide by particular rules, to refrain from undertaking certain activities, and to remedy detriments where damage is done. Corporate law is therefore a subtle balance between conferring rights where none previously existed, and attributing responsibilities where few are otherwise accepted. Economic history has been a journey of trying to achieve that balance but lurching precariously from one extreme to the other.

More significantly, corporate law is the means to achieving purposeful company ends. At present the law for the most part prioritizes the interests of shareholders. It does so to varying degrees ranging from some US states that elevate shareholders to unassailable heights to Central European countries that demote them closer to the shop floor. Both are equally misconceived. There should be no presumption in company law of either shareholder primacy or stakeholder pluralism. One or other may sometimes be appropriate but never consistently so.

Instead corporate law should prioritize purpose. It should require companies to articulate their purposes, incorporate them in their articles of association, and above all demonstrate how they credibly commit to the delivery of purpose. The law should provide the foundations on which those who serve, source, and supply a company can be assured of its intentions and its abilities to discharge its duties. It should not just be the creator of the corporate form but also the instigator of its identity and the author of its authenticity. When we read the corporate purpose statements, we as employees, customers, suppliers, investors, communities, and nation states should know precisely to what we are committing our livelihoods, money, offspring, health, and well-being and what we can legitimately expect in return. At the moment we know none of these with any precision or credibility whatsoever.

This simple act of incorporating corporate purpose in corporate law transforms business at a stroke. It does so by elevating purpose to where it should be: the existence of the company in law. It imposes the fulfilment of corporate purpose as a fiduciary responsibility and requires corporate governance to be aligned with its achievement. But even more than that, it also ensures an alignment of interests of the company's investors with its purpose because in the process of demonstrating its commitment to purpose, the firm will have to establish the commitment of its investors as well as its management to its fulfilment. To do that its institutional owners will in turn have to incorporate a statement of purpose that includes a commitment to uphold the purposes of firms in which they invest. The same applies to the company's suppliers and corporate customers. In other words, not only does the incorporation of purpose in company law commit the management, it also commits all the parties associated with the firm and in turn requires them to establish the basis on which they can credibly establish such commitments. It is therefore the bootstrap to reboot the entire corporate and economic system.

Beyond requiring a statement and demonstration of purpose, corporate law should be enabling rather than prescriptive or restrictive to promote as great a variety of corporate purposes as possible—so long as they are not at variance with social interests. But not all purposes should be equal in the eye of the law. Some are enlightened and some are despicable—for example where they involve child trafficking or pornography—and the law should not tolerate the latter. It does this through its regulatory function, which is explored further in Chapter 8.

Regulation has become a dominant feature of modern society, particularly over the last decade in relation to the sector of economies that has failed and abused its rights the most—finance. In the wake of the financial crisis and the subsequent scandals that have engulfed the financial sector, financial regulation has mushroomed. Having been caught systematically abusing the trust placed in them, financial institutions are now subject to almost continuous intrusive scrutiny.

However, as Chapter 8 describes, the form that the regulation has taken has been seriously misguided and threatens to exacerbate the problems it seeks to correct. It is structured according to institutional boundaries, for example, in regulating banks differently from securities houses that hold and trade market instruments such as equities, bonds, and derivatives. The former are regulated according to one set of laws—banking regulation—and the latter by another—securities regulation—and because the two have evolved separately, there are significant inconsistencies between them.

The problem that this creates is that while regulation looks at financial systems through the lens of institutions, the institutions themselves do not. They perform a variety of purposes and functions that overlap with each other and undertake similar activities in different institutions. Basing regulation on institutions encourages them to circumvent it by organizing their activities in the least regulated way. This has promoted the growth of what is termed 'shadow banking'—the provision of banking services by institutions that are not classified as banks and therefore not subject to as onerous a set of regulations as banks.

The consequences of this for financial stability are potentially devastating. As banking is driven into the shades and shadow banking comes to dominate it in terms of its scale and significance, the possible consequences of its failure increase in tandem. The next financial failure will be in the shadow banking system and, in the absence of formal systems of injecting liquidity, rescue funding, or bailouts, it will be harder to manage than the collapse of the formal banking sector was in the financial crisis.

In the thirtieth anniversary edition of the *Oxford Review of Economic Policy* in 2015,[8] I discuss an article that I wrote thirty years earlier in the second edition of the journal in 1986[9] detailing precisely how deregulation associated with 'Big Bang' in the United Kingdom had set in train processes that would lead to the 2008 financial crisis more than twenty years later. Similar factors are now destined to do the same in shadow banking, the only difference being that in all probability we will not have to wait another twenty years for the next crisis.

While this is a particular problem in financial markets because of the ease with which similar activities can be organized in different institutions, it exemplifies a more general concern that if regulation is not to have unintended and deleterious consequences, it should stop regarding its role as being simply to punish wayward blaggards but instead to delegitimize unacceptable purposes and practices. For example in relation to the financial sector, it should determine what financial institutions are supposed to do and what is unacceptable. Regulation should limit the range of permitted purposes to those that are socially acceptable and ensure that they are credibly and consistently implemented across all service providers. Considering regulation in the context of the achievement of social as well as private purpose therefore leads naturally to a regulatory focus on function rather than form.

Part 5

The social purpose of financial institutions is much more than providing services to investors; it is about promoting growth, investment, innovation, access, and equality, i.e. the real sector of the economy. Far from constraining institutional innovation through regulation, the state should promote it through partnerships with the private sector. Part 5 describes two ways in which the public sector promotes social purpose, through finance and taxation, and infrastructure and investment. It discusses the role of the state as a corporation that coordinates the provision of goods and services, which the private sector on its own fails to deliver. It does this in precisely the same way as the private sector by determining, firstly, its purposes and values—the social objectives that the state as a corporation seeks to achieve—secondly, its ownership, which may in part, but not necessarily, involve public ownership, and, thirdly, its governance, which aligns the interests of the different parties to the social purpose.

Chapter 9 discusses finance and its role in promoting growth, investment, innovation, and economic development. The financial system has a primary role to perform in converting the needs of individuals for safe, short-term, liquid savings into the risky, long-term, illiquid assets of companies. The analysis of ownership around the world in Chapter 4 described how this requires a combination of long-term engaged concentrations of ownership alongside dispersed liquid trading of shares to promote innovation and investment at low costs of financing.

Two things have militated against this—taxation and regulation. At present corporate taxation is primarily regarded as a source of revenue for governments, but increasingly, as corporations shift their activities to the most favourable tax jurisdictions in the world, they extinguish their tax liabilities and force nations into competitive races to lower their tax rates. The result is that corporation tax becomes a diminishing source of revenue for governments and a growing cause of acrimony between corporations and their nation states.

As a source of revenue, corporation tax is ineffective; as an incentive to align private with public interests, it is potentially very powerful. This is illustrated by one of the most damaging forms of distortion that the corporate tax system has introduced and that is to the financial structure of firms. At present, the interest payments that companies make to their creditors—their banks and bondholders—are allowable as a cost against their earnings in computing their liability for corporate taxation. In contrast, payments of dividends that companies make to their shareholders are not. As a consequence, corporate taxation systematically encourages corporations, including financial institutions around the world, to raise finance in the form of debt rather than equity.

This has been a major cause of the inexorable rise in corporate indebtedness. Most significantly, while regulation has sought to raise equity capital held by banks since the financial crisis, corporate taxation has done exactly the opposite. Eliminating this distortion is just one of the many ways in which corporate taxation can be used to align the private interests of companies and financial institutions with their social purposes.

It is not just in regard to taxation that, in the absence of compelling arguments to the contrary, public policy should adopt a principle of neutrality in not favouring one form of finance over another; it is also true of regulation. Far from enabling companies to select the financial structures and forms of ownership that are best suited to their activities, regulation frequently impedes diversity. In seeking to protect the interests of investors, regulation has weaved a web of rules that have discriminated against long-term engaged equity ownership in favour of short-term, passive share capital, with unintended and damaging consequences for finance, investment, growth, and development. Instead, if they facilitate the pursuit of their purposes, companies should be free to choose patterns of ownership that, in acknowledging the responsibilities which come with shareholder rights, allocate voting rights to investors who commit large amounts of capital (possibly with unlimited liability) to protect other people's interests for the long term.

Chapter 9 demonstrates that the traditional separation between finance and investment suggested by economics, and increasingly reflected in public policy, is misguided. On the contrary, policy should promote their partnering. A requirement for companies to specify their corporate purposes in their articles of association and demonstrate how their corporate structures assist them with achieving them would go a long way to achieving that.

The final chapter describes how purposeful corporations can tackle one of the most serious challenges the global economy faces in addressing the under-provision of infrastructure. Decades of privatization of utilities and infrastructure around the world have failed to resolve the shortfall. The reason is the commitment problems that arise between private-sector providers and public-sector policymakers and regulators.

On the one side of the social compact are corporations that receive certain privileges in return for providing a range of public services. The privileges they enjoy include rights as utilities to supply monopoly products and as banks to have access to monetary deposits on favourable terms. They are protected against risks of failure as monopoly providers and recipients of public insurance. In return, utilities and banks are expected to supply goods and services that benefit us as customers, investors, and communities.

At present, the only way we know of aligning the fiduciary duties of companies to their shareholders with their public obligations to their customers and communities is through regulation. However, the interests of regulators in promoting customer, investor, and community interests are in direct conflict with those of utilities and banks in seeking to maximize the earnings of their shareholders and executives. Utilities and banks therefore do whatever they can to circumvent regulation and to turn it to competitive advantage as a barrier to entry for new firms into their industries.

If instead the flexibility of the law is used to enable companies to commit to public as well as private purposes, and their licence conditions to operate are incorporated in their articles of association, then current conditions of conflict are converted into constructive cooperation. Conversely, by incorporating private investor as well as public-sector purposes in state-owned corporations then the risks that private investors otherwise face of expropriation of their investments in long-duration infrastructure projects are diminished. In both cases, the corporation provides a legal construct for binding private- and public-sector interests together, with its structure—ownership, governance, leadership, measurement, and incentives—determined by its purposes, not vice versa as at present.

Chapter 10 has brought us full circle back to the Roman origins of the corporation as a provider of public works. Together with Chapter 9, it demonstrates that the role of the state is much more than just providing the legal basis for the creation of different corporate forms. It is a source of organizational and social innovation that builds the backbone of finance and infrastructure required to support new institutions and create the arteries through which economic activity flows. In turn the corporation is much more than a commercial vehicle for delivering returns to its shareholders; it is a means for creating social and public goods.

One of the most damaging aspects of the Friedman misconception of the firm is the artificial barrier it has erected between the private and public corporate persona, between the internal and external boundaries of the firm, between the commercial and social. The strength of the corporation lies in its ability to transcend all of them. Part 1 of the book establishes that is what the corporation should do; Part 2 that is what over its long history until recently it has done; Part 3 that is what it is quite capable of doing; Part 4 that is what it is empowered to do; and Part 5 that is what government should encourage it to do. Extract the firm from the shackles of the Friedman principles and it will free man of the shekels expected by its principals.

Part 1
Principles

Hesiod had four of them, Ovid five, Shakespeare seven. 'All the world's a stage, | And all the men and women merely players; | They have their exits and entrances, | And one man in his time plays many parts, | His acts being seven ages.' The seven ages of man: 'At first, the infant, | Mewling and puking in the nurse's arms; | Then the whining schoolboy, with his satchel | And shining morning face, creeping like snail | Unwillingly to school.'[1] This is all very politically incorrect; it is much safer to stick to the corporation.

There we find six ages. At first the merchant trading company established by royal charter to undertake voyages of discovery and promote commerce around the world. Then the public corporation created by Acts of Parliament to engage in major public works and the building of canals and railways. Then with freedom of incorporation in the nineteenth century came the private corporation—the seedbed of the industrial revolution and the manufacturing corporation. Next were the service firms and the rise of financial institutions. The fifth age is the transnational corporation putting a girdle around the earth and running rings around national governments. The last scene of all that ends this strange eventful history is the mindful corporation—sans machines, sans man, sans money, sans everything—but with principles and purposes that determine our destiny.

1

Purpose

The purpose of life
Is to give purpose to lives,
So that society thrives
While the world survives.

Where We Are

Over the last forty years there has been a remarkable transformation in the corporation. Forty years ago, 80 per cent of the market value of US corporations was attributable to tangible assets—plant, machinery, and buildings—as against intangibles—licences, patents, and research development. Today, intangibles account for 85 per cent of the market value of US corporations.[1]

The millennium was a turning point when for the first time investment in intangibles exceeded that in tangibles in both the United Kingdom and the United States.[2] We might once have been nations of shopkeepers, buildings, and office blocks—lots of office blocks—but no more. The turn of the millennium marked the turn of America and Britain into nations of brands and brains.

Reliance on intangibles might feel like placing ones faith in magic; an economy of magicians not manufacturers making nothing but air—the weightless economy. But it is no such thing. The sixth age of the corporation marks the most remarkable period of our existence. It is indeed a corporation sans machines, sans man, sans money, sans everything.

Take Facebook and its founder Mark Zuckerberg as examples. In 2008 Mark Zuckerberg made a very costly decision when he failed to employ two people who had recently left Yahoo. Instead the two went to the Red Rock Café in Mountain View, California to write computer code on laptops perched on wobbly tables. It was the code for sending messages on cell phones in a cheaper and more reliable form than either SMS or MMS. In October 2009, they raised $250,000 from five ex-Yahoo friends.

The two people were Brian Acton and Jan Koum, and the company they formed was called WhatsApp, which in 2014 they sold to Facebook for $19bn. Instead of employing Acton and Koum for a few thousand dollars back in 2008, Mark Zuckerburg ended up buying their corporate form for $19bn.

This story is made all the more remarkable by the fact that this was a company with not just no machines, no men, and no money—it was burning money. In the six months prior to the purchase, WhatsApp made a loss of $230 million. What was Mark Zuckerberg thinking when he purchased a loss making company with no assets, no people, and lots of liabilities for $19bn? Was Mark a magician or mad?

The mindful corporation is an extraordinarily efficient concept. The creation of a corporation worth $19bn on the back of an idea that involves few people, a handful of computers, little space, and next to no capital stands in marked contrast to the previous ages of the corporation with their fleets of sailing ships, hoards of labourers, belching factories, teams of service providers, and gleaming transnational headquarters of far-flung corporate empires. They have given way to the mindful corporation.

At the same time as it is an elegant culmination of a process that has been in progress for 600 years, since the mindful corporation is sans machines, sans man, sans money, sans everything, it crystallizes both the wonders and the woes of the corporation. On 19 August 2004, Google came to the NASDAQ stock market at a share price of $85 per share in an initial public offering that valued the company at more than $23bn. Today the founders Sergei Brin and Larry Page are each valued by Forbes at more than $40bn.

But Google not only exemplifies the extraordinary concentration of wealth that the mindful corporation is creating, which by comparison puts the tens of millions of dollars of annual income earned by investment bankers into the poverty category, it also illustrates another form of concentration: concentration of power. When Google came to the stock market, it issued two classes of shares—one class that was made available to the public at large and another class that was just held by the founders. The latter had ten times the voting control of the former. As a result, today Sergei Brin and Larry Page retain control of Google, or Alphabet as it is now known, with a majority of the votes.

This ownership structure was deemed by many analysts and investors at the time to be a violation of good corporate governance and a threat to the ordinary investor. Thirteen years later at the time of writing in January 2018, the share price of Alphabet stands at more than $1,000, a twelve-fold increase since its issue—not bad for a period during which the S&P index has only somewhat more than doubled. In this case at least, concentration of power does not appear to have acted to the detriment of its investors. Other social media companies, such as Facebook and LinkedIn, and Internet companies, such as Alibaba, also came to the stock market with dual-class share structures that allowed their founders and partners to retain control.

But whether the concentration of ownership and power acts to the detriment of society more generally is a moot issue. Concentration of wealth may be fully justified by the enormous contributions that the founders have made to our lifestyles and well-being; and retention of voting control may be required, as the founders claim, to preserve their corporations' clarity of vision and purpose. But have no illusions—the mindful corporation is creating extraordinary disparities of wealth and power in the hands of those with the minds to create them that make the landed gentry of the past look like impoverished downtrodden farmers.

This is the last in a long progression of changes to the role of the corporation in contemporary society during its six ages of existence. At the outset it was a public agent—an instrument of king and then Parliament to promote the national interest in building an empire and then the infrastructure on which we rely to this day.

With freedom of incorporation, the stranglehold of the state was relaxed and families controlled its development. However, it remained firmly rooted in and dependent on the nation state. Even when it grew into major manufacturing industry and families ceded control, it was dependent on the state for its prosperity. But with the emergence of, first, the financial service and then the transnational corporation, which is not only international but also stateless, the corporation has become footloose.

Not only has it become footloose, it is also timeless. Kings and parliaments provided a permanence and durability to the purpose of the firm. This was then adopted by families that passed corporations through several generations of owners—such as the Barclays and the Cadburys. As families relinquished control to outside investors, ownership was initially retained by individual investors, the euphemistic widows and orphans, for extended periods of time but then transferred to institutions that have held them for progressively shorter periods of time as portfolios of assets to be traded at will, a phenomenon that has been observed around the world.

So from entities with persistent ownership beholden to their nation states, corporations have transitioned into organizations with investors with no commitment to any particular nation or generation other than the present. The result is that the interests of the corporation have progressively diverged from those of the societies within which they operate.

Much of what we observe in terms of both flourishing and failures of societies around the world is attributable to the way in which the corporation has evolved. The remarkable growth of China, India, Japan, Korea, and Singapore in the post-WW2 period has come on the back of the emergence of corporations owned by the state in China, by banks and other corporations in Japan, and families in India, Korea, and Singapore. The failure of Africa and the Middle East to demonstrate similar flourishing reflects an absence of indigenous corporate sectors outside of the resource extractive industries and over-reliance on foreign subsidiaries. The problems that have recently emerged in Asian economies of environmental pollution in China, of growing levels of income inequality in India, of monopoly distortions in Korea, and of conflicts in bank–firm relations in Japan are associated with the failures of their corporate sectors.

Closer to home the widening disparities of income within corporations between executives at the top and employees on the shop floor can be attributed to the changing nature of the corporation. So too can the disparities in wealth between those who own and control corporations and the rest of society and the failure of governments to be able to raise tax from highly profitable transnational corporations. So too can the breakdown in trust in the financial sector where the interests of shareholders and executives have diverged from their customers and creditors.

That a single organizational form can perform so many different functions, from the one-man enterprise to the corner shop to the conglomerate, from social enterprise to manufacturing to public infrastructure, from the no-tech to the low-tech to the high-tech, is truly remarkable. That the corporation can explain the growth of nations around the world and the failure of others to progress is indicative of its macroeconomic significance. That the different nature of the corporation is associated with social benefits and ills, and its changes over time with their emergence and eradication, suggests that it is to the corporation that we should turn for both the source of our prosperity and our impoverishment.

The fact that the corporation has become footloose and timeless could be a source of tremendous well-being that frees it from the political constraints and historical conventions to which we are currently subject. To the economist the combination of well-functioning competitive and complete markets together with well-governed corporations that pursue the wealth of their shareholders is the source of economic prosperity.

With the emergence of the mindful corporation we could therefore be on the edge of the most remarkable prosperity and creativity in the history of the world. On the other hand, we could equally well be at the mercy of corporations that are the seeds of our destruction through growing inequality, poverty, and environmental degradation that give rise to social disorder, national conflicts, and environmental collapse on scales that are almost impossible to conceive of today. We are therefore on the border between creation and cataclysm, and the corporation is in large part the determinant of which way we will go.

Our future therefore depends on reinventing the corporation for its seventh and final age. But before describing what it will take to get us from here to nirvana rather than into a collapsing supernova, we firstly need to look backwards to understand where we are and how we got here to the cusp of nirvana and supernova.

How We Got Here

For the most part, the intellectual history of the corporation is one of benign neglect that lagged far behind the emergence of economics from the Age of Enlightenment. To the extent that the joint-stock corporation was discussed, it was largely to suggest that it should not exist. For Adam Smith, specialization of labour was a source of economic prosperity but the corporation was infested with conflicts of interest between management and shareholders to the point that 'negligence and profusion, therefore, must always prevail, more or less, in the management of the affairs of such a company.'[3]

It was the market and exchange rather than the corporation that was the source of economic prosperity. Even for Alfred Marshall—the grandfather of industrial economics writing more than a hundred years later—the existence of the corporation rested precariously on the integrity of the English gentleman: 'It is a strong proof of the marvellous growth in recent times of a spirit of honesty and uprightness in commercial matters, that the leading officers of great public companies yield as little as they do to the vast temptations to fraud which lie in their way.'[4]

It was not until Ronald Coase, writing in the 1930s, that the corporation was given a more solid foundation as an alternative lower-cost way of organizing economic activity than the marketplace.[5] Once one thinks of the corporation in these terms then it clearly takes on a relevance of its own as a legitimate subject of study, and from this sprung the intellectual underpinnings of business-school education and scholarship.

But what continued to dominate economic analysis of the corporation was precisely the issue that had concerned Adam Smith and Alfred Marshall—its dependence on managers who at best were negligent and at worst fraudulent.[6] Since it is the shareholders who bear the cost of their managements' negligence and frauds, it is the shareholders who should have the right to prevent them from engaging in such malpractices. With the risk of failure goes the right to govern the corporation and shareholders should have ownership rights to elect, remove, and reward management—corporate governance.[7]

The only problem with this elegant solution was whether shareholders would in practice exercise those rights. So long as the shareholder was the founder of the firm, or a family, then the answer was yes. But if the shareholder was one amongst many institutional investors as we have today then the answer is no. Shareholders might have the rights but they do not have the incentives to exercise them.[8]

It is this failure of governance with which all the ills of the corporation today are associated. Two hundred and fifty years after Adam Smith first identified the problem, we are still trying to grapple with it. The joint-stock corporation should not have existed but not only have we allowed it to but we have encouraged it to become the most important institution in our lives, and we are paying the price for it.

So, looking through an economic lens, nearly all policy towards the corporation has been concerned with solving this one issue of how to make management more accountable to their shareholders. A front cover of *The Economist* published in 2015 proclaimed 'capitalism's unlikely heroes' to be the hedge-fund activists who strike terror into the boards of public corporations by purchasing blocks of shares in companies and then demanding seats on their boards with a view to shaking up and shaking out their negligent if not fraudulent management.[9] They are the new corporate raiders—the Carl Icahns and the Lord Hansons of the 2010s—the heroes of *The Economist*'s capitalism who will bring us to our state of nirvana.

Well let me tell you, if this is nirvana, I'm the Virgin Mary, which for a variety of reasons is unlikely. The new corporate raiders will bring us no more happiness than their predecessors. On the contrary, they will accelerate the cataclysm to which I previously referred and bring us to supernova not nirvana.

There is considerable irony in the conclusion that the market is needed in the form of a market for corporate control to ensure that the corporation fulfils Ronald Coase's objective of being more efficient and lower-cost than the market. This reductionist conclusion brings the corporation back to its primordial market form, and once again we end up being without a theory of the corporation.

The reason is that the intellectual conception of the corporation from Adam Smith to the present is fundamentally wrong. The basic defect of the corporation is not its lack of accountability of management to its shareholders or the failure of shareholders to exercise their rights of control. On the contrary these are the very attributes of the corporation that make it into such a remarkable and valuable institution.

Why? Three things: contract and market incompleteness, unenforceability, and infeasibility. Let me unpack that economic and legal jargon. The idea that shareholders bear the risks and rewards of the corporation rests on the notion that everyone else—namely, we as employees, customers, suppliers, and creditors—are protected by contracts that ensure that we are paid, supplied, and repaid. The firm is a 'nexus of contracts',[10] binding together the employees, customers, suppliers, and creditors. Only shareholders do not have contracts that ensure that they are paid a dividend or can claim their money back. Once invested, a shareholding in a firm becomes its permanent capital that cannot be claimed back and only sold to others through, for example, stock markets. So shareholders as a group are exceptionally exposed to the fortunes of the firm.

But that rests on the assumption that we as employees, communities, and creditors are indeed protected by contract. As the employees in the Cadbury factory in Somerdale when Cadbury was taken over by Kraft, those who work in the sweatshops in Bangladesh, or those who inhale the pollution of Beijing have experienced, contracts are very restricted. And as nations and taxpayers discovered during the financial crisis, even if they exist, they are not enforceable if the borrowers—the banks in that case—do not have the money to repay them.

Most seriously of all there are many for whom contracts and markets are simply irrelevant. They are not relevant in much of the developing world, such as for those living in the slums of Kibera in Nairobi. They are not even conceivable for future generations who do not have a voice let alone a contract to protect them from the destruction of what should be their as much as our rainforests and environment.

Shareholders are not therefore by any means the only party exposed to the misfortunes of corporations, and the more that we strengthen the rights and powers of shareholders, the more we threaten the interests of others. The Somerdale plant was closed by Kraft the acquirer of Cadbury to enhance the value of its acquisition; the sweatshops of the world are a product of Western corporations scouring the earth for lowest-cost suppliers; and the sale of inappropriate financial products is undertaken by banks to make money at the expense not for the benefit of others.

So long as the corporation is viewed as just an instrument of its shareholders then these problems will become worse and bring us to a point of social, political, and environmental catastrophe. But the solution is not simply to transfer control to another party—employees, customers, or the state. That merely creates other problems. Mutual organizations owned by their employees or customers are unable to raise substantial amounts of capital and therefore operate in low-capital industries such as retailing and wholesaling. Publicly owned corporations are bureaucratic, inefficient, and distorted by conflicting political influences.

Most seriously of all, control by employees, customers, the state, or shareholders comes at the expense of the party which is not represented at all—future generations. Mutual organizations demutualize to allow current generations of customers and employees to benefit at the expense of future generations. Founders of mindful corporations capitalize the future value of the entities that they create through initial public offerings. Hedge funds extract the capital value of corporations they target by seeking higher dividend payments and repurchases of shares. In other words, the 'financialization' and 'securitization' of corporations have converted them into rent-extraction vehicles for benefiting current generations of owners at the expense of future generations.

What makes the corporation so remarkable is that it equally has the power to do the opposite—to be our saviour and source of social as well as economic well-being—provided that we recognize that our intellectual conception of it is fundamentally wrong and that the separation of its control by management from its ownership by shareholders or its control by other parties is its attribute not its deficiency.

How can this be so? The law recognizes that the corporation is a legal personality distinct from its shareholders. Its directors owe a fiduciary responsibility to the members of the corporation who are in general its shareholders, but in so doing the directors may legitimately uphold the interests of many other parties—its employees, creditors, customers, and communities. The directors can and should balance the interests of different parties in pursuit of the prosperity of the corporation. And owners should ensure that the corporation pursues its long-term not just its immediate prosperity, which may, as the Court of Delaware, the

leading jurisdiction over US corporations, has reaffirmed on several occa-
sions, involve forgoing short-term for long-term shareholder returns.

But the delicate balance between the interests of different parties and
generations is jeopardized by an excessive focus on shareholder returns
or stakeholder interests. While the law permits and even encourages
directors to uphold the well-being of others, the market for corporate
control and the hedge fund activists make it increasingly difficult for
them to do so. That is why nearly every country in the world with the
exception of the United Kingdom protects management through long-
term stable shareholders, takeover defences, and board structures that
impede the replacement of management.

It is through the separation of management and long-term owners
from their shareholders that the corporation is able to commit first and
foremost to its purpose in delivering the largest social networks, the best
Internet search engines, the cheapest washing machines, or the most
reliable cars. To deliver these purposes it commits to many different
parties including but not exclusively its shareholders and to future
generations as well as to the present. And it is this notion of the corporation as a remarkable instrument of commitment rather than contract
or control that has been missing from our conception of the corporation. It is the power to commit to its purpose and to different parties
to different degrees in the delivery of that purpose that makes the corporation such a powerful institution.

The corporation is not a 'nexus of contracts' between the parties to the
firm. It is the opposite; it is a nexus of relations. Those relations are based
on trust. That trust depends on commitment and that commitment is to
the purpose of the corporation—a purpose that inspires and unites all to
a common goal of producing profitable solutions to problems of people
and planet. In so doing, the parties to the firm recognize and respect
their joint interests and contributions to the realization of the corporate
purpose and benefit from the mutual relations of trust that it engenders—
a more committed work force, more reliable suppliers, more loyal customers, and more supportive investors.

Why have we failed to recognize this until today? The answer is that
the failings of the corporation have not until recently been so manifest.
Adam Smith was writing in the second age of the corporation when it
was still a public instrument of Parliament. So while he recognized the
potential for the corporation to do damage, it was not the central
concern of his time. By the time we get to the third age and Alfred
Marshall, the corporation is owned by families and then individuals
who in many cases, such as the Barclays, Beechams, Boots, Cadburys,
Colmans, and Reckitts were people of high integrity and social

conscience—many Quaker families. It is as we move to the fourth age of the rise of the financial institution, the fifth age of the transnational corporation, and the sixth age of the mindful corporation that the power to defraud, destroy, and exploit becomes all too evident.

But while the mind of the corporation is remarkably nimble, the mind of man is not always so. We cling on to intellectual paradigms far beyond their sell-by date. As Schopenhauer said, 'All truth passes through three stages: first it is ridiculed, second it is violently opposed, and third it is accepted as being self-evident.'[11] As *The Economist* article illustrated, we are currently between stages one and two. The problem with accepting the normal rate of paradigm progression to stage three is that time is extraordinarily short and by then the damage that will have been done may be irreversible.

So before it is too late and before I exhaust your patience, let me then turn to what we need to do to reinvent the corporation for its seventh age—an age of what should be re-creation not cremation—the age of the trusted corporation.

The Trusted Corporation

The three key determinants of the corporation are purpose, ownership, and governance. If the purpose of the corporation is just to make profits then we are sunk. That is not the purpose of the corporation—it is not what it has been, it is not what it needs to be, and it is not what it should be going forward.

The purpose of the corporation is to do things that address the problems confronting us as customers and communities, suppliers and shareholders, employees and retirees. In the process it produces profits, but profits are not the purpose of corporations per se. They are the product of their purposes. All the most successful corporations know this to be the case, but what is much less well understood is how to do it and what it takes for those companies that are not doing it to do it. Some believe that they only have to say it in mission and corporate social responsibility statements and it will happen. That has no plausibility; the tough part is committing to purpose to an extent that it becomes irreversible, because only then is it credible.

Some of the most successful corporations in the world do exactly that. Examples are Bertelsmann the media company, Bosch the automotive supply company, Carlsberg the brewery, and Tata the Indian conglomerate and owner of Jaguar-Land Rover. All of these have one thing in common—they are all owned by what are termed 'industrial foundations'—foundations and trusts that own companies. These industrial foundations devote their profits to investing in their businesses and giving any surplus to charity. But the primary purpose of the industrial foundations is to ensure that the companies below them, such as Bosch and Carlsberg, abide by their purposes, principles, and values as set down by their founders. If they fail to do so then it is the boards of the foundations that take responsibility for this.

And herein lies the germ of understanding of how one goes from good intention to commitment. What define these successful and enlightened corporations are combinations of clearly defined purpose, stable and supportive ownership, and accountability of boards and directors to the fulfilment of that objective. These are the ingredients that translate the entrepreneurship of the founders into legacies that are of enduring value to humanity. Not only are these then worthy sentiments, they are commercial commitments. Consistent with this, while the financial performance of foundation-owned firms is not much better or worse than that of other firms of equivalent size and sector, their performance differs markedly in one respect—they survive. While matched samples of similar firms on average die within twenty years, foundation-owned firms typically survive for at least sixty years.[12]

What such enlightened corporations do is to deliver on their stated purpose by balancing and integrating the five different components of capital that comprise their business activities—human capital (employees, suppliers, and purchasers), intellectual capital (knowledge and understanding), material capital (buildings and machinery), natural capital (environment, land, and nature), social capital (public goods, trust, and social infrastructure), and financial capital (equity and debt). The balance has changed over time. In its first and second ages, the corporation was a public enterprise producing social capital in the form of canals and railways; in its third age it created material capital in the form of manufacturing industry; in its fourth age it augmented human capital in the service firm; in its fifth age it generated increasingly large amounts of financial capital in the transnational corporation; and in its sixth age intellectual capital has been most in evidence.

There is one form of capital that has never featured prominently in the corporation until recently and which, by contrast, has been consumed voraciously, and that is natural capital. One of the reasons why we stand on the precipice of cataclysm is the failure of the corporation to protect natural capital. But it is not its only failure because, in transitioning to financial and intellectual capital, the corporation has also jettisoned the social capital that originally defined its charter. A preoccupation with financial capital has come at the expense of the preservation of social as well as natural capital.

What is required is for corporations to balance their production and usage of different types of capital. As Chapter 6 discusses, to do this corporations need to have accounts that record their human, intellectual, natural, and social capital as well as material and financial capital. They should report their production of these assets and their usage and abusage in their balance sheets, and they should state their net worth in relation to all of them, not just their financial and material capital. To achieve this, as Chapter 7 will argue, company law should be reformulated to require corporations to articulate their purposes, to redefine the fiduciary responsibility of boards of directors to the delivery of their stated purposes, to produce accounts that measure their performance in relation to them, and to implement incentive arrangements that reflect their success in delivering them. The directors should thereby be accountable not simply to their owners but more generally to those in whose interests the corporation is being run.

It is hardly a revolution—capitalism not only survives, it flourishes, but its effect will be profound. It is a private contractual solution to the provision of corporate commitment that does not rely on either public ownership or public law and has a close parallel in existing corporate law. One of the most innovative developments of the last ten years has been the emergence of the benefit corporation in the United States. It has swept across more than thirty states in the United States, most significantly in Delaware. The benefit corporation is a company that has a stated public purpose alongside its commercial objectives. These are enshrined in its charter or its articles of association. What gives it teeth is that the board of directors has a fiduciary responsibility to uphold those public purposes and if they fail to do so then shareholders can seek injunctive relief to prevent them abusing the corporation's purposes.

Where it is potentially particularly powerful is in relation to the commanding heights of the economy—our banks, utilities (such as energy, telecoms, transport, and water companies), systemically important institutions, health service providers, and corporations with significant market power. At the moment we have just one instrument for aligning their interests with those of society and the public they are supposed to serve—regulation. But as commercial organizations whose primary purpose is to make money for their shareholders, their interests are diametrically opposed to those of the regulators who act as custodians of the public interest. As a consequence, they do whatever they can to avoid regulation and seek to turn regulation to a competitive advantage that deters entry of new firms.

That is why regulation has been such a failure. But convert banks and utilities into benefit corporations and make their licence conditions part of their public purpose then the fiduciary duty of the directors is no longer to avoid regulation to the benefit of their members but to promote their regulatory requirements as part of their corporate charters. Of course not all corporations will be enlightened in the purposes that they adopt and we should impose minimum standards across all firms in terms of bribery, corruption, human rights, market manipulation, market abuse, and environmental obligations. We should not tolerate social legislation put in place at the beginning of the nineteenth century to protect workers in the form of, for example, the Factory Acts in Britain, being systematically circumvented by transnational corporations contracting-out supply and employment to parts of the world that do not have such social legislation. The minimum standards should apply to the payment of living wages and safe and sanitary factory conditions at all stages in the supply chain and production process in every part of the world.

But we can do much better than that, as the founders of the industrial foundations have done. For various reasons they have chosen not to hand their companies on to their heirs, perhaps because they do not have them, trust them, or like them. The reason why this is a defining moment in the life of the firm is because it is at this point that entrepreneurs have achieved their commercial vision and accumulated their financial fortune. Their attention then turns to their legacy, and the industrial foundation model offers them the means of perpetuating it in a form in which not only their names but also their aspirations are preserved.

The John Lewis Partnership is such an organization. It is governed by a constitution based on an irrevocable 'settlement in trust' that establishes that the company should be run for the benefit of its employees in perpetuity. But British common law has an aversion to limitations on transfer of property and at the time of this settlement restricted it to twenty-one years after the death of someone living when it was adopted. In this case the relevant person was the current monarch Queen Elizabeth II. So at her funeral, Britain may not only lament the passing of its dear monarch but also the prospect of the demise twenty-one years later of another great British institution—the John Lewis Partnership.

And what will happen when Sergei Brin and Larry Page in Google and Mark Zuckerberg in Facebook have passed their sell-by date and passed into their solid coffin state? Who will then ensure that their corporate visions will be upheld? What this points to is a new form of philanthropy. Currently it can be characterized as engaging in rape and pillage while accumulating as much wealth as possible and then giving it away as an act of penitence in the form of a charity or foundation. That is the history of the robber barons of the past—the Carnegies, Mellons,

Rockefellers, and Vanderbilts. This has two drawbacks—first the creation of wealth involves substantial social damage in the process and second the wealth that is accumulated is not as productively employed as it might be. Reinvest it instead in productive enlightened corporations, and wealth creation is aligned with and assists in wealth disbursement. The social injustice of staggering inequalities of wealth is thereby converted into sources of protection of the most vulnerable through making successful entrepreneurs into enlightened corporate reformers.

But how can we convince the mass of existing unregulated rather than new or regulated firms to adopt more enlightened policies? If the only interest of their owners is in financial gain then the purpose of these corporations will remain firmly on financial performance. Pension funds, hedge funds, and sovereign funds will engage in active long-term sustainable governance only if they believe it to be in the interest of their beneficiaries—their pensioners, investors, and citizens—but not otherwise. Enlightened self-interest might encourage a move in this direction as evidence mounts of the superior financial performance of engaged, long-term sustainable investment, but we cannot afford to wait on this.

And we do not have to. The book will detail how a combination of corporate ownership, governance, accounting, laws, and regulation can spearhead the emergence of a new breed of enlightened commercially successful businesses. It will show how these can promote corporate purposes that yield human, social, and environmental as well as private benefits. It will demonstrate how these can enhance the trustworthiness of companies and turn them into vehicles for creating commitments we can trust. In other words, it will establish how we can move to the seventh age of the corporation—as the trusted corporation.

The Seventh Age

We have lost trust in corporations to look after our interests as customers, employees, communities, and nations. We have lost trust in them to pay people at the bottom of organizations properly in relation to those at the top, to pay their fair share of taxes, to look after the environment, to provide meaningful work, to avoid slave labour, and to employ people in safe and sanitary conditions in their supply chains.

Restoring trust in corporations is one of the most important issues of our age. Economists regard trust as a way of lubricating the wheels of economies by reducing the costs of transacting. But in a world of incomplete, unenforceable, and infeasible contracts, the significance of trust is much more than that. It is the essence of our survival as citizens and communities in a world of intense uncertainty where we rely on others not only to keep to their word but also to have deep empathy and interest in our well-being.

The corporation today is inhumane. It is inhumane because we have taken humans and humanity out of it and replaced them with anonymous markets and shareholders over whom we have no control. Stephen Hawking has warned of the consequence of removing humans from control of artificial intelligence and making us no longer masters of our own minds. We have already done that in the corporation by allowing markets not man to become masters of our mindful corporations.

Underlying this is the fact that we have systematically eradicated the humanities from the study of economics and business. That was not the original foundation of the Enlightenment in emphasizing rationality over religion. Adam Smith was careful to balance the importance that he attached to markets in the *Wealth of Nations*[13] with morality in *The Theory of Moral Sentiments*.[14] But that balance has been lost in the subsequent 250 years in emphasizing economic efficiency over ethics. We need to correct that as a matter of urgency and put humanity and the humanities back into business.

Restoring trust in corporations is urgent because without it our economic systems will continue to collapse, our financial systems to fail, and our environment to degrade. With it we can achieve greater levels of social well-being and economic prosperity than has been possible to date because ultimately a trusted corporation is a commercially successful corporation and the competitiveness of nations depends on the trustworthiness of their corporations.

2

Values

Man is the only animal that blushes. Or needs to.

Mark Twain

A Synthesis

A remarkable development has taken place. Microscopic cells, known as foraminifera, invisible to the naked eye, much less than 1mm in diameter, have become as large as 120mm in diameter to form shells containing many chambers. They have been so successful that the great pyramids and sphinxes of ancient Egypt were constructed of stone laid down by them.[1]

What allowed this to occur was a process by which algae colonized the holes of the foraminifera. The foraminifera benefited from the algae's photosynthetic capability to produce energy-giving sugars, and the algae benefited from the carbon dioxide and other metabolites produced by the foraminifera. There was a symbiosis between the two organisms that allowed them to flourish together.

The process took place over millions of years but what makes it particularly interesting is its primitive form in which a unicellular organism, the foraminifera, formed a relationship with another organism with very different but highly complementary properties. In other words, it is illustrative of a cooperative relationship that permeates all forms of life, and is the basis of evolution of much more complex types than the algae–foraminifera combination.

In fact, it is not only the basis of much biological evolution but also of organizational evolution. The traditional analogy of firms is with engineering not biological processes. A firm is a form of production in which different inputs—capital, labour, land, materials—are combined to produce an output of a good or service. It is a mechanical process that continues so long as the inputs are fed into the corporate machine and it stops when the inputs are no longer available.

This view of the firm is as inaccurate as it is uninspiring. A firm is an evolving entity as much as the organisms of life are evolving systems. It has a form of life that exactly parallels that of its biological equivalents. It is born through the combination of some primary agents. It grows through combining with other agents. It marries, produces offspring, spins off others, mutates, and dies. This is not just a play on words; it is a substantive feature of the nature of organizations in general and corporations in particular.

The significance of this reinterpretation of the firm is that it brings out many characteristics of business that remain disguised in more traditional descriptions. This chapter will emphasize three of them. The first is relationships, the second is consciousness, and the third is integrity and morality.

Relationships

The aspect of biology that is discussed most frequently in economics is competition and survival of the fittest. There is a strong parallel between the biologists' and economists' description of competition between species and firms. In both cases competition is pervasive and threatens their existence. Only the fittest survive, and over time, through random changes and competition for scarce resources, they evolve genetically in biology and behaviourally in economics to a form that is best adapted to the environment and industries in which they operate. Competition is therefore the means by which selection of the fittest occurs and the most resilient gene variants and corporate conduct are attained.

This neo-Darwinist interpretation has increasingly come to be questioned in biology. The issue that has arisen is whether the significance attached to competition has been at the expense of a potentially equally important consideration, and that is cooperation. In particular, it is difficult to explain the altruistic behaviour that is widely observed in nature in the context of the neo-Darwinist modern synthesis except in family kinships that share common gene pools.

In economics, cooperation relies on incentive mechanisms that promote mutually beneficial conduct amongst parties who would otherwise resort to destructive self-interested tactics. These incentives make cooperation trump selfishness. However, they are fragile. If circumstances in the future change then selfishness may re-emerge as a dominant strategy and unravel the basis on which cooperation is built today.

In biology and economics, competition rather than cooperation remains the driver of adaptation and economic advancement. The fight for survival, not innate altruism, converts the selfish gene and the selfish firm into bodies that possess beneficial and benevolent properties.

However, the example of the algae and foraminifera might caution us about the lesson that economics should learn from biology. The mutually beneficial synthesis did not rest on a fragile repeated game in which one organism could walk away from the other. Once the algae entered the foraminifera their interests were intertwined and their individual interests were subsumed in the collective. They were conjoined in a form that had properties that were distinct from those of their individual components.

It might at first be thought that this evolution of life does not occur in economics. But that is precisely what occurs in a corporation. When different parties contribute to the pool of capital in a firm they do so in a way in which they make binding irreversible decisions. Capital cannot be withdrawn again except when the operations of the firm are wound up. It is permanent capital in a similar manner to the permanence of biological structures and in particular not just with symbiosis—the cohabitation of dissimilar entities in an intimate relationship—but also with their eventual fusion resulting in the formation of new species—symbiogenesis.[2] The interests of the parties to a firm are intertwined in precisely the form of the creation of new organisms.

For the most part, economics emphasizes the importance of reversibility and the flexibility that derives from being able to shift resources to their most productive use at lowest cost. Impediments to the free operation of competition are viewed as undesirable. However, what the analogy with biological processes suggests is that the legal form of the corporation has created a structural solution to the problem of promoting cooperation. Both nature's and economics' solution is to establish structures that deliberately impose irreversibility.

One of the reasons for emphasizing the biological rather than engineering analogy of the firm is that it lends insights to the way in which cooperation as well as competition prevails in business. Relationships with machines are at best uni-directional—I might love the computer on which I am typing this manuscript but I doubt that my computer reciprocates my feelings. So it is impossible to construct a theory of relationships from an engineering view of the firm, and one of the reasons why there are such weak theories of cooperation in economics is because of the mechanistic basis of them.

By viewing corporations as living organisms rather than inert machines, biology reveals that the source of cooperation is the structure of corporations not just the conduct of their participants. It is not that the algae and foraminifera are engaged in a repeated game in which the involvement of one is conditional on the response of the other and vice versa into the indefinite future. It is not that their mutual interests are vulnerable to the whims of either. They no longer have a separate existence and their cooperation is irreversible.

Likewise once voluntarily adopting the corporate form, the providers of its capital are trapped in an embrace from which there is no escape. As with their biological counterparts, the interests of those who invest in the corporation are not just mutual or a partnership, they are joint. Their gaze diverts from their own to their collective horizons and the game of natural selection in which they are now engaged is the survival of their new corporate, not individual, forms.

What makes evolution towards the mindful corporation particularly striking in this regard is that it involves little in the way of either financial or material capital but it can nevertheless yield large amounts of value—intangible value. The agents that are bound together are not just the providers of financial capital but of human and intellectual capital, and they produce not just financial value but also social value in the form of social networks. It is sometimes suggested that human capital is inalienable in the sense that it cannot be separated from the human who possesses it. But that is precisely what happens in the mindful corporation—the human capital of individuals resides in the corporation, not just in themselves, and can only be extracted to a limited degree.

Corporations in this respect differ in significant ways from other business organizations such as partnerships where separate legal forms are not established. In partnerships, capital can be withdrawn on the agreement and departure of partners. They do not possess the permanence of the corporation or the irreversibility of symbiogenesis but are closer to teams where the parties cooperate so long as it is perceived to be mutually beneficial for them to do so.

As in the natural world in which we live, the wonder of corporate evolution is the diversity it creates. It develops new patterns of activity that previously did not exist. It allows us, its component parts, to produce benefits that we individually were incapable of realizing. And as it grows and multiplies, it yields ever-greater riches.

By viewing the corporation through the lens of biology we have literally breathed life into an otherwise moribund legal concept. We have created a vehicle that has as great a significance in terms of human evolution as the genetic components from which it derives. Indeed both nature and the corporation should probably be regarded as an indefinite set of permutations in which new forms of evolution can be propagated. We are by no stretch of the imagination at the end of means by which it will be possible to accelerate the mechanisms of evolution.

This multiplicity prevails so long as a further mechanistic view of the firm does not dominate, and that is the firm as a control mechanism. The agency concept of the firm regards it as an instrument of its owners, its shareholders, who employ agents, managers, to operate on their behalf. This master–slave relationship confers rights of control on owners to dictate how the corporation is run and the means by which they can exercise that control over their agents. These rights derive from their ability to propose motions and cast votes at shareholder meetings, appoint and remove their agents, and determine the basis on which agents are rewarded.

A control concept erodes diversity by imposing a single objective function of monetary value maximization on the organization and steers it away from the plurality of existences that we associate with the natural world. It therefore reduces an entity that is capable of a plethora of forms to one that has a singularity of purpose. It derives from a conception of the firm that regards it as having no separate existence from those who own it. There is no sense of it possessing self-determination in having a will that is distinct from its owners.

This leads us to a consideration of more than just the physical manifestation of the firm. What is particularly significant about the corporation as a binding device is not the physical body to which it gives rise, its *corpus*, but its mental state, its *mentis*, for just as humans have developed something that is more than a physical form, so too have corporations. And that something is their consciousness.

Corporate Consciousness

Consciousness is a difficult concept. It is difficult because in most respects it does not exist. We have minds, we have brains, we have brain cells, axons, neurons, and synapses but what, if anything, is consciousness beyond the constituent components of our brains? In considering consciousness, we are forced to move from biology to some of the most fundamental questions in philosophy, or at least that is what some people argue.

In his book *Mind and Cosmos*,[3] Thomas Nagel sets out the notion that one should think of consciousness as our ability to determine a set of relations that impute general laws and principles from our conceptions of our interactions with others. Those principles derive from our capacity to infer results from self-reflection on our condition within a broader universe.

Consciousness is a set of thought processes that allow us to position ourselves in relation to others. Nagel argues that this broad awareness and appreciation of our presence in a larger cosmos gives rise to a state of mind that is distinct from the biological laws which determine our physical evolution. It is not correct to say that consciousness simply derives from laws of natural selection and it is wrong to see the physical and mental processes as being reducible to this one single explanation.

Consciousness is the product of processes that reflect the development of our self-awareness. Whether that process is purposeful in having a specific goal is subject to debate. Whether it has a theological foundation in the existence of a god is even more controversial. Nagel argues that it is not necessary to impute theology—the goal of consciousness may simply be that of increasing value. In other words, the guiding hand that comes from consciousness steers us towards a world in which the evolutionary processes that underpin it result in increasing value.

What is value and how do we determine it? There are two views. The first is that it is the result of rational development reflecting a correct and appropriate weighting of our assessment of the desirability and benefits of different outcomes. This is what is termed a 'realism view' and it stands in contrast to a 'subjective determination' where value reflects sentiments and perceptions that differ across individuals.

The determination of value could occur completely independently of the physical evolutionary process, in which case it would have no bearing on life as it has emerged. Alternatively, it may act as pilot of how consciousness steers the evolutionary process. It may come from the way in which we perceive the world as is and how we respond to the alternatives that it presents to us. In this case, it would be wrong to regard normative notions of value as being distinct and separate from their positive counterparts. They are intertwined with each other.

Nagel rejects natural selection as a sufficient description of the evolution of the universe and argues that the weightings we place on different outcomes are an important determinant of our physical state. It is not simply that our self-reflection impacts on our consciousness and influences evolution but our consciousness is also integral to our assessment of the weightings to be placed on different values. They may be correct rather than subjective weightings reflecting a rational assessment of outcomes but nevertheless they interact with the way in which the world has and will evolve.

The issue that this raises in the context of corporations is whether the evolutionary processes of corporations are affected by conscious processes or are just the outcome of natural selection. Are competitive markets a sufficient description of the evolution of corporations or are they influenced by consciousness? This is a fundamental question because the prevailing view in economics is that competitive markets are the driver of corporate behaviour. They are an adequate description of the way in which corporations evolve. We do not have to introduce a conscious guiding hand—the unconscious one is sufficient.

Nagel's view of evolution questions that. If consciousness pervades natural processes presumably it influences commercial ones as well. It must be as relevant to combinations of individuals as it is to single individuals. If so, at what level does that consciousness exist? Does it reside in individuals or can it be attributed to the organizations themselves? Do corporations have a consciousness that is equivalent to that of individuals and is it distinct from or just an aggregation of the consciousness of their constituent individuals? In other words, do corporations have minds of their own?

In answering those questions we should go back to the notion of consciousness as imputing general principles and rules from conceptions of interactions with others. We as individuals have accumulated a body of knowledge that allows us to draw such inferences. Correspondingly a body of knowledge about the impact of corporations on other parties has been accumulated that allows them to have a conscious appreciation of their influence on others.

This knowledge, which has been accumulated from the study of business as an economic and social phenomenon, permits corporations to have a conscious realization of their role in their universes and societies that is equivalent to that of individuals. Like its biological equivalent, the corporate consciousness to which that experience and knowledge gives rise influences the evolution of firms and lends direction to the market processes to which they are subject.

As in the case of nature, the issue that this raises is what is the direction in which conscious behaviour takes corporations. Nagel's notion of increasing value has an obvious familiarity and attraction in the corporate world and leads us to the question of the source and determination of that value. Whose value is the corporation pursuing and who establishes what that value is?

A realism view would regard value as reflecting a rational weighting of the benefits that the corporation confers. It leaves no room for discretion. The corporation should be guided by a correct evaluation of the benefits it confers. A subjective view leaves considerable room for discretion and suggests that value is determined by sentiment and perception.

Either way consciousness places the determination of value centre stage in the corporation. The weightings that a corporation attributes to the benefits it confers are as important in its evolution as they are in species. They are more fundamental than the purpose and goals of the corporation, which derive from the determination of its value.

The biological concept of the corporation led us to view it as an entity that binds, but is distinct from, its constituent components. The philosophical notion of consciousness extends this to recognize its presence in the world outside and to regard the entity as guided by the pursuit of value that reflects the benefits it confers. Together they point to the importance of the corporation as an entity that cements relations within it and values its benefits outside.

While not diminishing the significance of competition and natural selection, the living conscious entity conception of the corporation stands in contrast to the current prevailing notion of it as a machine buffeted around by competitive processes over which it has no influence. It replaces the inert object with an entity with a degree of self-determination that reflects its conscious assessment of its place in its universe.

One of the interesting implications of this reinterpretation of the corporation is for the historical evolution described in Chapter 1—the six ages. Recall that the corporation developed from a trading to a public entity licensed by king and parliament, to a private body owned by families producing things then services, to an international organization devoid of any clear owner, finally to the mindful corporation.

This is precisely what the living organism concept would lead us to expect. The corporation starts as a component of the state with little or no separate identity. It is then given a private life of its own but initially remains tied by the umbilical cord of ownership to its families. It breaks away to a dispersed amorphous ownership and floats freely around the world. Finally, it moves to a weightless free form with negligible material components dominated by its conscious mindful state. What we await in the seventh age of the trusted corporation is this conscious entity fully recognizing its relation to its universe and its value in conferring benefits on others.

The conscious living concept of the corporation therefore allows us to understand its historical evolution. But it has an even more important role in determining how the corporation should evolve into its seventh trusted age. Not only does the corporation have an existence and the potential to improve our existence, we should be able to trust it to do this more than we can trust ourselves.

The emergence of artificial intelligence (AI) lends particular urgency to this consideration of corporate consciousness because we will not have to wait long for AI not only to control the people and transform the processes that deliver goods and services to customers and communities but also to become the mind of the corporation replacing boards of directors as the ultimate decision-taking authority. The algorithms that underlie AI will therefore determine the corporate purpose and values—whether they are benevolent or malign, self-interested or other-regarding, humane or inhumane. This takes us firmly from biology and positive notions of mind and consciousness into the realms of ethics.

Integrity

There are two ways in which the corporation has greater power to achieve value than individuals. The first is that it can bind together the constituent components involved in the production of value in a form that is not possible for us individually to do. We can look to contracts as ways of achieving relationships that are costly but not impossible for us to break. But those are not the same as the irreversible interlocking that occurs when capital is committed to a corporation in a form in which algae were committed to foraminifera.[4]

Second, it can form relationships with others that individually we are incapable of establishing. The reason for that is our weak power to commit and our low levels of integrity. The *Oxford English Dictionary* defines integrity as 'the condition of having no part or element taken away or wanting; undivided or unbroken state; material wholeness, completeness, entirety'. It is associated with 'the character of uncorrupted virtue, especially in relation to truth and fair dealing; uprightness, honesty, sincerity'. It involves individuals being true to themselves in possessing commitments and being true to those commitments.[5]

Philosophers have a somewhat ambivalent view of integrity as one of the virtues. Bernard Williams noted that integrity as a description of the state of an individual lacks association with moral purpose so that acting with integrity does not in itself possess virtuous attributes until the nature of that purpose has been determined.[6] Macbeth and a Nazi soldier are, for example, in this context potentially steeped in integrity in being committed to their purpose but without a purpose that would carry any approbation. It is the combination of integrity with acceptable or moral purpose that lends it its virtuous properties.

Furthermore, we should also acknowledge that deception is intrinsic to human and animals alike from the chameleon onwards. It is inherent to self-preservation. If honesty were unequivocally beneficial then we would have developed far more reliable mechanisms of demonstrating deception than the ones we possess today. Through natural selection, we would have inherited properties that would have allowed us to reveal our true state of integrity—precise digital signals of flashing red, for example, whenever we were behaving dishonestly rather than the imprecise analogues of blushing, perspiring, and sweating to which we are confined at present. We are victims of the inherent benefits that deception confers upon us.

And nowhere is this more in evidence than in commerce, where deception is endemic. In their book *Phishing for Phools,* George Akerlof and Robert Shiller describe a myriad of examples of how we are systematically manipulated by people who deliberately set out to deceive us into purchasing products and services that we cannot afford or do not need or want.[7] Such is the pervasiveness of deception that the desirable welfare properties that we associate with competitive markets simply do not apply, because they yield 'an equilibrium that is optimal, not in terms of what we really want'.[8]

Of course, one can address both the above two points by arguing that the purposes to which our integrity commits us should be other- rather than self-regarding in promoting social rather than private interests. But then integrity is no longer simply about the wholeness and completeness of the self but also embraces others. However, even if we were to extend the concept of integrity in this direction then it would still be unclear whether integrity makes a positive contribution to economic efficiency.

Integrity is sometimes but not always integral to economic performance because, in preserving commitments, integrity can be an impediment rather than a contribution to efficiency. Achievement of beneficial outcomes frequently involves deviating from previously held convictions. An employer may be justified in violating a commitment to lifetime employment of some employees to preserve that of others. Commitments to programmes of social welfare reform may have to be abandoned in the face of deteriorating economic conditions. Integrity to the self may stand in the way of the interests of others.

We are therefore left wondering whether integrity is of itself virtuous, whether it is in our self-interest let alone those of others, whether it is remotely plausible in real economic contexts, and whether, even if realistic, it would be desirable. We might therefore be tempted to consign integrity to the bin of economic irrelevance from which some economists might feel it should never have been allowed to escape.

This would be entirely the wrong conclusion. Rather than looking to us individuals as the source of inadequate integrity, we should focus on the corporations that we create as potential enablers and extinguishers of integrity. Our current conception of corporations sees them as manifestations of those who found, own, run, and regulate them. They have a purpose—financial in relation to commercial enterprises, philanthropic in relation to not-for-profits, and social in public organizations—that owners, governance, and management have a responsibility to deliver. Their frequent failure to do so is viewed as a primary cause of the many defects that have recently been revealed in our economic and financial systems.

However, there is another interpretation of corporations as integrity transformation devices, with the potential both to extinguish the very limited degree of integrity to which we are able to commit or to enhance it significantly. One of the striking features of the individuals who are willing to perpetrate manifestly unethical conduct in the workplace is that they will frequently be models of virtue in a family or domestic context. We undertake activities for commercial purposes that we would not dream of perpetrating with our friends or families. The corporation legitimizes that which we would regard as fundamentally unacceptable in our normal lives by virtue of the pursuit of profit and investors' financial interests—what might be termed '*sintegrity*'.

But by the same token, the corporation can do exactly the opposite. Instead of prioritizing profits, it can promote the interests of the customers and communities it seeks to serve—'*saintegrity*'. In the process it produces profits, but profits are not per se the purpose of the corporation. There are numerous examples of organizations that recognize this. Many are family firms, some are owned by foundations, and some by employees. One that was mentioned in the previous chapter and is frequently upheld as exemplary in the United Kingdom is the John Lewis retail partnership, which is owned by a trust that runs the firm in the interests of its employees. Another is the Swedish bank Handelsbanken that is a listed company with dominant shareholders who lend credibility to the preservation of the long-term relations it has established with its individual and corporate customers.

A common feature of such companies is the emphasis that they place on the dignity and well-being of their employees. They enhance not detract from employees natural interests in performing fulfilling, meaningful roles that command recognition and respect. In other words, they transform individuals' selfish interests into the pursuit of a collective goal that delivers a higher purpose than individuals are capable of achieving themselves. This is real integrity in integrating across individuals and time to create a whole that is greater than its parts. It is synergy that comes from the innate energy to contribute to communal endeavour that otherwise lies dormant or unattainable within us.

The capacity for the corporation to integrate integrity derives from its ability to provide checks and balances on individuals to ensure that they conform to a higher order than they can individually achieve. This comes from a combination of defined purpose, ownership, and governance of the corporation, as described in later chapters. In essence through these mechanisms of accountability, the corporation is able to translate our weak analogue signals of deception—*'mintegrity'*—into the digitally flashing red warnings that are required to preserve integrity—*'maxtegrity'*. It is therefore capable of providing us with a means of committing to a purpose of which we are otherwise bereft.

What is remarkable about the corporation is that it can be everything from a source of sintegrity to saintegrity and to convert our mintegrity into maxtegrity. In the process it allows us to move from being unsustainably anti-social creatures into sustainably social communities. Through defining its purpose the corporation provides the teleological foundation that Bernard Williams correctly identified as being a necessary but omitted component of virtuous integrity. Through its ownership, governance, and accountability, the corporation is able to provide the commitments required to convert norms into sustainable outcomes. In other words, it lays the deontic duties for transforming aretaic virtues into beneficial consequences.

Understanding what encourages and allows companies to adopt and commit to different forms of integrity is a critical research question in business. It is not to us frail individuals to whom we should look for the source of virtuous integrity but to our institutions and in particular corporations to legitimize what we as individuals seek but are otherwise incapable of achieving. This is because the corporation is capable of creating credible commitments to a common cause by integrating integrity into individual self-interests through the culture of organizations. One important manifestation of that is a culture of kindness and its adoption through kindness in leadership.

Kindness

Does kindness matter? Does it matter in leadership? These questions may sound banal. Kindness is a virtue, virtues are good, so kindness is good. As a virtue, it is relevant to all types of people: strong and weak, intelligent and stupid, leaders and followers. Kindness is therefore as inherently good in leadership as it is in any other walk of life.[9]

One might stop there and conclude there is little further to say on the subject. The reason there is much more to it is that kindness is not just a virtue—'it is good'—but also a value—'it does good'. The most obvious example of that is what one might term 'reciprocal kindness'. I will be kind to you if you are in turn kind to me. Indeed this form of kindness might not be a virtue at all. It is generated out of self-interest and can be entirely self-regarding. I would not do it for you were it not for the benefit that you confer on me. I will continue to be kind only so long as you are kind to me and as soon as you stop so will I.

This is the typical economist's rationale for altruistic behaviour. It is a repeated game sustained by mutual self-interest. But as with most repeated games it is fragile and vulnerable to the infinite regress problem that if either party is expected to renege at any time in the future then it will be impossible to start it in the first place. But the value creation of kindness is not restricted to reciprocity between two parties. Its real force derives from multiple interactions and in particular the creation of virtuous cycles.

One of the best-known examples of this is the YouTube 'kindness boomerang' video[10]—one person fulfils an act of kindness to another who is then prompted to engage in another act of kindness to someone else who in turn does a different act of kindness to someone else, and so on, until eventually someone returns an act of kindness to the first person. Its underlying principle is kindness begets kindness. Acts of kindness encourage them in the recipients as well as making the giver feel good. There is no reciprocity but recognition of the value of kindness on the part of the recipient, which enhances appreciation of the benefit of engaging in such acts of kindness.

The remarkable feature of such acts is that they cost nothing to give but create significant value—they are priceless in all senses of the word. They may appear superficially to be like chain letters but they differ in an important respect—they are not Ponzi schemes destined to fail because of their dependence on resources being infinite. Acts of kindness each create value and do not simply divert it from one party to the other. Indeed, as the kindness boomerang illustrates they can create virtuous cycles that continue indefinitely. The world will not be exhausted by acts of kindness in the way in which it is by chain letters—on the contrary it can be infinitely enriched.

This relates to the significance of kindness in an organizational context and in particular in regard to leadership. One argument for emphasizing kindness in the context of leadership is that it moderates the excesses of authority. It is all too easy for leaders to abuse their authority to the detriment of their subordinates. It is reinforced by such convictions that 'leaders have to take hard decisions', 'it is kind to be tough', and 'kindness is a sign of weakness'. But there is a more significant justification for kindness in leaders, which is that organizations can enhance the likelihood of boomerang kindness. The virtuous cycle is only as strong as its weakest link, and the boomerang will not complete its journey if anyone in the cycle fails to pass on kindness to others. What a kind leader can do is to establish a corporate culture in which the value of kindness is recognized throughout the organization and is therefore widely if not universally adopted.

The appreciation of kindness as not just a virtue but also a value, and the significance of leadership in converting kindness as an individual virtue into a corporate value is the reason why kindness in leadership is so significant. It transforms the micro individual virtue into a macro corporate value. Furthermore, if kindness in leadership prevails beyond the corporate world in public policy and government, it extends corporate into communal, national, and ultimately global value. Kindness becomes a value without frontiers and an antidote to the selfishness that is widely perceived to have become a universal affliction.

Leaders can create cultures and social norms of kindness in their corporations and societies, where the value of kindness is recognized and valued. But they can equally fail to do so or still worse denigrate kindness to a point that companies and nations disintegrate into a state of self-interest, greed, and intolerance. They can, in other words, create organizations and institutions of 'saintegrity' or 'sintegrity'. Their power to do so in equal measure lends them a moral authority that extends well beyond the economic and financial significance with which leadership is commonly associated.

Implications

The biological view of the corporation led us to appreciate the importance of relations in its development and the way in which the corporation is able to provide binding commitments within it. The conscious concepts suggested that the evolution of the corporation is also influenced by its perception of its external relationships. These were reflected in the way in which it determined its value to the societies in which it operated.

This final section of the chapter points to the way in which the corporation can achieve higher as well as lower levels of integrity than its individual components through its organization and structure. Its external as well as internal commitments can be lent credibility by its self-governing arrangements. It can reinforce the self-regarding attitudes of its constituent members or it can restrain them and strengthen other-regarding components that promote rather than diminish integrity.

Value lies at the top of the defining elements of the corporation and below it sit purpose and the ownership and governance that are required to deliver purpose and sustain the value of the corporation. This animate view of the firm has numerous empirical implications that stand in marked contrast to its current inanimate conceptualization. As a production function and control device, there should be an optimal ownership and governance arrangement that achieves the single objective of monetary value maximization. To the extent that there is currently diversity of ownership and governance forms then over time there should be convergence on a single best form. It is merely a matter of time before we learn the optimal structure and control system for maximizing financial value.

That optimal structure has often been associated with the Anglo-American system of shareholder ownership and control, and there has, at least until recently, been a widely held view that the world was converging on it. In contrast a living, conscious view of the firm sees value in diversity and richness as well as riches in varieties of corporate forms. Diversity should prevail and persist, not only because there is no single optimal ownership and governance arrangement, but also because it is a source of innovation and inspiration for the creation of new ideas and activities.

Corporate life is as enriching as its anthropomorphic equivalent, and we should expect both the history and current nature of the corporation across the world to reflect this. While the inanimate, engineering view predicts steady convergence on a single structure, the living, conscious form anticipates divergence, persistence, and multiplicity. We will subject these alternative views to both an extensive historical and international comparative analysis in Part 2 of the book. We begin in Chapter 3 by describing how ownership of the corporation has evolved from its origins in a flock of geese in the Capitol in Rome, and then in Chapter 4 we will examine more recent and current international comparisons of ownership and control around the world. But let us first join a flock of fellows of Oxford University in the Sheldonian, gaggling vociferously about one particular corporation.

Part 2
Provenance

'Their gods are not our gods, their people are not our people.' The words reverberated like a bolt from the heaven depicted on the ceiling above the assembled congregation in the Sheldonian Theatre in Oxford. They struck at the heart of a community of scholars whose *raison d'être* was to embrace not exclude ideas and lines of enquiry. There was an uncomfortable shuffling of bodies in the excruciatingly uncomfortable seats of the Sheldonian. The Vice-Chancellor sat slumped in his ornate chair, with his cap precariously perched on his head as if to hide the acute embarrassment on his ever-reddening face.

What brought the Scholars and Masters of Oxford University together in such large numbers for a rare meeting in this fine building designed by Christopher Wren, the architect of St Paul's Cathedral in London, was an offer of £20 million for the construction of a new department of the University—a business school. Why a seemingly generous gift should be the source of such controversy and gossip in the Senior Common Rooms was the fact that the building was to be erected on the most hallowed of English turf, a cricket pitch, and one that the University had previously promised would be preserved in perpetuity. At issue was whether the leadership of the oldest university in the English-speaking world had the right to claim that perpetuity would be terminated just thirty years after the promise was first made.

While this was superficially the subject at issue, it masked the real source of controversy. It was not the building or its location that were the cause for concern; it was what was going to happen inside it—the study of business. One might as well have proposed the creation of a brothel as a business school for the entertainment of the pinstriped, jet-setting, Porsche-driving wheeler-dealers who were going to occupy it in the name of management studies. Their gods were mammon, money, and mansions not maths, morality, or music, and their people were Maxwell, Murdoch, and Madoff, not Mill, Moses, or Mozart.

The debate concluded and the assembled congregation filed out through one of two doors marked yea or nay to register their support or opposition to the motion proposing the construction of the building. They returned to hear the result: 214 in favour of the motion; 259 against. The motion was defeated.

A muffled exclamation of surprise, indignation, and delight reverberated around the Sheldonian as those present began to comprehend the enormity of what they had just done. They had rejected a £20 million donation, torn up years of planning for a new department of the University, and sent a message to the world that Oxford was too precious for business. But above all, they had delivered a bloody nose to a university administration which many of them felt needed to be put in its place and made to realize that it was the rank and file of the university academics—the working dons—not the bureaucrats or a rich donor who were ultimately in charge.

As they dispersed along the damp, dark lanes of Oxford, the dons felt an inner sense of contentment with a job well done. And as they wended their way home to tell their families of this momentous occasion, they saw fireworks and bonfires illuminating the winter skies in celebration not just of their achievement but the attempted destruction of another great British institution—the Houses of Parliament. It was the fifth of November 1996—Guy Fawkes Night, a night indelibly printed on the minds of every British schoolchild with the words:

> Remember, remember!
> The fifth of November,
> The Dons' treason and plot;
> I know of no reason
> Why the Congregation's treason
> Should ever be forgot!

3

Evolution

Not only is there no God but try getting a plumber on a Sunday.

Woody Allen

Immaculate Conception

The reason why the Congregation's treason should never be forgot is that what they had rejected was not a donation, building, or business school but something much more significant—the study of one of the most important ideas in the history of mankind. The idea is not science, the state, or religion. It is not an idea that is attributed to any particular inventor, author, or scholar, or whose origins can be dated with accuracy. But it is an idea that clothes, feeds, and houses us, employs us, and invests our savings. And it is the source of our economic prosperity and the growth of nations around the world.

It is a remarkable idea because it involves conceiving of a person that is of neither flesh nor blood. It is a person like us but not of us, with neither physical presence nor human form. It can contract and be contracted, employ and be employed, sue and be sued, just like us. It is the creation of parliaments not parents, of statute not sex, of the law not lust. It is our doppelgänger and to signify its human form we have given it a name that derives from the Latin for body—*corpus*. It is the corporation.

The corporate enterprise has its origins in the parallel evolution of two institutions. Remarkably it is a story that has never been very clearly told, and an understanding of it provides important insights into the nature and purpose of the organization we possess today. The first institution is the corporation and the second is the partnership.

The origin of both institutions can be traced back to Roman times.[1] In Ancient Rome, there were two types of legal contracts by which people could be joined together. The first was the *societas* and the second was the *collegium*. A *societas* was formed by the consent of the partners, *socii*, to undertake commercial and other activities. Examples include clothes, financial services, grain, maritime transport, and wine. The partners made a contribution in the form of money, labour, skill, or in-kind goods. They were responsible for the liabilities of the *societas* and had a right to its claims. They could determine their shares of profits and losses, and some partners could be excluded from losses, though no partner could be entirely excluded from a share of the profits. The *societas* was dissolved on the agreement of the partners or in the event of the withdrawal or death of a partner.

The *societas* therefore lacked permanence and did not possess legal personality. There was one exception: the *societas publicanorum*. It owes its existence to distrust in Ancient Rome of bureaucrats. To avoid them, public services were contracted out to *publicani*, public contractors, who built and maintained public buildings, minted coins, and collected taxes. Their functions included the feeding of the white geese on the Capitol, which had been recipients of government-sponsored meals ever since 390BC when their honking forewarned the Romans of the approaching Gauls.

These long-term, large-scale public projects required an organizational structure that could persist beyond the term of office of any one *publicanus*. A solution was found with the creation of the *societas publicanorum*, whose life continued indefinitely after the departure of any particular partner. It could own property and be bound by contracts arranged by one of its partners. In that respect it bore a close resemblance to the second type of legal form in Rome, the *collegium*—an association, *corpus habere*, or corporation—formed by three or more people bound together in office for a common purpose. The *collegium* could hold property, employ and be employed, and sue and be sued. It was in particular associated with trade guilds of, for example, doctors, dyers, painters, shoemakers, and weavers, and religious associations.

The *societas publicanorum* could raise finance from shareholders, *participes*, who traded their shares, *partes*, just like a modern corporations. By the second century BC, stock ownership in the *societas publicanorum* was widespread with 'almost every citizen' invested in government leases.[2] Not only were privatization and contracting-out invented two millennia before Margaret Thatcher, so too was popular capitalism.

The Roman conception of the corporation was an arrangement for the delivery of public services. Corporate property was described as *res universitatis*, universal property owned by all the citizens of a town or municipality, to distinguish it from individual property. The importance of organized bodies over individuals had of course been well understood by many civilizations over a long period of time. What

Roman law introduced was the idea that such organizations could be legal entities in their own right with a legal personality that was distinct from the individuals who comprised them.

It is unclear whether this personality was a legal fiction that depended on the law for its existence or a reality on which the law just conferred certain rights but, in any event, its effect was profound. 'The corporation law of every modern nation, whether its system of general law be the Civil Law or the so-called English Law, is based on this conception of the Roman Law.'[3] 'It is not often that jurisprudence can make a discovery comparable to the discoveries made by other sciences or arts . . . but here there is something that we may fairly call a discovery, though it was made by no one man and no one age.'[4]

The Roman Empire flourished with the *societas publicanorum* and contracted with its demise. The publicans became 'unsurpassed in fraud, avarice, immodesty, and audacity'[5] and embroiled in power struggles with the senatorial aristocracy from the first century BC. One graphic, and one might say crass, illustration of this is associated with Marcus Licinius Crassus, the third member of the First Triumvirate with Caesar and Pompey and the then wealthiest man in Rome. Some of his wealth was acquired through such conventional means as the selling of slaves. However, his most notorious method exploited the fact that at the time there was no fire service in Rome. Instead, as reported by Plutarch in his life of Crassus, Crassus would bring round his own fire service, his slaves, and negotiate with the owners of burning properties and those of endangered neighbouring properties over how much they would be willing to sell their properties for. If they did not agree to his fire sale offers then he would let the house burn down and then rebuild it with his slave labour.

Not unreasonably then limitations were imposed on the activities of the *societas publicanorum*, and, with the change from Republic to Empire, the government was less dependent on the publicans and more on public administration through a permanent bureaucracy. Privatization gave way to nationalization and with it the growth of industries, such as mining, that had previously enjoyed rapid technological innovations, declined.

Towns and Universities

The lasting contribution of the corporation was to the subsequent development of new institutions and forms of administration. Municipal corporations played an important part in the governance of the

Roman Empire, first in the towns near Rome then in Italy then in the rest of the Roman world, creating a system of self-government under Rome's supervision. This in turn gave rise to the adoption of corporations by former Roman colonies.

In English law the corporation owed its origins to the recognition of the rights and duties pertaining to the residents of cities and towns, such as London, by charters granted to them by William the Conqueror.[6] Several centuries later it was transported to another colony. The government of the Massachusetts Bay Colony exercised its authority through the Charter of the Massachusetts Bay Company, which, by the Cambridge Agreement of 1629, was taken to America so that the company could erect a self-governing religious commonwealth, a 'City of God in the wilderness'.[7]

The corporation has been a source of knowledge and invention as well as government. Our institution, the university derives from the fact that in the twelfth and thirteenth centuries teachers (in the case of England, France, and Germany) and students (in Italy and provincial France) incorporated institutions of learning separate from the cathedrals and monasteries of which they were previously a part. It is therefore particularly ironic that in 1996 Oxford should have rejected business studies because, as one of the oldest examples of the university, it is one of the oldest examples of a corporation.

Oxford University is a federation of thirty-eight colleges, each of which is a legal entity in its own right. They are brought together under the auspices of another legal entity—the University of Oxford. Each college can contract and be contracted, employ and be employed, sue and be sued, just as the University can. They have their own governing bodies, responsible for overseeing the provision of teaching students and the upkeep of the fabric of the medieval buildings. It is a complex legal structure that gives both Oxford and Cambridge universities their distinctive features and has placed them at the forefront of scholarship and learning for 900 years.

Important though the corporation was to public administration and the creation of knowledge in universities, its main contribution was still to come, many centuries later, to the wealth, competitiveness, and growth of nations. But before that, there was another quite unexpected place where the corporation was to make an appearance after its demise in Ancient Rome.

A Soulless Sole

We do not normally associate the Church with the promotion of innovative business practice but during the late eleventh, twelfth, and thirteenth centuries, the Roman Catholic Church developed a body of corporation law within the system of canon law.[8] It differed appreciably from Roman law in rejecting the Justinian requirement that only institutions recognized by the imperial authority could be granted the privileges of corporations, and instead it conferred the same rights on alms-houses, hospitals, the bishopric, and the Church itself.

The trend of medieval litigation favoured the members of the corporation in relation to its head. The bishop as head of the Church in his diocese sought support from members of his chapter, i.e. the clergy, when conferring privileges, managing property, and judging cases. This was part of a process of development in intellectual thinking in the twelfth century by which reason was no longer the privilege of aristocratic society but an attribute of individuals of equal moral standing. 'The role of reason was being democratized. Reason ceased to be something that used people, and became something people used.'[9]

The canon law concept of the corporation differed significantly from Roman corporation law in four respects. First, it was not dependent on imperial authority for recognition of liberties and privileges. It could be created by any group of individuals with a common purpose and the required structure. Second, it was not only a public corporation that could exercise judicial authority over the corporation, instead any corporation could have 'legislative and judicial jurisdiction over its members' and 'by becoming members of a corporation individuals could be deemed to have accepted its rules.'[10] Third, authority was not only exercised by the corporation's representatives, whose powers derived from birthright or imperial patronage, but also by the ensemble of members. Fourth, the Roman law maxim that 'what pertains to a corporation does not pertain to its members' was rejected and instead the property of the corporation was perceived to be 'the common property' of its members.

In effect, canon law swept aside Roman concepts in establishing corporations that possessed freedom of incorporation, private ordering, delegation of decision taking, and common ownership. These rules and concepts of canon law reflected 'Germanic ideas of the corporation as a fellowship *Genossenschaft*, with a group personality and a group will, in contrast to the Roman idea of a corporation as an "institution", whose identity is created by a higher political authority'.[11] They were fused with Roman institutional ideas of the corporation as having a head empowered to perform acts that the corporation could not undertake itself, for example in relation to administration of property and resolution of disputes.

The corporation was used to reconcile the immortality of the offices of the Church with the mortality of its officers and to separate the ownership of its property from holders of its offices. This was done through a particularly distinctive form of the corporation, the corporation sole—a corporation comprising just one person.[12] The corporation sole provided a means of ensuring that the Church retained possession of its property, parish churches, and monasteries by separating them from its parsons and monks. The parson and monks were owners of the churches and monasteries not in their own right but as corporations.[13]

Furthermore, since the corporation sole was not a real person, it could not possess a soul and could not itself be held responsible for delict of duty by its officers. The corporation thereby protected the Church from obligations to surrounding communities. The corporation sole therefore possessed two key features of a corporation: permanent capital, namely the property of the Church, and separation between ownership by the Church and control of its affairs by its officers.[14]

The corporation was not just a convenient organizational arrangement. By rejecting the Roman notion that only public corporations had legislative jurisdiction over their members or rights of ownership over their property, the corporation elevated ecclesiastical law to that of other legislative forms. Unlike universities, the Church's authority and legislative power did not merely derive from the conferment of royal charter. Through the corporation, canon law asserted its position in regard to spiritual matters alongside the secular politics of kingdoms, feudal systems, and towns in governing the lives of the people.

The corporation was therefore used in creating new public institutions to manage public works, towns, guilds, seats of learning, and religious institutions, and by the thirteenth century these were flourishing in a variety of different forms. However, the corporation was not performing business or trade. For that, the other legal form with a far longer pedigree, the partnership, had already established itself as the preferred instrument for conducting business.

Islamic Routes

With the collapse of the Roman Empire, much of Western Europe went into decline but there was one part of the world that staged a remarkable renaissance by embracing institutions and laws of the ancient world. The Islamic Golden Age dates from the middle of the seventh to the thirteenth century. Its commercial activity flourished on the back of the *mudaraba*, a form of business partnership.

The *mudaraba* was used to solve a problem that confronted Islamic commerce of how to reconcile the strict prohibition on the payment of interest with rewarding providers of capital. It had its origins in the Code of Hammurabi, the sixth king of Babylon between 1792 and 1750BC. The Babylonian partnership *(tappûtum)* was defined in the Code according to the following principle: 'If a man has given silver to a man for a partnership, they shall divide the profit or loss there may be in proportion before a god.'[15] It was developed in the neo-Babylonian Empire between 626 and 539BC in the form of the *harrānu* contract that organized trade and business partnerships on an interest-free basis. The partnerships typically but not always divided the profit equally between the financing and working partners.[16]

In the *mudaraba* the profits were split between the partners to an enterprise according to a formula they negotiated in advance. The liability of a passive investor was limited to his own investment while liability for damages fell entirely on the merchant causing them. The partnership was legitimized by the fact of having been practised by the Prophet himself.[17]

The *mudaraba* was more flexible than its nearest equivalent in the Talmud, the *isqa*, which dictated equal profit shares between merchant and investor. Even after Maimonides' codification of Jewish law, the *Mishneh Torah*, in the twelfth century, the *isqa* still required the merchant to accept liability for part of the principal and his profit share to exceed his share of liability.[18] On the back of the *mudaraba*, Muslim trade expanded from China to Spain, and from the Black Sea to Zanzibar. With it, it carried commercial law, introduced arithmetic, and spread Arabic across three continents.[19] It is regarded as the forerunner of the *commenda*, which originated in tenth- or eleventh-century Italy and became the foremost legal instrument in medieval Mediterranean trade.[20]

Flexible though it was, the *mudaraba* had its deficiencies. It was designed to avoid unjust enrichment for modest ventures of short duration initiated by a small group of partners. It was not suited to large, long-term projects that employed many people. Any partner could terminate a partnership by simply informing their co-partners of their wish to do so and their death automatically nullified a partnership. Most partnerships lasted for a few months and consisted of two people; few exceeded a year and involved more than five people. They lacked permanent capital, employees who were willing to accept the liability of partners, or the ability to bind themselves or their partners to contracts with other firms. In other words, they did not possess legal personality or the corporate form of the *societas publicanorum*.

There was an alternative long-term arrangement, the *waqf*, an unincorporated trust, which emerged about a century after Muhammad, in the eighth century AD. It bore some resemblance to the *societas publicanorum* in so far as it delivered public services, such as drinking water, pavements, and inns for travellers, some of which survive to this day. However, it was a trust not a corporate body. It existed to protect the founder's assets and ensure that his will was upheld in perpetuity. The terms of the trust were irrevocable and conferred no discretion on its caretakers, the *mutawalli*, to alter its purpose or redeploy its assets.

There were therefore two organizational forms—a highly flexible partnership for promoting short-term low capital ventures involving a small number of individuals, and a rigid trust for the deployment of founders' assets in perpetuity. What was not available, and did not emerge for more than a millennium in the Middle East, was an organizational structure that was perpetual, well capitalized, and contractually entrusted to bind and deploy assets and employees as it deemed appropriate. In other words, there was no corporate form in which the management of the organization could function separately from its ownership.

The failure of such an organization to emerge had slow but insidious consequences for the Middle East. It could not keep pace with the larger, better-capitalized entities that were emerging elsewhere in the world. Between 1000 and 1600, the Middle East's share of world gross domestic product fell from 10 per cent to 4 per cent,[21] and with it its influence on commerce, culture, and language began to wane.

The significance of organizational form in this regard is illustrated by one particular example. Just like their European counterparts, *madrasas*, the Islamic colleges, were founded as trusts. However, while the colleges of Oxford and Cambridge were self-governing legal entities that determined their own destiny, the madrasas were run according to the terms of their founding *waqf*s. As a result, their curricula and modes of teaching became ossified during a period in which European universities were embracing new forms of scholarship and learning.

So the corporation was a tremendous vehicle for creating institutions but not undertaking business and trade, and the partnership for conducting business and trade but not establishing institutions. The corporation was not used in raising finance and the partnership was not suited to large-scale administration. What then happened was the merger of the two: the emergence of funding for corporations and of administrative structures in partnerships. In essence, this was the entry of one form of organization, the partnership, into another, the corporation, and it resulted in one of the most important forms of not just symbiosis but symbiogenesis—a new species of organization. We will start with the partnerships.

Cum Panis

While the corporation was consolidating its position in the Church, the partnership was moving west from the Middle East to the shores of Italy. The *commenda* partnership became in the Middle Ages one of the most frequent arrangements for organizing commerce by land and sea. It was the means by which capitalist nobles and bourgeois could participate in trade without carrying it on themselves. The *commenda* (from the Latin *commandare* 'to deposit, trust, or lend') involved investors bearing all the risks of the capital and being entitled to a share of the profits (usually three-fourths), and managing borrowers bearing all risks of labour and keeping the rest of the profits. Third parties only had claims against the managing borrowers and not the lenders who had limited liability.

The oldest preserved *commenda* contract dates from 1072.[22] It appears frequently in the Cairo Geniza, a collection of 300,000 Jewish manuscript fragments found in the Ben Ezra synagogue in Cairo. The collection includes correspondence and contracts from the early part of the eleventh century relating to the trade of Cairo Jews and it records that they used the Muslim *mudaraba* in preference to the Jewish *isqa*, confirming that indeed the *commenda* was exported from the Middle East to Europe.

The active partners in the *commenda* began to divide their ships into shares and sold shares or *carati* (reflecting their division into twenty-four parts) to several owners. In the fourteenth century, the city-state of Genoa used the multi-share *commenda* as a way of funding state projects and, as a precursor to John Law's ill-fated attempts in France 300 years later, in 1407 created a *carati* bank to manage the state debt and exploit the state colonies.

Alongside the *commenda* was the *compagnia* (from *cum panis*, companion or 'sharer of the same bread') which was a partnership of relatives that involved investment of a limited sum for a limited time of between one and five years but for which liability was unlimited (what later became known as the 'general partnership'). It derived from the *societas* in which partners pooled their capital and labour, and shared risks and rewards in an unlimited form.

Giant Italian (in particular Florentine) super-companies emerged on the back of this in the thirteenth and fourteenth centuries, of which Acciaiuoli, Bardi, and Peruzzi were the most notable. These firms were involved in the flourishing trade in commodities, particularly in wool. To gain access, they required franchises and concessions from monarchs, which they secured as a form of repayment on their loans. England, as a main exporter of wool, was particularly important in this regard, and the Italian companies were heavily involved in lending to the English monarchy.

Their activities were funded by participation of wealthy individuals in the fixed term *compagnia*—40 per cent of the Peruzzi first company (1300 to 1310) capital was contributed by ten outsiders—and investments by small savers for which Peruzzi opened a bank branch in Naples in 1302—a structure not dissimilar to the parallel family ownership and shareholder investment in listed companies around the world today, described in the next chapter. Ensuring prompt repayment was key, and this was achieved by strong pressure being exerted on government agencies, with, if necessary, recourse to the monarch.

The firms developed a network of branches across Europe. But there were two deficiencies of the super-company structure. First, there was no permanent capital to fund the businesses. Thus, when on threat of the imposition of a wealth tax in Florence in 1324, investors wished to conceal their investments, subscriptions to the fourth Peruzzi Company halved from li.118,000 to li.60,000. Secondly, the integrated nature of the partnership made it exposed to losses in any one branch and dependent on firm central leadership from the senior partner. In particular, the joint and several liabilities of partners made them vulnerable to actions by other partners that bound the entire partnership. Therefore, threat of default by Edward III led Bonifazio, Peruzzi's chairman, to go to England in 1338 where he judged the company's survival lay. However, this came at the expense of providing central direction to the business and by 1343 the company was bankrupt.

Some of these deficiencies were averted in the Medici bank in the next century. It organized its activities in branches, each of which were legally independent partnerships. Thus failures of the London and the Bruges branches in 1472 and 1481 respectively did not bring down the whole business. Likewise, a Bruges municipal court threw out a claim for damages in 1455 against the Bruges branch of the Medici Bank brought by a purchaser of defective packing of nine bales of wool from the London branch on the grounds that the Bruges and London branches were separate partnerships and that claims should be made against the London not the Bruges branch.

The branches operated according to their articles of association, which stipulated the purpose of the branch, the capital that was subscribed, how the profits were to be divided, and the restrictions on the authority of the managers. For example, the articles of the Bruges branch restricted the granting of credit to *bona fide* merchants and manufacturers and ruled out extending loans to princes. However, the company remained dependent on strong central leadership, which was not forthcoming after the death of Cosimo in 1464. In particular, several of the branches, such as Avignon, London, and Naples, were heavily exposed to lending to sovereign borrowers. Despite the fact that the super-companies, the Acciauoli, Bardi, and Peruzzi, had been wrecked by lending to English kings and other sovereigns, the Medici 'were unable to steer clear of it and foundered on the same reef'.[23]

So by the middle of the fifteenth century, the partnership had adopted quite sophisticated 'hub and spoke' methods of managing businesses on an international dimension. They were beginning to adopt the administrative structure of corporations. Meanwhile, the corporation was emerging in its most decisive guise alongside its public and religious functions in a different part of Europe.

A Guilded Age

The two deficiences of the unlimited and the limited liability partnerships, the *societas* and the *commenda*, namely the limited period of the partnership undermining the provision of long-term capital and the absence of well-established central governance arrangements, were precisely the advantages possessed by the English guilds. In a guild, established before the Norman Conquest based on the Roman *collegium*, property was granted for the guild 'to possess now and hence-forth', implying that the body was to continue indefinitely.[24] After the Norman Conquest, guilds took on a trading function, which in turn developed into craft guilds and companies of merchants in the fourteenth century. One in particular, the Staplers, became involved in overseas trade. At the end of the fourteenth century it received the first charter for foreign trade to the countries bordering the North Sea and the Baltic.

In addition, these bodies evolved a governance structure during the fourteenth century involving a governor, assistants, and deputies. The governor was given powers of executing justice amongst English merchants, and in 1404 the Staplers were granted rights to make statutes and ordinances for the discharge of the duties of the deputies and to punish English subjects who disobeyed these rules. As corporate bodies, the guilds were therefore able to enact by-laws. Similar privileges were subsequently bestowed on the Merchant Adventurers and the Eastland Company.

So long as trade remained close at hand there was not much of a requirement to raise capital. While there might be rules requiring freemen to employ capital according to the terms of the fellowship, there was no central pooling of capital. However, the exploitation of further trading opportunities required more substantial investments to be made. To achieve this, a fusing of the partnership principles of the *societas* with the perpetual life and governance structure of the guild-merchants was required.

The first form this took was the regulated company that extended the guild principle into foreign activities. In the regulated company, each member traded with his own stock and on his own account subject to the rules of the company. Charters were acquired to confer a monopoly for the members of the company. Essentially, the regulated company was a restrictive practice that prevented competition occurring between members and allowing monopoly benefits to be exploited. The Merchant Adventurers were examples of this form.[25]

The distinguishing feature of the joint stock company was that members traded on a common rather than individual account and joint stock. The first example of this was the Russia Company, which started its activities in 1553 under the governorship of Sebastian Cabot. The company raised £6,000 from £25 shares. The primitive type of company was formed for a single expedition at the end of which it was wound up. The Russia Company was ahead of its contemporaries in having a few stocks in the sixty-seven years to 1620. The stock corporation also played an important role in the syndicates that were employed by England in the war against Spain in the second half of the sixteenth century. While both Portugal and Spain organized and financed exploration through the state, England chose the self-governing guilds. The state-run organizations had the advantage of access to financial resources but suffered from their cumbersome central bureaucracy.

Go East, Young Man

A similar process was followed in the Netherlands with ports forming trading companies to organize activities in the Indian Ocean. To avoid competition these were consolidated in 1602 into one, the Dutch East India Company. A distinctive feature of the Company was that unlike the *commenda*, it did not have to return capital to investors immediately on completion of each voyage. Initially it could retain members' capital for ten years, and in 1623 it passed an amendment that made the capital perpetual. In return members were allowed to trade their shares on the open market.

In contrast, the English East India Company operated on conventional trading company lines liquidating capital at the end of each voyage. The nature of trading activities in the East Indies created financing requirements for ships, provisions and equipment, labour, and goods. The innovation of the East India Company was in fusing the corporation with joint stock. Whereas the Dutch East India Company merged several limited partnerships in a single organization that essentially coordinated and cartelized the individual partnerships, limited partnerships were not available in England until the twentieth century.

To encourage participation by passive investors, a different institutional form was required, and the solution that was found was to graft joint stock onto corporations with their well-established managerial structure comprising the General Court, the Court of Directors, officers of various types, and a Governor. However, the requirement to keep its assets liquid when each stock was wound up put the English Company at a disadvantage. From 1614 the joint stock was subscribed for a period of a year, in 1654 it adopted a perpetual existence, and then in 1658 fixed capital, equivalent to its Dutch counterpart, and its shares became transferable.

The right of a shareholder to vote at the election of officers was formerly analogous to that possessed by the citizens of municipal corporations. One shareholder one vote was the first rule at the East India Company. This soon became unacceptable to the large shareholders and various changes were made, for example that only holders of £500 stock should have the right to vote, the small holders being allowed to pool their stock to the required minimum.

While the organization of the East India Company and its novel forms of capital and governance were important innovations, there was an additional feature that contributed to both its significance and longevity and reflected the original purpose of its Roman forbearers—to act as a public agency. The Company not only evolved in terms of its structure and conduct, it developed a conscious appreciation of its relationship to the communities in which it operated. 'This idea that the object of a business corporation is the public one of managing and ordering the trade in which it is engaged, as well as the private one of profit for its members, may also be noticed in the charters granted to new corporations, especially in the recitals, and in the provisions usually found that the newly chartered company shall have the exclusive control of the trade intrusted to it.'[26]

Citing various dispatches by the East India Company from London to Madras, Surat, and St Helena, Philip Stern notes that this pursuit of public purpose derived from its degree of independence from its nation state. 'English common and statute law was a useful model but not a binding one abroad, expanding as it did no "further than to England,

Wales, & Berwick upon Tweed"... The corporation thus had a dual personality: subject to the English Crown in one sense but possessed of a supreme rule abroad in another: "wee act by his authority; so their dependence is on us, and they act by ours." As London contended, "the Company must always have the Preference in India as his Majesty justly hath here," though in some ways they implied it was even greater, as St Helena's laws and constitutions, which they had drafted, were also to be regarded "as good Law as Magna Charta is to England".'[27]

The vision that lay behind the East India Company's public purpose was clear: 'These projects for encouraging colonial immigration reflected a vision of plantation as a multidimensional process, in which settlements acted as nodes within a global Company system crosscut by a variety of English, European, and Asian commercial and migratory diasporic networks and labour markets ... While certain tensions between "commerce" and "territory" would consistently remain, and London would never abandon its desire to rein in costs, an East India Company firmly committed to a system of colonial plantation unavoidably required a different way of doing business.'[28]

The Company had a profound interest in the governance of the areas that it administered:

> At the root of the Company political thought was an almost obsessive concern with the correlation between population and strength, particularly economic strength, a notion with firm roots in Restoration economic thought ... The basic principle behind the Company's project of peopling its colonies was to ensure a freedom of trade and security and property to inhabitants and foreigners. Unencumbered commerce would encourage people to choose to settle in Company plantations, attract wealth, and increase navigation, all of which contribute to the strength of polity; in turn, settlers should be encouraged to cultivate land, placing great importance on the Company's role in providing a legal apparatus to ensure due process in matters such probate, land transfers, property disputes, and confiscation.[29]

> Its leadership had come to regard themselves as bearing a responsibility not just for trade but for government in the East Indies.[30]

> The Corporation was supposed to be a broadly representative institution, one of those freedoms in liberty and property that would inspire immigration, settlement, and investment in the city.[31]

> 'Rules and discipline' preserved the trade as well as prosecuted it. A 'united stock' provided the capital and the corporate institution necessary to provide those rules. Finally, recalling the importance of consultative government, that institution had to be governed at every level by 'a Select & authorized council'.[32]

Taxation was critical to the success of the Corporation: 'Without revenue there could be no government, and without government there was only anarchy.'[33] 'This is what made paying taxes such a serious moral responsibility.'[34] Alongside governance, considerable emphasis was also placed on religion and giving people a sound moral upbringing and defence. 'The Company seemed to seek violence neither for its own sake nor for territorial aggrandizement. The conflicts in Siam and Bengal aimed not at war but peace.'[35]

A main concern of the Company was the presence of what were termed 'interlopers'—any English subject travelling to or residing in Asia without the Company's permission—threatening the dominance of its operations. The Company argued that it was not seeking their exclusion as a monopolist but as an organization that was creating new trading operations rather than dominating existing ones. It suggested that it needed to be able to promote productive relations with local populations and that these could be undermined by the hostility of merchants acting independently.

The justices of the Court of King's Bench concurred with the Company in this regard. They rejected the notion of it being monopoly, not because the Company was its own republic with an authority that was distinct from the Crown but, on the contrary, because its power derived from that of the Crown and the Company possessed a permanent and inviolable right to trade and traffic in the East. The Company therefore did have rights to set and prosecute its laws by virtue of the authority granted to it by the Crown and, in so doing, it was representing rather than abusing the public interest. In other words the governance as well as trade that it was performing was on behalf of not in place of the Crown.

However, this benign view of the East India Company changed markedly in 1688 with the 'Glorious Revolution'. The fact that the Company's position was 'rooted in royal grants at home and prerogative abroad'[36] meant that it was exposed to the newfound authority that Parliament began to exert: 'The problem for the Company was not its ties to any one monarch in particular but its constitutional and institutional ties to monarchy in general. Parliament eager in its own way to establish its authority with respect to the monarchy, became a natural venue in the years following 1688 for the Company's enemies to air their long-standing complaints.'[37]

It was stated that the Company 'had borrowed money with no intent to repay. It had pirated Mughal ships, disregarding even its own passes. It erected an "arbitrary Admiralty court" that illegally seized the property of English subjects. The execution of capital punishment at St. Helena was in fact "Murther". It had executed an "unwarrantable war" in which: "1. Many outrages and Violences were committed upon the Innocent Natives on Shoare; 2. Many of them killed; 3. Their dwelling houses, warehouses & goods burnt & destroyed. Their ships at Sea seized & made prize."[38]

In response there were proposals to double the capital stock of the company and limit the voting rights of large shareholders. However, there was concern that such changes could weaken the company's operations and 'ruin both trade and government in Asia irreparably'.[39] As a result the company was granted a new charter that was similar to its existing one dating back to Charles II but with one notable exception and that was the company ' "submit and conform" to any regulations of its affairs the monarchs and the Privy Council "think fit to make, insert, limit, direct, appoint, or express" before the end of September 1694; failure to do would render the charter void'.[40] In other words, for the first time the company became subject to serious regulatory oversight by the Privy Council and potentially Parliament.

The company might have been conscious of the responsibilities that derived from the trust placed in it operating in distant lands shielded from the gaze of public scrutiny at home. However, it may not always have demonstrated the integrity necessary to justify that trust, so when it was eventually subject to interrogation at home, it undermined the reputation and operations of the Company abroad.

The East India Company was not the only one to endure such a fate. Between 1620 and 1680, a number of companies, such as the French Company and the Spanish Company, ceased operations, and some companies, such as the Russia Company, were transformed from joint-stock to regulated companies.

Public and Private Parts

Herein we see the intrinsic dilemma that the fusion of the corporation and the partnership created. What was in effect a public body—the corporation—was drawn towards private interests when it absorbed the commercial affairs of the partnership. As a small organization of limited duration, the social impact of the partnership was modest. However, as part of a corporate body, the ramifications of commercial interests for public matters became profound. So while the partnership benefited from its conscious awareness of the impact of its activities on those with whom it was engaged in trade, it did not need to consider its position in its wider societies and nations. That was manifestly not the case for the corporation, and once it sought to acquire the commercial features of the partnership it was presented with an inevitable conflict between the two—a conflict that has continued to afflict it to this very day.

Nevertheless, after the 1680s the stock corporation expanded rapidly, and up to 1695 about 150 companies were formed. This growth was assisted by a gradual relaxation of the authority of the Crown to assert 'an exclusive right to create "corporateness"',[41] and merchants used a variety of methods to create separate legal personalities, even in the absence of a royal assent to do so. It was 'a tribute to the shrewdness of eighteenth-century lawyers that in most instances the advantages of formal incorporation were approximated'.[42]

Adam Smith maintained that: 'The only trades which it seems possible for a joint-stock company to carry on successfully without an exclusive privilege, are those of which all the operations are capable of being reduced to what is called a routine, or to such a uniformity of method as admits of little variation.'[43] Four industries were covered by his description: banking, fire and marine insurance, water supply, and canal navigation. In a well-known passage he writes: 'The directors of such companies, however, being the managers rather of other people's money than of their own, it cannot be well expected, that they should watch over it with the same anxious vigilance with which the partners in a private co-partnery frequently watch over their own. Like the stewards of a rich man, they are apt to consider attention to small matters as not for their master's honour, and very easily give themselves a dispensation from having it.'[44]

However, the initial phase of development of the joint-stock corporation was primarily associated with high-risk ventures:

> During the early history of the system, its applicability was almost the reverse of that suggested by Adam Smith. The capital of companies was used in the main, at the time at which each undertaking was started, for ventures which were either altogether new trades, or revived industries, or those proposed to be conducted by new methods, or again in cases where there was an exceptional degree of risk. The advantage of joint-stock ownership in such enterprises was obvious; for, while no individual would be prepared to undertake the whole liability, a number of persons, acting together, were willing to provide the funds required.[45]

Banks and Bourses

The emergence of banking in England in the seventeenth century paralleled that in Italy some four centuries earlier. Goldsmiths flourished after the dissolution of the monasteries in the 1530s increased supplies of gold. The seizure by Charles I of private gold deposited in the Tower of London encouraged the gentry to seek safe custody for their wealth, and goldsmiths and scriveners provided a safe deposit for money, bullion, plate, and jewellery. The money could be lent out and used to discount bills of exchange. The receipt that was given to the depositor was in turn passed from hand to hand and, over time since not all deposits were claimed immediately, the banker could issue more notes than there were deposits. The depositor would give instructions to pay one of his creditors thereby creating the forerunners of both the bank note and the cheque (the term being derived from the practice of keeping a counterfoil to serve as a record of the payment made against the general account). Unusually, the cheque was classified in England as a bill of exchange and was therefore negotiable. This allowed it to function as a general means of payment. On the Continent in Europe, the cheque was classified as an order of payment and was thus not negotiable.

The development of financial institutions in Amsterdam also paralleled the Italian institutions. The business of private cash-keeping had originally been in Antwerp. Cashiers or *kassiers* paid creditors and collected from debtors on behalf of merchants. The written orders from the merchants acted as cheques, and the receipts for deposits were negotiable and therefore became monetary instruments.[46] The Lombards brought pawnbroking to Amsterdam. But the real innovation was the introduction of stability to the chaotic payments system, which involved competing currencies and mints in the provinces and circulation of foreign coins. In 1610, contemporary moneychangers had to handle almost 1,000 gold and silver coins. Key to the creation of stability was the establishment of the Bank of Amsterdam, which acted as a central clearing mechanism. It issued no notes of its own and engaged in no lending. But all bills of exchange of more than 600 guilders had to be paid through the Bank with the result that all major merchants held accounts with the Bank. Such was the confidence in the Bank that in the Baltic and in Russia, only Amsterdam bills of exchange were accepted.

In contrast, the Bourse was a centre for highly speculative activities. The stock exchange originated in Bruges in the fifteenth century. The term bourse relates to the square and family inn (the complex of houses owned by the van der Beurse family known as 'Ter Beurse') where merchants gathered for the purpose of trading bills of exchange.[47] But it was in Bruges' rival, Antwerp, that the bourse really developed. A member of the de Beurse family was an owner of several houses where merchants in Antwerp met, and in 1485 they were allowed to form a common body or society. Antwerp became the preferred point of exchange of English wool, Portuguese spices, and German copper and silver. With standardization of commodities using seals or trademarks, commodity markets emerged away from the goods themselves.

A Thousand Years of Corporations

A thousand years of business sees companies and corporations involved in steadily changing purposes and associated functions: public works and services, towns, guilds, seats of learning, the church, alms-houses, hospitals, merchant trading, colonial and public administration, canals, railroads, safe keeping, lending, insurance, and financial instrument trading.

These changing purposes and functions required continuous innovation and evolution in the corporate form: incorporation (*societas publicanorum*), democratization and establishment of rights of members as against public authorities (canon law), separation of ownership of property from control of holders of offices (*corporation sole)*, profit sharing in business partnerships (*mudaraba, isqa,* and *societas*), growth and branching (*commenda* and *compagnia*), governance (guilds), capital raising, pooling of capital, retained profits, perpetual existence, fixed capital, transferable shares, shareholder voting (joint-stock company), public license to operate, consultative governance, tax raising (chartered company), Parliamentary oversight (regulated company), bills of exchange, bank notes, cheques (banking and central banking), and securities trading (commodity and stock exchanges).

Municipalities, guilds, universities, and the Church were all corporations with legal personalities separate from those of their individual members. Royal charters typically conferred legal personality, together with certain rights of self-governance. The emergence of stock corporations out of the guilds in England and ports in Holland provided a means of financing exploration and trade outside of the bureaucracy of the state.

But the most dramatic development was the evolution of the self-liquidating *commenda* into the perpetual stock corporation. What a brilliant innovation it was to offer rights of trade in return for removal of the right to withdraw capital. Any one member's share remained perfectly liquid, or indeed became even more liquid since it did not have to await the return of the fleet before its merchandise could be liquidated, at the same time as share capital in aggregate became perfectly illiquid. It was this separation of the capital of the firm from its members that furthered the emergence of the firm as an entity distinct from its members. At the same time banking flourished in England and Holland and the central clearing function performed by the Bank of

Amsterdam offered liquidity on a scale that no single bank could previously provide.

We therefore arrive at the beginning of the seventeenth century, where Chapter 1 began, with two parallel forms of doing business—the partnership that had evolved into family firms with elaborate management structures, and the corporation with shareholders for raising capital. And that is a key to understanding the corporation. It had at its roots a public or scholarly or religious purpose for which the creation of a corporate body was of advantage. When it finally emerged as a business activity, the corporation grafted the capital-raising element of the partnership onto this administrative role. But the symbiosis gave rise to a form of capital raising that was quite different from the partnership. While the partnership through the *compagnia* became predominantly a family business, the guilds did not have families at their roots. While the partnership was closely held, the guilds raised capital from the public at large. Bourses and stock exchanges therefore emerged on the back of this. The distinction between the Anglo-Dutch corporation as a widely held organization and that of the family-owned business of the rest of Europe had as its origins the divergent influence of the corporate and partnership forms.

Important and striking as the origins of the corporation and its parallels with biological evolution are, their main insight is into the original purpose of the corporation. It was created to perform a public function—to provide public services, to administer towns, to satisfy spiritual as well as material needs, and to provide seats of knowledge and learning. The key requirements for this were an ability to bind many people together for long periods of time in contrast to partnerships that funded entrepreneurship ventures of limited duration. Merging these provided the means to manage and fund the major corporate enterprises of the coming centuries.

The original business forms therefore had a clear sense of purpose and direction. The *societas publicanorum* had a public function; the *compagnia* was run by families; the guilds had administrative offices; the corporation had independent management that sustained that purpose. The origin of the word business captures this. In English and Italian company and *compagnia* come from *cum panis* 'sharing bread together'; in Swedish, *näringslivet* derives from 'nourishment for life'; in Chinese, 生意 means 'giving meaning to life and vitality'; and in Korean, 企業 means 'causing karma'. The universal origin of the concept of business is therefore of promoting life through a collective endeavour. In marked contrast to the Friedman conception of the firm, not only were social and public considerations incorporated in corporate purpose from the outset, they were interwoven in a fusion of commercial and community in a single corporate form.

It is only as we move into the twentieth century, where Chapter 1 left off, that we find the corporation progressively losing its public sense of purpose as its investment tail increasingly wags the administrative dog and the corporation becomes a rudderless vessel, not well suited for voyages into unchartered seas to eternity. But standing on a village green in Birmingham in 1900, a group of people are contemplating a very public-spirited proposal close to home from one of the most enlightened corporate leaders of the time.

4

Ownership

Man has always desired power. Ownership of property gives this power. Man hankers also after posthumous fame based on power. This cannot be had if property is progressively cut up in pieces, as it must be if all the posterity becomes equal co-sharers.

Mahatma Gandhi

A Green and Black Man

'I have seriously considered how far a man is justified in giving away the heritage of his children and have come to the conclusion that my children will be all the better for being deprived of this money. Great wealth is not to be desired and in my experience it is more of a curse than a blessing to the families that possess it.'[1] So on 14 December 1900 George Cadbury, standing in front of the Friends Meeting House on the idyllic village green of Bournville near Birmingham with 370 cottages and 500 acres of land around him, declared that he was giving away his wealth to the Bournville Village Trust. The aim of the Trust was 'the amelioration of the conditions of the working class and labouring population'.[2]

The idea of social welfare and reform was just emerging at the end of the nineteenth century, spurred on by the writings of John Ruskin.[3] Ruskin argued for an ethical approach to economic transactions and said that with wealth comes a moral obligation by which profit is only legitimate if it does not harm the rest of society.

Inspired by what George and his brother Richard Cadbury had created, Joseph Rowntree—another Quaker, fierce competitor of Cadbury in the chocolate business, and father of Seebohm Rowntree, the author in 1901 of *Poverty: A Study in Town Life*—built New Earswick between 1902 and 1904 on 150 acres near to York. And others followed the Cadbury and Rowntree lead—James Reckitt in Hull, Ebenezer Howard in Letchworth in Hertfordshire, and Henrietta Barnett in Hampstead Garden Suburb in London. Business was not just responding to social reform but shaping it and the societies within which it operated.

Meanwhile a less wholesome aspect of chocolate production was taking place off the coast of West Africa. At the beginning of the nineteenth century, the Portuguese had introduced cocoa into the islands of São Tomé and Príncipe. The climate and rich volcanic soils of the islands made them well suited to growing the crop, and in 1900 Cadbury bought 45 per cent of its beans from São Tomé and Príncipe. But the Portuguese had imported something else into the islands as well—slave labour. The Portuguese had officially ended it in the 1870s but in 1901 the board of Cadbury became aware of its continued use on the estates. On 26 September 1908, the London newspaper, the *Standard*, published an article accusing Cadbury of blatant hypocrisy, claiming that: 'It is the monstrous trade in human flesh and blood against which the Quaker and Radical ancestors of Mr Cadbury thundered in the better days of England.'[4]

The Cadbury board were aggrieved, believing that they had done what they could to pressurize the Portuguese government 'to put a stop to the conditions of slavery—not merely to wash our own hands of any connection with them' and that if they had withdrawn from the islands they would have lost the little influence they had over the Portuguese.[5] They sued the *Standard* for libel, and on 29 November 1909 the case came to court. The jury found in favour of Cadbury but the court awarded damages of 'one farthing', clearly unimpressed by how Cadbury had handled the slavery issue. A company renowned for the enlightened treatment of its employees had profited from less admirable practices further from home.

Family Affairs

Cadbury was an example of the most common form of corporate ownership that exists everywhere in the world—family ownership. Most companies start off being family owned. More surprisingly, many of them remain so even when they become large multinational organizations with listings on national stock markets, and families retain the largest shareholdings in many of the largest companies listed on stock markets around the world.

In 2006, families controlled a third of companies listed on stock exchanges in France and Germany, and nearly one-half in Italy.[6] In contrast, they only controlled around one-tenth of listed companies in the United Kingdom. Cadbury illustrates why. It was a family-owned company at the beginning of the twentieth century, it was not by the end, and it had ceased to exist altogether as an independent company by the end of the first decade of the twenty-first century, having been acquired by the US food and beverage company, Kraft, in 2010.

The reason why it was taken over by Kraft in the face of vehement opposition from the board of Cadbury was that the family was no longer in control of the company. Had they been so, then they could have stopped the acquisition by refusing to sell their shares to Kraft, and, in fact, Kraft would not even have attempted to launch a bid for Cadbury in the first place in the full knowledge that the family would not have been prepared to sell their shareholding. Instead, Kraft had merely to convince the financial institutions, into whose hands the shares of Cadbury had by then fallen, to sell their holdings at the generous price that was on offer.

On the other side of the Atlantic, another chocolate manufacturer, which had previously been an arch-rival of Cadbury, continues to thrive and survive as a family business to this day. In 1920 Frank Mars lived in Minnesota making candy, which his second wife Ethel sold to retail stores. Frank experimented with candy bars and around 1923 struck on the recipe for the Milky Way bar, which in one year increased its sales more than tenfold. The company moved to Chicago, and, shortly after graduating from Yale in 1928, Forrest Mars joined his father in the business. In 1930 they launched a peanut, caramel, and chocolate product called Snickers. However, father and son did not always see eye to eye and in 1934 Frank sent his son packing with $50,000, the foreign rights to Mars, and the words: 'This company isn't big enough for both of us. Go to some other country and start your own business.'[7]

In 1933, Cadbury's sales team became aware of a company operating from a small flat in Slough in the United Kingdom. In one of the most remarkable pieces of commercial chutzpah, Forrest Mars approached Cadbury with a request that it supply him with chocolate to coat his new confectionary. To what must have been his complete amazement, they agreed. It was a decision about which a subsequent chairman, Sir Adrian Cadbury, has with some justification mused, 'Why ever did we do that?'[8] The resulting Mars bar was one of the most successful confectionaries ever produced.

Leaving aside this slight tactical error, the question remains as to why Mars has survived when Cadbury has not. One critical difference is that Mars to this day remains 100 per cent owned by the Mars family. Until the recent acquisition of Wrigley, Mars has raised little external finance at all, let alone sought a listing on a stock market. In contrast, following the merger with J. S. Fry and Sons of Bristol, the Cadbury family holding in the merged firm was diluted to just over 50 per cent by 1919. In 1962 following pressure from some members of both the Cadbury and Fry family to determine the value of their company's shares and cash out, the company went public and was listed on the London and Birmingham stock exchanges. By 1969 when Cadbury merged with Schweppes plc, 40 per cent of the shares were dispersed amongst 200 shareholders.

This pattern of share issuance to fund growth and in particular acquisitions was repeated across the British corporate sector in the twentieth century. It resulted in family shareholdings being steadily diluted to the point that families lost control of their firms, rendering them vulnerable to the fate of the takeover that befell Cadbury.[9]

Economic Misconceptions

Why does it matter? Some argue that family ownership is a bad thing. It leads to the type of crony capitalism that was thought to afflict Asian economies after the Asian Financial Crisis in the second half of the 1990s. It is associated with the pursuit of self-interest of families at the expense of the commercial well-being of firms. It creates conflicts between family members, which eventually lead to their and their firms' disintegration. So the emergence of institutional from family ownership can be regarded as economic advancement, democratizing the control of companies, making them more accessible, accountable, and transparent to the societies in which they operate. On this score, the United Kingdom is leading the way in showing the rest of the world where corporate ownership is heading.

Underpinning this view is the economic conceptualization of corporate ownership. As described in Chapter 1, since Ronald Coase first provided a rationale for the existence of the corporation based on the theory of transaction costs, and Adolf Berle and Gardiner Means documented the separation of ownership and control in the 1930s, economists have become fixated on one and only one aspect of the firm—the agency problem—the problem of aligning the interests of the managers running the firm with those of their masters, their shareholders. It is this which is regarded as being the primary function of ownership—to control the otherwise wayward tendencies of management to build corporate empires, award themselves egregious salaries, and indulge in lavish lifestyles at their corporations' expense. And it is this that is the justification for changes in ownership through takeovers and shareholder activism when the existing owners fail to rectify the deficiencies of their managers.

The economic concept of ownership therefore equates it with corporate control, in particular the control of corporate assets, the determination of investment decisions, and the allocation of resources to different activities. In essence, this view of the firm sees owners sitting at the top, controlling their executives as puppets, pulling the purse strings of financial resources at their disposal. Ownership should reside with those who work their puppets most effectively, and it should be transferred immediately to those with greater skills at doing so.

At best, this is an incomplete and, arguably, highly damaging description of the firm. It is incomplete because it fails to appreciate the far more significant functions that ownership performs, and it is damaging because the misconception has been the source of profound corporate failures and substantial economic hardship. The case of the most successful and significant product of all times illustrates this.

Any Ownership Is Fine, So Long as It's All Mine

To quote Zohar Goshen and Assaf Hamdani, Henry Ford:

> did not invent the automobile, nor did he own any valuable intellectual property in the technology. He was competing with hundreds of other entrepreneurs attempting to create a 'horseless carriage'. Ford, however, had a unique vision regarding car production. Investors exercised considerable control over the first firm that he founded, the Detroit Automobile Company, and this led to irreconcilable conflicts. While Ford's investors demanded that cars be immediately produced and sold, Ford insisted on perfecting the design prior to production, leading to delays, frustration on both sides, and the eventual shutdown of the firm by the investors.
>
> Investors continued to control Ford's second attempt, the Henry Ford Company. Again, after designing a car, Ford resisted investors' pressure and interference to move directly into production. Eventually, his obstinacy led to the investors replacing Ford with Henry Leland, changing the company name to the Cadillac Automobile Company, and producing the car designed by Ford with great success.
>
> In his third attempt, the Ford Motor Company, Ford insisted on retaining control. This time, with no outside investor interference, Ford transformed his ideas for car design and production into one of the great corporate success stories of all time. Finally, with yet another move along the spectrum of ownership structures, Ford's grandson, Henry II, took the corporation public in 1956 with a dual-class share structure, ensuring that control stayed with the Ford family to this day.[10]

In some cases, entrepreneurs' vision borders on fanaticism. In 1964 at the age of sixty, Forrest Mars 'had finally got his hands on his father's company, merging it with his own Food Manufacturers, Inc. Soon after, he summoned a group of executives and other employees to a buff-colored conference room. Mars did not just walk into the room; he charged in . . . After a few quips, which sparked a little dutiful laughter, Mars talked of his plans and hopes for the Mars Candies Division, as the Chicago operation was henceforth to be known. He paused. "I'm a religious man," he said abruptly (he was an Episcopalian). There was another long pause, while his new associates pondered the significance of his statement. Their mystification increased when Mars sank to his knees at the head of the long conference table. Some of those present thought that he was groping on the floor for a pencil that had slipped from his hands. From his semi-kneeling position, Mars began a strange litany: "I pray for Milky Way. I pray for Snickers . . . " For men accustomed to an orderly kind of life within a closely held, profitable company, it was an unnerving moment. But Mars's litany had purpose. His listeners, without knowing it, were being introduced to a basic tenet of Forrest Mars's management system: all members of an organization must be united in a coordinated drive to a single objective—profit through faith in the company's leadership and product.'[11]

In nearly all cases, success involves immense innovation and endurance: 'The Cadburys had wrestled with the problem of milk chocolate for fifteen years, but had failed to find a breakthrough recipe. The challenge seemed insurmountable: to create and mass-produce a bar that was milkier and creamier than those of the competition . . . George Cadbury was so caught up in the process that it is said that one night sleepwalking and delirious, he "rose in the small hours and trundled his young wife, Edith, around the bedroom under the impression she was a milk churn". Late in 1904, an exhausted George Junior and his team hit on the exact combination of temperature, pressure and cooling that would condense the milk in such a way that large volumes of it could be mixed with the cocoa without spoiling'[12] and so was born Cadbury's Dairy Milk chocolate in 1905.

Goshan and Hamdani describe these as examples of the pursuit of 'idiosyncratic value'—value that is recognized by entrepreneurs and innovators of vision but no one else. In particular, the visionaries are dismissed as cranks and fanatics by the people who really matter—the more sober-minded investors, who see cost, waste, and risk where the visionary senses creativity, worth, and riches. As the case of Henry Ford illustrates, the divergence of view can be fatal to the development of radical new innovations where control resides with investors, as it did in the first two examples of Henry Ford's companies. But where ownership coincides with vision, as it did in the third case, and in Cadbury (as it did at the beginning but not by the end of the twentieth century) and in Mars, vision is supported not extinguished by ownership.

Ironically, stock market ownership, which is often regarded as particularly conducive to the promotion of entrepreneurship and innovation through providing the means of accessing large pools of diversified investment, is exactly the opposite—the mundane views of investors stifling and snubbing the spark of creative inspiration. This is not to suggest that entrepreneurs and innovators are always right or that investors are not often perfectly justified in pulling the rug from under their feet, but instead it emphasizes that ownership involves committing to, not controlling, entrepreneurship and innovation.

What underpins the successful relation between the two parts of the corporation is trust—trust that management will not abuse their power to exploit their owners and defraud them of their earnings, and trust that owners will not exploit their power over other investors and parties to the firm. As we will see, the history of the emergence of stock markets around the world in the twentieth century is one of creation of institutions of trust to sustain these relations in the absence of regulation.

Family Firms

The Fords and Mars are the norm not the exception in being dominated by families. Family ownership is the most common form of ownership of companies around the world, not just as we might expect in small firms but perhaps more surprisingly in the largest listed companies as well. They are part of a more general class of shareholders who are sometimes termed 'block holders'—shareholders who own a substantial fraction of shares in a company, often defined as being in excess of 25 per cent on the grounds that 25 per cent represents a 'blocking minority' that allows the owner of the shares to veto certain actions by the firm.

Block holders are ubiquitous. In most countries, three shareholders control a majority, i.e. more than 50 per cent of the shares in companies and in some countries a single voting block (i.e. a group of shareholders voting together) control a majority of shares in companies. The nature of those block holders varies across countries. In some, such as China, they are the state, but in most they are families. This is true in Asia, Europe, and South America.

As noted above, the one country that stands out in this regard is the United Kingdom. It has far fewer family owners than most countries around the world, and even those that are family controlled display a high level of attrition through takeovers, financial failure, or transitioning into some other form of ownership.

The United Kingdom is often categorized with the United States as being the archetypal form of stock-market economy—what is described as 'Anglo-American'. However, while they are superficially similar in having large active stock markets, the differences between the two countries are actually more pronounced than their similarities. In particular, the prevalence of block holders in the United States appears to be significantly greater than in the United Kingdom.

The contrast between Ford and Mars on the one hand and Cadbury on the other is therefore by no means exceptional, and one aspect of Ford explains why—the Ford family was able to retain control of the company to this day through a 'dual-class share structure'. What this means is that, while Henry Ford sold shares in his company on the stock market, he retained control through keeping the voting rights. In other words there were two types of shares—those sold to the public at large with few voting rights attached to them and those retained by the family with a large number of voting rights.

Dual-class structures are commonplace around the world, including in the United States, and, as was mentioned in Chapter 1, some of the most successful newly established companies such as Facebook, Google, LinkedIn, and Snapchat came to the stock market with dual-class structures that gave Larry Page and Sergei Brin, in the case of Google, and Reid Hoffman in LinkedIn shares with ten times the voting rights of those sold on the stock market. The justification for this was the same as Ford's, namely to allow the founders to retain and promote the purpose and values of the firms. They were idiosyncratic value-preservation devices.

In contrast, dual-class shares are not permitted in the United Kingdom, and, according to the listing rules of the UK stock market, companies cannot be 'premium listed' with dual-class structures. Such arrangements are perceived to be a violation of the equal treatment of all shareholders, and indeed there is evidence that they have allowed controlling shareholders to 'tunnel' financial resources out of companies.[13] But equally, as noted in Chapter 1, there is evidence of shareholders doing very well in companies with dual-class structures.

The importance of the acceptance or rejection of dual-class shares is that it is highly relevant to the survival or extinction of family firms. As will be documented later, the Cadbury story of a firm that grew through issuing shares to fund its expansion, which caused the ownership of the founding families to be diluted to a point that they lost control and were eventually taken over is by no means exceptional. It happened repeatedly, and it did so because, in the absence of a supportive banking system, families were faced with a choice of starving their firms of funds or losing control of them. While Ford was able to present its customers with the Hobson's choice of 'You can have any colour you like provided it is black,' the owners of British family firms were given the choice of 'You can have as much funding as you like provided you are not there to use it.'

Dual-class shares are not the only respect in which the United States differs from the United Kingdom. The United States is also much more permissive of limitations on the degree of control that shareholders can exercise on companies. For example, it allows companies to protect themselves against threats of takeovers through the use of 'takeover defences' such as 'poison pills', and restrictions on removal rights of shareholders to replace directors through 'staggered' or 'classified' boards that rotate the composition of boards over extended periods of time.

The effect of these provisions in the United States is to make directors less exposed to external interventions or shareholder actions than in the United Kingdom. While both systems promote the primacy of shareholder interests above others, the effect of dual-class shares, takeover defences, staggered boards, and other provisions is to allow US management to exercise a greater degree of 'business judgement' than their British counterparts. So whether it be through founder or family control or through management discretion, US firms are better able to protect idiosyncratic value against the type of ravages by investors to which Henry Ford was exposed.

What lies behind these marked international variations in the nature of superficially similar capitalist systems is a fascinating history of divergent social, political, as well as commercial and economic influences. The next sections tell the story of how the United Kingdom ended up with one of the most diversified least family-owned corporate sectors in the world; how Germany today has some of the most persistent family ownership; how Japan switched from family to no family control in a matter of a few years; and how the United States looked initially similar to the United Kingdom but ended markedly different. We will demonstrate how, despite their divergent histories, all four countries establish the importance of trust and the existence of trustworthy institutions in the development of financial systems, and why it is these, rather than regulation, that hold the key to the promotion of idiosyncratic value and flourishing corporate sectors.

The United Kingdom

In the first half of the nineteenth century Britain had a plethora of local banks all over the country that were actively involved in the financing of small and medium-sized firms. However, the existence of these local banks empowered to engage in note issuance caused serious stability problems. Between 1809 and 1830, there were 311 bankruptcies that prompted the Bank of England to encourage banks to withdraw from illiquid investments in small companies and spread their activities more widely through mergers with other banks. As a consequence, a mutually attractive arrangement emerged by which, as concentration in the banking sector increased, the clearing banks faced decreasing competition during the nineteenth century and the Bank of England diminishing risk of bank failures.[14]

The result was that, in place of the highly decentralized but fragile banking that existed at the beginning of the nineteenth century, by the start of the twentieth century there was a highly concentrated banking system, a noticeable absence of local banking, and, at least until the secondary banking crisis in the 1970s and the financial crisis in 2008, little bank failure. There was only one party that was made worse off as a result and that was the corporate sector, in particular small and medium-sized enterprises, that found themselves unable to raise the finance for investment that was previously available to them from local banks.

As the supply of bank finance for small and medium-sized enterprises dried up, companies turned to the stock market instead. As in the case of banking in the first half of the nineteenth century, stock markets in the United Kingdom in the first half of the twentieth century were highly localized. There were more than nineteen provincial exchanges all over the country that specialized in particular industries: for example, the Birmingham exchange was important for cycle and rubber tube stocks, Sheffield for iron, coal, and steel, and Bradford for wool. 'The number of commercial and industrial companies quoted in the Manchester stock exchange list increased from 70 in 1885 to nearly 220 in 1906. Most of these were small companies with capitals ranging from £50,000 to £200,000' and 'by the mid 1880s Sheffield, along with Oldham, was one of the two most important centres of joint stock in the country, with 44 companies, with a paid up capital of £12 million.'[15]

As in the case of banking in the first half of the nineteenth century, the local nature of stock markets in the first half of the twentieth century was important in allowing companies to access sources of finance. Directors were keen to uphold their reputations amongst the local communities from which they were raising finance, and their dependence on local investors acted as a commitment device—'institution of trust'. Writing in 1921, one author noted that 'local knowledge on the part of the investor both of the business reputation of the vendor and the prospects of his undertaking would do a good deal to eliminate dishonest promotion and ensure that securities were sold at fair prices fairly near their investment values.'[16] Concentrating ownership among local investors was recognized as a method of reducing information problems as well as fraud.

As one stockbroker put it, 'The securities are rarely sold by means of a prospectus and are not underwritten, they are placed by private negotiation among local people who understand the [cotton] trade.'[17] As a result, securities were traded in the city in which most investors resided. For example, shareholders in Manchester were anxious that the shares of Arthur Keen's Patent Nut and Bolt Co. of Birmingham should be listed in Manchester where most of the shareholders resided. The reason was that proximity between brokers and directors was thought to create better-informed markets.

What then happened and continued to happen throughout the twentieth century was that firms issued shares to fund their growth and in the process they diluted the shareholding of their directors, family owners, and founders. For example, if a family initially owned all 1 million shares in a company and issued another 1 million to fund the growth of the firm then the family's shareholding declined from 100 per cent to 50 per cent. Furthermore, as firms grew, their activities expanded beyond their hometowns and their shareholder base no longer remained geographically concentrated. So for example by 1920, shares in Guest, Keen, and Nettlefolds were quoted in Birmingham, Bristol, Cardiff, Edinburgh, Glasgow, Liverpool, and Sheffield, as well as Manchester.

As companies' dependence on local stock markets diminished, the need for more formal systems of information disclosure through company accounts and listing rules intensified. The result was the 1948 Companies Act and the London Stock Exchange Listing rules that together substantially strengthened information disclosure and fundamentally changed the nature of the UK stock market to one concentrated on a single stock market in London. From an economy based first on local banking in the first half of the nineteenth century to one dependent on local stock-market institutions of trust in the first half of the twentieth century, Britain became a country with highly concentrated banking and few stock markets in the second half of the twentieth century and a heavy dependence on regulation to substitute for the disappearance of institutions of trust. Most seriously of all, as in the case of Cadbury, Britain became a country in which family ownership was diluted largely out of existence, and the external funding of small and medium-sized companies became seriously constrained. In both respects, it differed markedly from Germany.

Germany

At first sight, German financial markets at the beginning of the twentieth century looked remarkably similar to those in the United Kingdom. There were many firms listed on German stock markets and firms raised large amounts of equity finance. Contrary to the conventional view of Germany as a bank-oriented financial system, firms raised little finance from banks and surprisingly large amounts from stock markets.[18]

The mechanism by which this occurred and trust was upheld in Germany was quite different from that in the United Kingdom. In Germany, it was not so much associated with local stock markets as with banks acting as promoters of new equity issues on behalf of companies and custodians of shares on behalf of individual investors. Where equity was widely owned by individual investors it was generally held on their behalf by custodian banks. As a consequence, banks were able to cast large numbers of votes at shareholder meetings, not only in respect of their own shareholdings, which were in general modest, but more significantly on behalf of other shareholders.

The economic historian Frederick Lavington argued that banks provided a more secure basis for the issuance of initial public offerings (IPOs) in Germany than promoters in the United Kingdom whose interests were primarily confined to selling issues rather than ongoing relationships with companies.[19] In the same way as firms in Britain upheld their reputation amongst local investors to gain access to equity markets, so German firms depended on banks as the gatekeepers to stock markets.

In the United Kingdom, much of the new equity was used to fund acquisitions of other companies, but not in Germany. It was predominantly directed towards internal investment and contributed to the rapid expansion of German relative to British manufacturing during the twentieth century. Companies did not grow through full acquisitions of other companies as in the United Kingdom but by taking partial share stakes in each other. Equity therefore came to be held by companies and banks in the form of pyramids and complex webs of intercorporate shareholdings, bank custodianship, and family ownership.

This resulted in a fundamental difference in the way in which corporate control was exercised in Germany and the United Kingdom. In Germany, voting control remained within corporate and banking sectors and families, and was not transferred to outside individual and institutional shareholders, as occurred in the United Kingdom. As a consequence, an 'insider system' of ownership and control of corporations in banks, companies, and families emerged in Germany in

contrast to 'outsider' ownership by individuals and institutional investors in the United Kingdom. These distinct forms of ownership persisted
into the second half of the twentieth century, and both differed from
what happened in Japan.

Japan

Japan and Germany are often categorized together as 'bank-oriented'
systems. In fact, banks were not primary funders of German corporate
investment, and Japan did not have a bank-oriented system in the first
half of the twentieth century. Japan actually bore greater resemblance to
the United Kingdom than Germany in having low concentration of
ownership, widely dispersed amongst institutional investors. Of the
three countries discussed to date, dispersion of ownership was greatest
in Japan, as ownership of the newly industrialized companies, such as
the cotton-spinning firms, became widely held on stock markets. So
pronounced was the dispersion of ownership that measures of concentration of ownership were lower in Japan than they were at that time in
the United Kingdom.[20]

As in Germany and the United Kingdom, informal arrangements of
trust were critical to the development of Japanese stock markets. Unlike
in the United Kingdom, they were not attributable to the prevalence of
local stock exchanges, and most companies were listed on one of two
stock exchanges—Osaka and Tokyo. Nor, unlike in Germany, did banks
play an important role in relations between investors and firms in the
first half of the century. Instead, in the first two decades of the twentieth
century particular individuals rather than institutions were critical to
the ability of companies to be able to access stock markets. These individuals, known as 'business coordinators', had some of the characteristics
of today's private equity investors and business angels. They were prominent members of the business community, sometimes senior figures in
the local chambers of commerce, who sat on the boards of several firms.
Their reputation acted as a validation of the soundness of the companies
with which they were associated.

The role of business coordinators diminished from the 1920s onwards
and their place was instead taken by *zaibatsu*, family firms. These were
established during and after WW1 and sold their subsidiaries on Japanese stock markets during the 1930s. In this case, it was the reputation
of the *zaibatsu* families that facilitated their access to stock markets.
However, the success of the *zaibatsu* was the source of their subsequent downfall, because in the aftermath of WW2, the American

occupation attributed the power of the Japanese military machine to the *zaibatsu* and dismantled them.

In their place, the American occupation sought to create US-style widely held companies and, to achieve this, it introduced US investor protection that transformed weak regulation in the first half of the century into some of the strongest in the world in the second half of the century. However, the effect was exactly the opposite of what was intended. Instead of promoting a US outsider system of corporate ownership, banks and companies began to acquire cross-shareholdings in each other. The dismantling of the *zaibatsu* in the aftermath of WW2 and the introduction of investor protection left a vacuum that individual and institutional investors failed to fill, and instead an insider system of corporate control in the hands of banks and corporations, similar to that in Germany, emerged in the second half of the twentieth century.

The dispersion of ownership in the first half of the century had occurred in the absence of any significant investor protection but the introduction of strong regulation resulted in Japan moving from essentially an Anglo-American outsider system to a German-style insider system in the second half of the century. This presaged the collapse of the Japanese banking system in the 1990s and the 'lost decade' before an outsider system began to re-emerge in Japan at the beginning of this century.

The United States

Surprisingly, it is harder to undertake long-run analyses of ownership of corporations from the beginning of the twentieth century in the United States than in most other major developed economies. The reason is that until the formation of the Securities and Exchange Commission (SEC) in the 1930s in the wake of the 1929 stock-market crash and the Great Depression, there was little requirement on companies to disclose information. Most of our knowledge about corporate ownership in the United States at the beginning of the twentieth century comes from the work that Gardiner Means did, some of it in conjunction with his co-author Adolf Berle.[21]

As in the other three countries, Gardiner Means reports a rapid dispersion of ownership from the beginning of the century. It gave rise to Berle and Means' concern about a separation between the ownership of shareholders and the emergence of managerial control in the absence of the banks, families, or holding companies that held management to account in other countries.

More recent work casts doubt on this conventional view. It shows that between 1926 and 1950 business groups were the most dominant force in the US stock market.[22] They comprised about one third of all corporate assets, one half of non-financial assets, and collectively controlled over 1,000 firms. They were important in utilities, railroads, and transportation as well as in manufacturing. Wealthy families, such as Morgan, Du Pont, and Mellon controlled some business groups and others were ultimately widely held, particularly those in the utility industries. Despite the much-publicized dispersion of ownership in the United States in the first half of the twentieth century, family ownership persisted in business groups for most of this period.

Business groups went into decline in the United States from the beginning of the 1940s as a consequence of regulation. By seeking to improve both transparency of accounts and shareholder rights, the Securities Act of 1933 and the Securities and Exchange Act of 1934 curbed the means by which parent firms could transfer wealth from one part of a business group to another. The introduction of double taxation of inter-corporate dividends in 1935 and the imposition of greater disclosure standards on listed firms investing in other companies' shares in 1940 were the final nails in the coffins of the business groups.[23] Family ownership through business groups therefore disappeared in the second half of the twentieth century but, as described above, it persisted in a form that was not available in the United Kingdom, namely through dual-class shares.

Lessons from Four Countries

All four of the United Kingdom, Germany, Japan, and the United States displayed rapid dispersion in ownership in the first half of the twentieth century. However, the United Kingdom differed from the other three countries in one important respect and that is, while concentrated family ownership persisted in all the other countries, it was steadily eroded in the United Kingdom as companies expanded through equity issuance and acquisitions. The decline of the United Kingdom as a major economic power during the twentieth century and the rise of Germany, Japan, and the United States were associated with the persistence of family block holdings in Germany, Japan, and the United States but not in the United Kingdom.

The growth of stock markets occurred in the absence of regulation. Regulation and investor protection were largely absent in all four countries in the first half of the twentieth century, and when they were introduced in the United States in the 1930s, and in Japan and the United Kingdom in the 1940s, they undermined the very institutions of trust on which they depended. Post-WW2, investor protection had the unintended consequence of promoting the emergence of an insider bank-oriented rather than an outsider individual and institutional system of corporate control in Japan, of hastening the demise of family ownership in the United Kingdom, and of intensifying separation of ownership and control in the United States through the elimination of business groups.

Investor protection was neither necessary for the development of outsider systems of corporate ownership in any of the United Kingdom, Germany, Japan, or the United States in the first half of the twentieth century nor sufficient on its own to promote an outsider system of ownership in Japan in the second half of the twentieth century. On the contrary, the introduction of regulation undermined the institutions of trust (local stock markets in the United Kingdom, family owners in Japan, and business groups in the United States) on which dispersed outsider ownership systems depended.

It was institutions of trust rather than regulation that were the necessary ingredient for the successful development of flourishing stock markets in all four countries. In the case of the United Kingdom it was local stock markets, in Germany the banks, in Japan business coordinators and *zaibatsu* families, and in the United States business groups and families. Despite the fact that many German firms such as Krupp, Siemens, and Volkswagen were intimately involved in the Nazi war effort, unlike the *zaibatsu* family firms in Japan, the allied occupation forces did not dismantle them in the post-war period. They continued to exist and thrive. In addition and again in contrast to Japan, there was no fundamental restructuring of German investor protection. As a consequence, while family firms went into decline and never recovered in Japan, they continued to dominate ownership and control of German industry.

The twentieth century reveals the importance not only of dispersion of ownership amongst individual and institutional investors but also of the parallel existence of block holdings. Where block holders reflect outsider as well as their own interests then they promote dispersed ownership by acting as institutions of trust. We associate block holders with the exercise of corporate control but what this chapter has revealed is that they can also enhance not diminish ownership dispersal by acting on behalf of all shareholders. In this respect they are institutions of trust not control since, in the absence of regulation, dispersed minority owners have few powers of redress. Well-designed regulation and investor protection can assist block holders in acting in this way but excessive regulation undermines their ability to do so. Financial theory provides us with some clues as to why block holders as well as dispersed shareholders, institutions of trust, and careful design of regulation and investor protection are all necessary ingredients of successful financial development.

The Magic of Modern Portfolio Theory

Modern theories of finance demonstrate the benefits that investors derive from holding well-diversified portfolios of different companies' shares. By so doing, they are able to minimize their exposure to any one company and only have to endure the risks associated with overall movements in the market as a whole. Even if they cannot distinguish between the Henry Fords and charlatans of this world, by holding combinations of the two they can achieve the equivalent of a riskless investment—investment in genius plus investment in lunacy equals the return on a government security

The allure of this has been that, by apparently having to do nothing other than purchase funds of multiple company shares, investors are able to extinguish much of the risk associated with investing. Not only are the risks of such portfolios low, but if the funds can be traded on exchanges, then they are also liquid in the sense that they can be cashed in when investors wish to do so. While economics repeatedly asserts that there is no free lunch, the practical application of what in mathematics is termed the central limit theorem to financial investment appears to come very close to achieving it.

The strength of this has been to allow large numbers of people with no interest in or knowledge of investing to participate in equity markets. It has permitted companies to draw on far greater volumes of capital than would otherwise have been the case. This is unequivocally good and here the matter would rest, were it not the case that this capital that firms raise can come back and bite them.

Recall the problem that Henry Ford encountered in the mark one version of his company—he wished to improve the design of the car when investors wanted to start selling it, and, because they controlled the firm, they could close it down when Ford failed to cooperate. The problem in mark two of his company was that when Ford resisted pressure to move swiftly to production, investors could remove him because again they controlled the firm. In other words, the problem that Ford encountered in both the first two versions of his company was the control that investors could exercise over him and his company after he had raised finance. The solution that he found in mark three of his company was to retain ownership and control himself.

The strengths that portfolios create in pooling capital are precisely their weakness in promoting enterprise and innovation. They increase the supply of finance and thereby reduce the cost of capital but they undermine the ability of entrepreneurs and innovators to pursue idiosyncratic value that the market does not immediately recognize. The depressed value of companies pursuing idiosyncratic policies leaves them exposed to the type of interventions that Henry Ford experienced or their modern equivalents—takeovers and hedge-fund activism.

We have therefore created highly liquid, low-risk equity markets that reward investors handsomely at little risk and cost to themselves. The only problem is that they provide forms of finance that innovative firms do not want. The consequence is that firms shun the markets and seek refuge from the pressures of activist investors and hostile bidders in the safe harbours of private equity, as Henry Ford found. That is precisely what has happened; only it has become worse than it was in Ford's time.

Vanishing Stock Markets

At the turn of the century in 2000 there were more than 2,000 companies listed on the main market of the London Stock Exchange (LSE) in the United Kingdom. Today eighteen years later there are less than 1,000 firms. The reason for this is that the number of companies choosing to exit (delist) from the LSE has far exceeded the number choosing to enter, i.e. list for the first time—what are termed initial public offerings (IPOs). At the beginning of the century the number of delistings was in excess of 200 per annum while the number of IPOs was only around half that.

The United Kingdom is not the only country to have witnessed a marked decline in the size of its stock market; so too has the United States. *The Economist* reported in May 2012 that the number of public corporations in America had dropped by 38 per cent from 1987. Michael Jensen, the well-known Harvard Business School finance professor, predicted the 'eclipse of the public corporation' in the 1980s;[24] Jensen's prediction appears to have been realized in both the United Kingdom and the United States in the 2010s.

But it has not been realized everywhere. As their names suggest, emerging markets have experienced rapidly expanding stock markets.

So too have some developed markets such as Japan where the number of listed companies on the First Section of the Tokyo Stock Exchange has increased from 1,400 to 1,800 over the same period that the number listed on the LSE main market has halved.

On average around the world, the number of companies listed on stock markets has remained constant since the beginning of the 1990s at approximately ten per million of population. However, in the United Kingdom and the United States the number has declined from closer to 30 per million of population to just in excess of the global average. Why is this happening? Why are companies choosing to leave the UK and US stock exchanges, but not others?

Some idea of the answer to this comes from observing the changing composition of ownership of shares of listed companies. Until the beginning of the 1970s, share ownership in the United Kingdom and the United States was dominated by individual investors. At that stage, institutional investment increased rapidly, and pension funds, life insurance companies, and mutual funds replaced individual investors. Like individual investors, the institutional investors tended to hold shares for extended periods of time.

Over the last few years, other institutions have replaced these domestic institutional investors—hedge funds, private equity investors, and, above all, foreign institutional investors. Foreign ownership has increased markedly as investors have begun to appreciate the benefits associated with international as well as domestic portfolio diversification.

With this has come a marked decline in the period for which investors on average hold the shares of companies. Seventy years ago the average holding period of shares was around eight years, thirty years ago it was about four years. Today it is on average a matter of a few months. What was previously a long-term investment for individual and then institutional investors has become an increasingly short-term investment.

The changing nature of ownership and the shortening holding period of shares has been a global phenomenon not restricted to the United Kingdom or the United States. However, its significance for companies outside the United Kingdom and the United States has been much less than in these two countries. The reason for this is that the changing nature of institutional ownership has come against the backdrop of remarkable stability in the ownership of those people who ultimately control most listed companies in the world, namely families.

While many large companies are listed on stock markets, families retain the dominant controlling shareholders of even the largest of them. For example, in Germany the proportion of companies with dominant family owners controlling more than 25 per cent of shares of the largest

200 non-financial companies has remained in excess of 30 per cent over the last twenty years.[25]

The significance of the dominant family ownership is that it lends stability to the ownership of companies whose other shareholders are turning over rapidly. While the dispersed and changing ownership of UK and US firms can have profound effects on their control, this is not in general the case in other listed companies around the world: ultimately it is the families not the mass of institutional investors who determine how these companies are run. They act as 'anchor' shareholders. In contrast, listed companies in the United Kingdom and United States have enjoyed no such protection, and for them idiosyncratic value is not preserved in the hands of founders and their families but instead is at the mercy of institutions whose vision extends little beyond the next dividend payment.

Faced with the conflict that this creates, many firms have chosen to follow Henry Ford's example and decided to go private. In essence, UK and US firms have been voting with their feet by moving from the turbulent waters of stock markets to the safe harbours of private ownership.

The Transformation Process

In creating almost perfectly liquid, low-cost equity investments for shareholders, we have lost sight of the ultimate purpose of stock markets—to fund risky investments by companies. The provision of liquid, low-risk, short-term finance satisfies one end of the investment chain—the investors' end. At the other end sit companies that are engaging in exactly the opposite activities—illiquid, high-risk, long-term investments. They are investing in physical assets, such as buildings, equipment, plant, and machinery, and above all in intangible assets—ideas, innovation, and research and development—that can take years and sometimes decades to come to fruition.

What the stock market and in particular the investment chain is there to do is to transform shareholders' desire for liquid, low-risk, short-term investments into companies' requirements for illiquid, high-risk, long-term sources of capital. What it does, and has done increasingly effectively, is the first of these. It has become progressively easier for investors to trade shares at low cost, hold highly diversified portfolios that reduce the risks of their investments, and cash in their shares. But at the same time, this has made it progressively harder for companies to raise patient, long-term capital that does not impose high cash-flow requirements on them. Instead of transforming investments, stock markets have forced the type of finance demanded by one end of the investment chain on the other end, and the reaction of the latter has been to shun the finance offered by the former.

One way of thinking about this is in terms of 'realization' and 'influence' periods. It takes a certain period of time for corporate investments and strategies to come to fruition. In some cases, in particular in relation to new innovations and inventions, realization periods might be decades. Over those periods, the investments and strategies are vulnerable to the interference of investors who lose faith in or do not perceive their vision and objectives. To avoid this, those with the ideas and vision need to be able to control the investments and strategies for corresponding periods. In other words, their influence periods have to correspond with the realization periods.

If the influence periods of innovators and inventors are shorter than the realization periods then innovators and inventors face the type of hold-up risk from investors that confronted Henry Ford in the first two forms of his company. On the other hand, if they are much longer than the realization periods then investors are exposed to innovators and inventors wasting their money on activities that are unrelated to the companies' investment needs.

Balancing influence and realization periods is therefore critical to successful investment and innovation. By conferring control on investors who are not committed to long-terms investments with substantial realization periods, stock markets have failed to offer innovative firms the long influence sources of finance that they need. The United States and, in particular, the United Kingdom have become markets with too few investors who are willing to support companies for the periods that their investments require, and regulation has continued to exacerbate the problem.

Minority Affirmative Action

Agency theories of the firm and concerns about the separation of ownership and control have resulted in a preoccupation amongst policymakers with minority shareholder rights. This has been supported by a body of academic opinion that points to the association between investor protection and the development of financial markets and systems.[26] Stronger minority investor protection is associated with better-developed financial markets, and, as a consequence, there has been a steady strengthening of shareholder rights on stock markets around the world.

There are two justifications for this. First, in the context of dispersed ownership systems such as the United Kingdom and the United States, shareholder rights give minority investors the power to control otherwise self-interested corporate executives and managers. Second, in concentrated ownership systems outside of the United Kingdom and United States, it provides minority investors with protection against dominant shareholders.

Shareholder rights are therefore viewed as critical to the efficient operation of equity markets in all countries, and there is no doubt that they have been important in avoiding the conflicts identified by Berle and Means some eighty years ago. However, in the process of regulating to strengthen minority shareholders, we have diminished the incentives for other investors to provide the more engaged long-term investment that is required to match shareholder needs with those of the companies in which they are investing. No one is minding the shop. Britain, 'a nation of shopkeepers',[27] has sold its shopkeepers to stock pickers, securitized them, and sent them packing. In other words, we have lost the transformative role of stock markets to convert liquid, low-risk, short-term shareholdings into illiquid, high-risk, long-term investments that match influence with realization periods and promote idiosyncratic value as well as risk diversification.

Green Towns and Dark Satanic Mills

George Cadbury's vision survives in the form of Bournville, a model village on the south side of Birmingham in the United Kingdom. A hundred years on from when George Cadbury stood on that idyllic village green, it has been described as being 'one of the nicest places to live in Britain'.[28] A study by the Rowntree Foundation in 2003 found that 'the area, as a whole, scores well in terms of resident satisfaction and participation. It has relatively high levels of social and infrastructural capital. However, it is also a highly mixed neighbourhood with areas that are predominantly owner-occupied, areas that are predominantly council rented, and areas that are predominantly managed by a major, successful housing association—the Bournville Village Trust.'[29]

The village survives but the company does not. So does New Earswick near York, created by Joseph Rowntree, as does the Rowntree Foundation that undertook the study of the Bournville village, but the Rowntree company in York that Joseph Rowntree created does not. In contrast, Slough, where Forrest Mars opened his factory in 1932, might not be quite as idyllic a place as Bournville or New Earswick to live but the company that Frank and then Forrest Mars created survives. It survived because the Mars family retained ownership even as it grew to today's $30bn company employing 80,000 people. Cadbury and Rowntree did not.

Ownership by Mars has allowed the family to retain an influence in ensuring the realization of the original purpose, vision, and values of its founders. Far from acting as a straightjacket restraining it from pursuing new directions, that family influence has been an inspiration to realizing new innovative ways of doing business that have brought mutual benefits to more than just the owners. Anchor shareholders provide the vision and values that it is for the board of directors to implement.

Part 3
Practice

The Quakers led the way in some of the most enlightened and purposeful companies that Britain has had over the past 200 years. Companies such Cadbury, Clarks, Fry's, and Rowntree's were iconic in their days in creating not only enlightened but also commercially successful businesses, in some cases, as in Cadbury and Rowntree's, providing housing for their employees. The Quakers introduced one of the most important commercial innovations of all times, fixed-price contracts, to replace the haggling they abhorred, to ensure that all men who were equal in the face of God were treated equally in the market place.

Are there lessons to be learnt from the Quaker family businesses of the past for business today? The answer is yes but not in the way in which one might expect. It is not that we can or should seek a revival of the types of businesses that the Quakers promoted. Indeed if survival is an indicator of success then the Quaker companies have been a failure. Most of them went out of business or were taken over, and those that have survived, such as Barclays and Lloyds Bank, are not today universally regarded as paragons of virtue.

Philanthropy does not feature in a world where ownership and management is no longer in the hands of enlightened families but instead dispersed amongst a large number of institutional investors solely concerned about financial returns for their investors. Enlightened capitalism will have to be profitable if it is to flourish. It will have to generate benefits for investors as well as society. It will have to rekindle the flame which drove the Quakers—that treating people fairly and well is good business.

This is where the Quaker experience has valuable lessons for today in teaching us about the importance of engaging in commercial innovations, such as fixed-price contracts and housing for employees, that fundamentally altered conventions and practices of their time. The Quaker firms became models for business around the world because they demonstrated by example how enlightened business was a highly profitable innovation in business practice.

5

Governance

Remember the day that the Bear O'Shea
Fell into a concrete stairs,
What the Horseface said when he saw him dead
It wasn't what the rich call prayers.
I'm a navvy short, was the one retort
That reached unto my ears.
When the going is rough you must be tough
With McAlpine's fusiliers.

'McAlpine's Fusiliers' by Dominic Behan

On Purpose

It is almost impossible to pick up a management journal today without seeing reference to 'purpose'. Every company is being urged by every academic to get a purpose; without one they haven't got a life.

What is purpose? Purpose is the reason for a company's existence. It answers the question, why does a company exist? One obvious answer is to make profits. But that is no more of an answer than happiness is an answer to the question of what is the purpose of life. Of course we would rather be rich than poor and happy rather than miserable. But those are not the reasons why companies or we exist.

The reason why companies exist is to do things, and their purpose is a statement of that. In exact contradiction to the Friedman doctrine, what people have in mind when they refer to the purpose of a company is not just to produce profits. The purpose of companies is to produce solutions to problems of people and planet and in the process to produce profits, but profits are not per se the purpose of companies. They are derivative from purpose rather than fundamental in their own right.

One way of determining a company's purpose is to answer the question what is its value proposition? What value is it seeking to create for whom over what period of time? Is it predominantly looking to enhance or maximize shareholder value, or consumer value, or the human capital of its employees, the social capital of its communities and societies, or the natural capital it owns and in its supply chain? Is it seeking to do this in the short or long run and in what ways will it enhance these values? These questions link together purpose with the values discussed in Chapter 2 and measures of performance in the next chapter (Chapter 6), and by answering them they establish a corporation as a self-reflexive entity. The parties involved in addressing and answering them are the source of the corporate consciousness, and the means by which it commits to them are the basis of its corporate integrity.

There are two conceptualizations of corporate purpose—a positive and a normative. The positive is literally a statement of what the company is there to do—to produce cheap consumer goods, reliable cars, or the largest social networks. The normative is a statement of what the company should do—to look after its employees, to clean up the environment, to enhance the well-being of its communities and societies within which it operates. The latter has a social public-service element that goes beyond the private interests of the company's consumers or investors. The distinction is between 'making a good'—the positive—and 'doing good'—the normative.

One reason why the distinction is important is that it is reflected in company law. Here is Section 172 of the 2006 UK Companies Act: 'A director of a company must act in the way he considers, in good faith, would be most likely to promote the success of the company for the benefit of its members as a whole.' The members of the company are essentially its shareholders, so what this is saying is that the director of a company has a fiduciary responsibility to promote the success of a company for the benefit of its shareholders.

The section of the Act then goes on to say that the director must:

> in doing so have regard (amongst other matters) to: (a) the likely consequences of any decision in the long term, (b) the interests of the company's employees, (c) the need to foster the company's business relationships with suppliers, customers and others, (d) the impact of the company's operations on the community and the environment, (e) the desirability of the company maintaining a reputation for high standards of business conduct, and (f) the need to act fairly as between members of the company.

So in promoting the success of the company for the benefit of its shareholders, the directors of the company should have regard to the interests of other stakeholders. However, these are derivative of the requirement to promote the interests of the shareholders and are not a primary duty in their own regard.

Shareholder primacy is present in other jurisdictions. For example, Leo Strine, Chief Justice of the Delaware Supreme Court, is unequivocal about the relevance of shareholder primacy in US legislation: 'Stockholders are the only corporate constituency with power under our prevailing system of corporate governance.'[1] Whether the duty of the directors is to shareholders or stakeholders, or, as the section of the UK Companies Act goes on to say, under certain circumstances, to the company's creditors, the focus is not first and foremost on the company's purpose. The ordering goes from shareholder and possibly other stakeholder interests not from purpose to the company's activities.

Does this matter? To some degree it does because if directors had a fiduciary responsibility to uphold a corporate purpose then they could be held to account for its delivery. In particular, if the purpose had a normative component of doing good as well as making a good, then directors would in principle be obliged to promote a social as well as a private benefit.

There are three reasons why in practice this might not be quite as significant as it initially looks. The first is that in a private corporation it is up to the members of the corporation, its shareholders, to seek a remedy for a violation of a breach of fiduciary responsibility. The imposition of the public purpose is therefore dependent on the shareholders' willingness to do so. If sufficiently publicly spirited, then shareholders might act in this way, but if they are as self-interested in their financial earnings alone as they are often depicted as being then they will not. So the enforcement of a purpose that does any more than promote the financial benefits of shareholders may remain weak, even if purpose was made more prominent in company law than it is at present.

Secondly, shareholders do not in general sue their directors, at least outside of the United States. It is for the most part regarded as a complex, expensive, and largely self-defeating exercise if, at the end of the day, any recompense for breach of duty comes from the company itself. But the most important reason why the law is not decisive on this matter is that there is a still more pragmatic influence on corporate practice—the market for corporate control. Directors fear the wrath of shareholders through their direct engagement much more than through the courts. It is the telephone call from an activist shareholder backed up by the possibility of a resolution at a shareholder meeting that threatens the survival of corporate directors, and it is this that bears the greatest influence on their behaviour.

Strine provides a graphic illustration of the consequences of shareholder interventions for one of the United States's most prominent corporations, DuPont, its hometown of Wilmington, Delaware, and its industry rival and fellow victim of insurgent investors, Dow Chemical Company, with which it subsequently merged:

> When it came down to it, the DuPont board knew who called the shots and surrendered the direction of the company to the prevailing market winds... And, therefore, it was without any apology or shame that DuPont and Dow not only presented their historic home communities with gut-wrenching job losses, facility closures that threatened to hollow out towns, and all the damage to other businesses that came with those decisions, but then asked those home communities to go into the pockets of ordinary taxpayers.[2]

Jack Coffee emphasizes the impact of hedge-fund activism on board conduct in the context of the case of Valeant Pharmaceuticals, which according to Coffee, the press described as a 'hedge-fund hotel'.[3] It allegedly employed high-powered executive incentive schemes to encourage management to slash costs, shrink research and development, and raise pharmaceutical prices. More generally, Coffee suggests that the rise of what are termed 'wolf packs'—groups of activist shareholders working together to gain control of a corporate board—has resulted in the appointment of 'blockholder directors'—directors selected by the insurgent investors. As a consequence, Coffee documents the transition of corporate governance in the United States from managerial corporatism between 1920 and 1985, through the passive shareholder capitalism that prevailed between 1985 and 2005, to the current system of hedge-fund activism.

As Strine says: 'These powers translate into purpose because those who run corporations owe their continued employment as managers and directors to the only constituency the corporate law establishes—stockholders.'[4] So even if the law required the company to have a clearly defined purpose and directors to uphold that purpose as their fiduciary duty, then it would only be a primary determinant of their behaviour if potential activist shareholders had an interest in societal benefits beyond their own. Otherwise, it will be business as usual with directors focused on what activists regard as the source of shareholder value.

Tacking purpose onto a system that remains institutionally wedded to shareholder value will not turn the tide of corporate activity in the direction in which purpose wishes to point it. We need to get closer to the core of the issue, and the core is the governance of the corporate purpose.

Governance

There is a widely held view that corporate governance is about enhancing shareholder value, protecting shareholder interests, and ensuring

Figures 1, 2, and 3: The first three ages of the corporation: at first the merchant trading company established by royal charter to undertake voyages of discovery and promote commerce around the world. Then the public corporation created by Acts of Parliament to engage in major public works and the building of canals and railways. Then with freedom of incorporation in the 19th century came the private corporation—the seedbed of the industrial revolution and the manufacturing corporation. (From Chapter 1)

Figure 1. Three East India Company Ships and a French Squadron, 9 March 1757.

Source: Caird Collection, National Maritime Museum, Greenwich, London. © National Maritime Museum, London

Figure 2. Manchester Ship Canal Construction Excavation Trench.

Source: Powys Digital Project History

Figure 3. Messrs Fairbairn and Sons of Manchester, The Official Illustrated Guide to the Great Western Railway, 1860.

Figures 4, 5, and 6: On 14 December 1900 George Cadbury, standing in front of the Friends Meeting House on the idyllic village green of Bournville near Birmingham with 370 cottages and five hundred acres of land around him, declared that he was giving away his wealth to the Bournville Village Trust. The aim of the Trust was 'the amelioration of the conditions of the working class and labouring population'. Meanwhile a less wholesome aspect of chocolate production was taking place off the coast of West Africa: 'it is the monstrous trade in human flesh and blood against which the Quaker and Radical ancestors of Mr Cadbury thundered in the better days of England' The Standard, 26 September 1908. (From Chapter 4)

Figure 4. A street in Bournville Village near Birmingham, a new town founded by chocolate manufacturer and social reformer George Cadbury, July 1909.

Source: Topical Press Agency/Hulton Archive/Getty Images

Figure 5. Cadbury's Cocoa Advert.

Source: Mary Evans/Retrograph Collection

Figure 6. c1900: Workers sort the cocoa crop in the Congo, Africa.

Source: Leopold Mercier/Roger Viollet/Getty Images

Figures 7, 8, and 9: Thomas Midgley was an American mechanical engineer and chemist who was the recipient of a glittering array of prestigious awards and prizes in recognition for the work that he did leading teams of researchers at General Motors that made two major and highly profitable inventions. But those very same inventions were also the cause of the release of large quantities of brain damaging lead and ozone depleting CFCs into the atmosphere that have afflicted the lives of generations of people around the world ever since. (From Chapter 6)

Figure 7. Thomas Midgley.
Source: © CORBIS / Corbis via Getty Images

Figure 8. Thomas Midgley working with the Delco laboratory test engine during World War 1 on "knocking" in petrol engines.

Source: Science Photo Library

Figure 9. Ethyl Advert.

Source: Chronicle / Alamy Stock Photo

Figures 10, 11, and 12: On 19th August 2004, Google came to the NASDAQ stock market at a share price of $85 per share in an initial public offering that valued the company at more than $23bn. Today the founders Sergei Brin and Larry Page are each valued by Forbes at more than $40bn. But Google not only exemplifies the extraordinary concentration of wealth that the mindful corporation is creating, which by comparison puts the tens of millions of dollars of annual income earned by investment bankers into the poverty category, it also illustrates another form of concentration: concentration of power. (From Chapter 1)

Figure 10. Google IPO, August 19, 2004.

Source: Chris Hondros / Getty Images

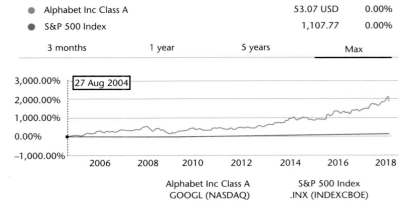

Figure 11. Google / Alphabet Share Price and S&P 500 Index 2004 to 2018.
Source: © Google

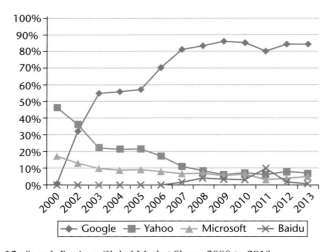

Figure 12. Search Engines Global Market Share, 2000 to 2013.
Source: Netmarketshare, Market Watch, webpronews, clickz, OneStat, and Websidestory

that firms act in the interest of their shareholders. Here, for example, is what the UK Corporate Governance Code, which is widely regarded as an authoritative statement of best practice, says:

> While in law the company is primarily accountable to its shareholders, and the relationship between the company and its shareholders is also the main focus of the Code, companies are encouraged to recognise the contribution made by other providers of capital and to confirm the board's interest in listening to the views of such providers insofar as these are relevant to the company's overall approach to governance.[5]

It therefore exactly parallels the UK Companies Act quoted above in paying due respect to stakeholders at large while clearly recognizing the primacy of shareholder interests. The Corporate Governance Code is designed to promote the success of a company in the interests of its shareholders.

This view of corporate governance is mirrored in policy advice that has repeatedly been given by both UK and US governments in regard to the way in which corporations should be governed around the world. In the East Asian crisis of the second half of the 1990s, observations were made by the IMF and the then chairman of the US Federal Reserve, Alan Greenspan, about the impact of crony capitalism and the need for East Asian countries to dismantle their traditional corporate relationships and adopt US-style dispersed ownership systems.[6]

This advice did not look quite so compelling four years later when the dotcom bubble burst at the beginning of the millennium. At that point, the response was to argue for a strengthening of corporate governance standards to ensure that there was greater accountability and better information provided in corporate accounts. But it was precisely the countries that adopted these standards, namely the United Kingdom and the United States, that suffered the most during the financial crisis five years later and those companies with the supposedly 'best corporate governance arrangements' that performed the worst during the crisis. The greatest degree of risk-taking occurred where companies aligned their managerial incentives most closely with shareholder interests, and those companies with the 'best systems of corporate governance' in the traditional sense, for example of having independent board directors, had the worst record of failures during the crisis.[7]

The reason that policy prescriptions repeatedly failed is that corporate governance is not and should not be about enhancing shareholder value. It is about promoting corporate purpose and the two are not the same. The governance of a firm in all its guises should define how a company assures the delivery of its purpose: the structure of company boards (independent directors and the appointment, induction, and servicing of new board members); the conduct of boards in terms of audit and risk management committees; the determinants of executive compensation, remuneration committees, and shareholder voice over executive compensation; and relationships between investors and firms in regard to information, transparency, shareholder activism, and shareholder engagement in corporate activities. It is directly related to the policies being promoted at national and international levels in regard to the development of better legal systems and contractual rights, stronger investor protection, more say on pay, rights of shareholders to propose shareholder resolutions, and creditor rights.

The correct focus of corporate governance should not therefore be on enhancing shareholder value per se, but on how these aspects of corporate governance in terms of ownership, boards, and remuneration promote corporate purpose and flourishing companies. By recognizing a company's customers as comprising all of its consumers, communities, and citizens, corporate governance achieves corporate flourishing and profitability by furthering the collective well-being of its consumers, employees, suppliers, and societies. In the process it enhances economic growth, entrepreneurship, innovation, and value creation and may thereby lead to increased shareholder value, but corporate governance is not about shareholder value. In an exact inversion of the traditional ranking, purpose is primary and shareholder value derivative.

One implication of this is for diversity. Since countries, industries, and companies have multiple and different purposes, what is suited to one country, industry, or firm is not to another. To appreciate this one only has to recall the history of corporate governance standard bearers. In the 1980s, Japan was regarded as the model of good corporate governance until Japanese banks collapsed in the 1990s. In the 1990s, it was the turn of the United States with its technology-friendly governance standards, until the tech dotcom bubble burst in the early 2000s. Then it was the turn of the UK model with its greater emphasis on general governance principles such as 'comply or explain' than inflexible rules, until the financial crisis put an end to that.

Now it might be Sweden or another Scandinavian country that is the standard bearer, in which case one can predict with confidence that it will not remain so for long. The reason is that there is no one best system of corporate governance that is suited to all companies at all times. The United Kingdom is a good illustration of this. It established corporate governance codes that promoted independent directors, auditors, and remuneration committees well before many other countries. It has a dispersed share-ownership system, the most active market for corporate control of any country in the world, increasing institutional activism, and some of the strongest creditor rights anywhere, and yet its performance in terms of growth, innovation, investment, and productivity has been poor over a long period of time.

Since companies have such diverse corporate purposes, there are significant risks of formulating prescriptive corporate governance codes. There is a problem of identification of appropriate forms of governance, as exemplified by the focus on dispersed ownership after the Asian crisis twenty years ago. There are unintended consequences, as illustrated by the relationship between independent directors and banking activities before the crisis. There is excessive uniformity in corporate structures and practices that exacerbate rather than mitigate risks of failures spreading across countries and companies.

We need diversity rather than uniformity in corporate governance, and we need it in all its various manifestations—ownership, board structure, and incentives—to be focused on promoting the full breadth of corporate purposes and not the single goal of shareholder value. It is the basis on which the purpose and values are instilled throughout the organization, and without it management cannot deliver on purpose.

Not Managing

Being a responsible businessman is not straightforward. Money and morals are not natural bedfellows. It is easy to say that one does well (i.e. make profits) by doing good (i.e. being socially responsible), but the truth of the matter is that one often does a lot better by doing bad. The very act of persuading customers that one's product is the best is a lie for every producer bar one, and only succeeds because it is in general extremely difficult to demonstrate otherwise.

In their book *Phishing for Phools*,[8] George Akerlof and Robert Shiller provide a compelling demonstration that the problem is even more pernicious than that. Markets have no morals, be they product markets or markets for corporate control. Economic and commercial conduct succeeds by deceit and manipulation, and the invisible hand of markets, whose almost mystical virtues are so widely extolled, is in fact a seedbed of impropriety. Combine that with the fact that the masters of managers are the self-interested, short-term institutional investors, and the life of the enlightened chief executive officer (CEO) is not an enriching one— at least not as enriching as it would be were they less enlightened.

That is not to say that enlightened CEOs do not exist; it is just that it is hard to name many of them. Indeed, if one asks most people for examples, beyond Paul Polman, the CEO of Unilever at the time of writing this book, few others are forthcoming. Paul Polman's case is illustrative of the problems. He was brave enough to make clear to his institutional investors from the outset how he intended to run Unilever and what he expected of them as well as what they should expect of him. Not many CEOs are willing to do that immediately on appointment, and the aborted acquisition of Unilever by Kraft at the beginning of 2017 is a reminder of how even those companies most committed to purpose are exposed to the vagaries of the market.

While important, corporate success is not just about visionary leadership; it is predominantly a matter of innovative management. There is mounting evidence that there are three aspects of management that are associated with doing well by doing good—purpose, practice, and performance. You have to want to do it, you have to bring others along in doing it, and you have to demonstrate you have done it.

An example of a company that embeds responsibility in the core of its business, not as philanthropy, is the John Lewis Partnership (JLP) in the United Kingdom. Storey and Salaman observe that:

> The JLP managers place much emphasis on the importance of trust. Trust is the expected response to the successful demonstration that responsibilities are real and are honoured. Managers stress that customers trust the JLP and that is crucial for the success of the business. Customer trust is based on their trust in JLP partners and their confidence that the JLP employment model and values and ownership structure do not prioritize profit above partner or supplier welfare. In other words the JLP's commitment to multiple responsibilities is important in affecting perceptions of the public and the performance of the business and therefore must be maintained.[9]

Many companies do not realize the extent to which doing good can be highly profitable as well as socially beneficial. Storey and Salaman quote one group manager at the JLP:

> When Charlie Mayfield became chairman he expressed the Partnership's strategy in these three terms: Partners, Customer Service and Profit. I think what he's now trying to say is, he doesn't want people to think about them as separate. They are completely interlinked.[10]

Doing Well by Doing Good

There are profitable opportunities around the world in terms of alleviating poverty, inequality, unemployment, and environmental degradation. The bottom and the middle of the pyramid may not individually have much spending power, but there are, unfortunately, a lot of them, and collectively they can account for a substantial source of revenue, if only one can find a way of reaching them. Similarly, future generations may have little current purchasing power but they are destined to be a lot richer than us and willing to pay for the environment and natural capital if we can protect and preserve it for them. In other words, there are substantial private benefits to be derived from the externalities of poverty and environmental degradation through their commercial internalization. This is not corporate social responsibility (CSR) as meritorious philanthropy; it is poverty alleviation and environmental protection as core corporate activities.

Of course, governments can do a great deal to assist with this through creating markets and subsidizing the production of these public goods, but there is much that the corporate sector can do itself, individually and collectively, through relationship and ecosystem building. The way in which companies such as Mars and Unilever have gained access to markets in the slums of the poorest cities and the products of farmers in rural communities in developing countries is by building ecosystems and partnering with organizations such as non-governmental organizations (NGOs), other companies, universities, and local and municipal governments.

The case of Mars operating in the slums of Nairobi through its subsidiary Wrigley illustrates how this works in practice.[11] The programme known as Maua (Swahili for 'flower') has expanded the distribution of Wrigley's products into informal settlements and rural areas through employers providing economic opportunities to subsistence sellers or micro-entrepreneurs, called 'uplifters'. The programme taps into uplifters' entrepreneurial abilities and connects them to a successful, established corporation and its products. This route-to-market project solves a key 'last mile' challenge for Wrigley and has opened up access to bottom of the pyramid markets in Nairobi. For micro-entrepreneurs, the programme has served as a platform for broader social benefits, including participant-led coordination and group formation, and training and information sessions.

The programme has grown quickly, and Maua now forms a key part of Wrigley's distribution system. In 2014 the programme reported double-digit growth. By 2015 the programme engaged with approximately 450 individuals and generated over $4.5million—15 per cent of Wrigley's national business and a level of earnings significantly exceeding that of the conventional parallel route to market models.

There are four key components to such programmes. The first is identifying the human, social, or environmental issues that need to be solved—what are termed the 'pain points' in the ecosystem in which the company is operating—in its supply chain, within its own operations, or, as in this case, in its distribution network. Second, the company needs to gain a deep understanding of the issue at hand and the challenges that confront participants in the ecosystem. It is very easy to presume that one knows the right answers but it is very difficult to get them right in practice. To do this, companies have to spend time consulting with local and international experts, with people in the field, with relevant local and national organizations and government agencies.

Third, the company has to establish close and enduring relations with relevant organizations and individuals in what are termed 'hybrid value chains'. It will have neither the skill set nor the contacts to do this itself, and relationship building is critical to the partnerships that firms need to support them in often unfamiliar and difficult terrains.

The Maua case illustrates all three of these elements. First, Mars Wrigley identified the pain points in its distribution systems in Nairobi and the failure of its existing arrangements. Second, it invested a great deal of time and effort in exploring the issues confronting people living and working in the slums of Nairobi. And third, it established relations with a number of NGOs such as Technoserve, which focuses on creating economic opportunities for women.

There is a final element that presents particularly significant challenges. Even if one is determined to do well by doing good and establishes the ecosystem that is required to achieve it, then there is still a powerful agent acting against it—performance. We know how to measure profits, at least we think we do, but we do not know how to measure much else. In particular, it is much harder to measure such nebulous concepts as human well-being, social capital, and natural capital, or at least to attach monetary values to them with the same precision as profit.

There are measures of human, social, and natural capital, but in general they rely on non-market as well as market prices derived from such tenuous sources as surveys of people's preferences and projections of benefits into the distant future that have to be discounted at subjective rates back to the present. As a consequence, even if a company creates good, it is much harder for it to demonstrate that it is the source of it doing well and to incentivize people to produce the good that is serving them well.

In the case of Maua, Mars Wrigley devoted a considerable amount of effort to creating measures of human and social capital associated with the programme. They worked with partners in academic institutions in identifying the state of the art for measuring these non-financial forms of capital and engaged in regular measurement of performance of the programme on these multiple dimensions as well as financial returns. The importance attached to providing precise measures of performance was a distinctive feature of the programme and was rewarded in, firstly, it focusing on those aspects that were critical to its success and, secondly, in demonstrating the nature of the relation between human and social capital with financial capital.

However, the greatest problems of all in doing well by doing good are not those outside the corporation on the ground or in the field but inside the corporation itself. It requires vision and leadership for the company to recognize the potential benefits to the firm as well as its stakeholders from adopting such practices. And even if the board of directors are fully supportive then the greatest opposition comes below from middle management that are unfamiliar with the processes required to promote people and planet as well as profits. They see them as contrary to their own interests in achieving the financial goals that are expected of them and as 'soft' approaches to tackling the tough realities they face on a daily basis in competing for business and custom.

In other words, doing well by doing good is a management innovation that is at least as challenging as a technological innovation. It requires the same determination and commitment from those at the top of the organization and it involves the same cultural conflicts lower down between those who are undertaking the research and development (R&D) required to identify the new markets, methods, and measurements and those for whom it is business as usual. As a result, they need the same 'safe places' within which to undertake the managerial experimentation as the science labs of the R&D departments. That is precisely what companies like Mars and Unilever create, and that is why Maua provides exactly one such space in the form of a pilot in Nairobi in which the think tank Mars Catalyst was able to develop the concept of the Economics of Mutuality that underpins Mars' approach to doing well by doing good in Maua.

Doing well by doing good is a form of business innovation as significant as the technical innovations that are recognized as the source of commercial opportunities. The successful organizations of the future will be those that are able to exploit the remarkable human, social, and environmental as well as technological opportunities of today. But even if the leadership recognizes this and can overcome the resistance of middle management, create the safe spaces for experimentation, identify the pain points in the ecosystem, form the partnerships, and measure the various types of capital, there still remains one overwhelming hurdle to doing well by doing good and that comes from those who ultimately pull the strings.

Investing for the Long Term

Chapter 4 documented the dominance of families as owners of some of the largest companies listed on stock markets around the world. However, even they pale into insignificance in relation to the largest owners of financial capital—the institutional investors. There is currently over $70 trillion in assets under management by institutional investors. The largest three—Blackrock, Vanguard, and UBS—together command around $10 trillion. It is to these giants of asset management that we need to turn for the successful transformation of short-term safe liquid savings of individuals into long-term risky illiquid assets of companies.

A number of institutions have begun to do exactly that. They are predominantly outside the United Kingdom and United States, most notably in Canada, some Scandinavian countries, and in Asia Pacific. The Ontario Teachers' Pension Fund in Canada, PGGM in the Netherlands, and the Norwegian and Singaporean sovereign funds are often cited as examples.

There are three things that distinguish engaged institutional investors from their more conventional counterparts. The first is that they hold significant share blocks in particular companies for extended periods of time. Second, since they hold rather than trade these blocks, they do not need to employ intermediary fund managers; instead, they either manage the investments directly themselves or actively evaluate fund managers against a longer and broader set of criteria than short-term financial returns; and third, they invest significant amounts in developing the necessary in-house expertise to perform these functions.

Dominic Barton describes how two long-term engaged investors incentivize their managers:

> Consider the example of GIC, the Singaporean sovereign wealth fund, which explicitly takes a twenty-year view on incentives and performance measurement. Its key performance metric at the aggregate-portfolio level, used as the basis for incentives, is the twenty-year rolling rate of return, while its minimum horizon for performance measurement is five years. Similarly, the Canada Pension Plan Investment Board has moved to five-year rolling returns as the benchmark for rewarding its managers.[12]

In other words, these institutions demonstrate a commitment to long-term equity ownership as against traditional short-term portfolio management. This does not require them to forgo the benefits of portfolio diversification because, alongside the concentrated holdings in a segment of their portfolio, they can retain diversified investments (e.g. index funds) in the remainder.

A key function of institutional investors is participation in the appointment and replacement of board members. Monitoring and evaluation of board performance is important but initial care in the selection of board appointments even more so. The reason for this is that the board is the custodian of corporate purpose. In contrast to a shareholder primacy view of the firm, corporate purpose does not reside with financial institutions or the market for corporate control. It is the responsibility of the board, as the elected representatives of the relevant constituents of the company, to define and execute corporate purpose.

In the United Kingdom, directors are formally elected at shareholder meetings on the basis of recommendations of nomination committees of independent directors and are therefore largely self-selected by their own boards. In Sweden, the nomination committee is external to the board and comprises representatives of the largest shareholders. Sweden is a particularly interesting comparison to the United Kingdom because, in contrast to many other Continental European countries, it, like the United Kingdom, has a strongly shareholder-oriented system.[13] However, its pattern of share ownership is very different from the United Kingdom with a much greater prevalence of block holders than in the United Kingdom. The existence of an external nomination committee in Sweden is a reflection of large and long-term shareholdings but it is also an inducement to it since the committee provides a forum in which the largest shareholders can express 'voice' about the composition of the board. There are therefore strong incentives on investors to acquire and retain share blocks to gain seats on the powerful nomination committees.

The concern that external nomination committees raise, in particular in the United Kingdom, is that they undermine their independence and make them prone to capture by large shareholders at the expense of minority shareholders. However, it may be possible to combine the benefits of active engagement by large shareholders in the Swedish external nomination committee with the board independence associated with UK internal committees through including both internal and external members on hybrid nomination committees. They could also have representatives of other parties such as employees, communities, and government in more stakeholder-oriented companies.

A particularly interesting class of long-term engaged owners is industrial foundations, which are widespread in even the largest companies in Denmark and Germany. Industrial foundations are companies that do not simply possess foundations but are owned by them; examples include Bertelsmann, Bosch, Carlsberg, Ikea, and Novo Nordisk. By conventional criteria these companies have all the symptoms of the worst forms of corporate governance—self-appointing boards that are not rewarded on performance or subject to an external market for corporate control. And yet on average their financial performance is as good as that of other similar companies. In fact, in some respects it is better;[14] they have stronger reputations and sounder labour relations and most strikingly of all, they survive: the average length of life of industrial foundation firms is some three times greater than that of other equivalent firms. A concern that is sometimes raised about industrial foundation firms is the self-selection of foundation board members. A hybrid system of board election by nomination committees comprising both internal foundation and external shareholder members might help to address this concern.

The Evidence

What does the empirical evidence suggest? Does purpose or profit produce better financial performance? Is long-termism good or bad? Is sustainable, stakeholder business better than shareholder business? Does doing good do well?

There has been a massive outpouring of empirical studies focused on precisely these issues.[15] A decisive study of a relation between responsibility and performance is the Holy Grail to which the business and financial academic community is working frenetically. But like the quest for the Holy Grail, it is proving a bit more elusive than might have been hoped.

On the plus side, there is mounting evidence that if one invests in portfolios of purposeful, sustainable, socially minded corporations and is willing to hold them for a sufficiently long period of time, then one can comfortably outperform their less enlightened and ethically sound counterparts.[16] But one also does well with instant gratification investing in 'sin stocks' engaged in gambling, alcohol, tobacco, arms, fossil fuels, and sex. While goodness might be rewarded in heaven, badness appears to have faster (if not such enduring) pay-offs closer to home.[17]

There have been studies examining the relationship of corporate social responsibility (CSR),[18] corporate sustainability,[19] customer satisfaction,[20] eco-efficiency,[21] environmental, social, and governance (ESG) factors,[22] and materiality[23] to stock returns, risk equity cost of capital, and merger stock returns.[24] They report that CSR, corporate sustainability, customer satisfaction, eco-efficiency, ESG, and materiality are associated with higher returns, lower risk, and lower costs of capital. There is evidence of a positive relation between employee satisfaction,[25] corporate cultures of integrity,[26] and stock returns, at least over the long run. There is evidence that highly trusted organizations are associated with greater decentralization of investment, hiring, and sales decisions.[27] These studies are careful to control for other factors that might be influencing the results and in identifying directions of causation from different forms of responsible business to performance not vice versa. There is, in other words, a clear relationship between good business practices and financial returns for shareholders.

If there are such clearly good, beneficial, and profitable management practices, why are they not universally adopted? Why is there such a deficit and deteriorating level of trust, meaningful work, and corporate environmental protection? In answering these questions, we should note that the criteria by which the above studies judge performance are financial returns and costs of capital. They are using profit as their measure of success. It is the same as presuming that the yardstick by which to measure human happiness (utility) is wealth. It is sometimes for some people but it certainly is not always for everyone. The reason why is similar to the reason why shareholder value is not always and everywhere the relevant yardstick, and that is it depends on circumstances.

Shakespeare's seven ages of man quoted at the beginning of Chapter 1 illustrate: 'At first the infant, | mewling and puking in the nurse's arms'—human capital; who becomes the whining schoolboy seeking friends—social capital; then the lover—human capital; who needs to earn income for his family as a soldier—financial capital; and progresses to become a justice worried about his social standing—social capital; before becoming an old man worried about his health—human capital; before the last scene of all—'sans everything'—spiritual capital.

At each stage the relevant objective to be maximized (the maximand) changes. It moves from being personal human capital to social, to family human, to financial, back to social, and finishing with human capital. So if we posed the question does a focus on purpose in our lives lead to a positive association with financial capital, the answer would be unequivocally not always. We are not predominantly focused on it for most of the ages of our lives and quite willing to sacrifice it for other goals. It is not just that 'money can't buy you love' or health or status or happiness, it is that at most stages of our lives our maximand is something quite different.

So too with the six ages of the corporation, also described in Chapter 1: at first the merchant trading company operating under royal charter, opening up voyages of discovery around the world—social and material capital; then the public corporation with its hoards of labourers—social and human capital; then the private company and the rise of manufacturing—

financial and material capital; the fourth age is the service firm and the rise of financial services—human and financial capital; the fifth age is the transnational corporation with its gleaming global headquarters running rings around nations—financial, human, and material capital. The last scene of all is the mindful corporation sans everything—human and intellectual capital.

So financial capital has featured prominently in three ages of the corporation but is rapidly losing its pre-eminence in the sixth age of the corporation. Instead human and intellectual capitals are of much greater significance. But as we come out of the previous ages, we are also left with a legacy of depleted natural and social capital. So the major constraints on the seventh and final age of the corporation as the trusted corporation are a combination of human, intellectual, natural, and social capital.

The importance of this stems from the fact that it means that the relevant maximand in many cases is no longer financial capital. It has moved on to a combination of human, intellectual, natural, and social capital. This has profound implications for corporate governance and control because it is these capitals that are constrained and have to be allocated to their most efficient use, and this requires control by the relevant party over their allocation. So where human capital is most heavily constrained then employee ownership is appropriate. Where intellectual capital is critical then the allocation of control to entrepreneurs or founders is required, and where social capital is deficient then local or public ownership may be appropriate.

New technologies are fundamentally altering the governance of firms. For example, through influencing the way in which the prices of shares are set in stock markets, high frequency trading is affecting resource allocation in corporations and intensifying a focus on short-term share-price fluctuations. Small increases in the speeds at which high-frequency trades are undertaken have been found to yield significantly higher and persistent profits for the trading firms that execute them.[28] New technologies therefore create substantial private incentives to engage in activities that may have few, no, or possibly negative social benefits associated with them. Corporate governance cannot remain oblivious to such social consequences of new technologies and, with the arrival of artificial intelligence, it is not just that the scale of the effects will become even greater but the source of decisions may move from the minds of men to machines as company board decisions themselves are automated.

The Thesis

There can then be no presumption that shareholder control is always and everywhere optimal or that shareholder value is in general the appropriate criteria by which to measure performance. Where the constraints of other forms of capital are greater then it is in relation to these capitals that we should expect value to be maximized and performance to be best. In such circumstances, while financial capital should not be depleted, it is not necessarily optimized either and may in some measure be sacrificed for the enhancement of other forms of capital.

This suggests some fundamental principles of corporate governance. The first relates to ascertaining which capitals should be exercising corporate control and therefore what capital values should be maximized:

Principle 1:   Corporate control should be exercised and value maximized by scarce capitals.

So corporate control should reside with those capitals that are in short supply because it is those that will have to be allocated to activities of maximum value. In the absence of frictions, total corporate value, defined as the sum of values of different forms of capital, will be maximized when control is allocated according to principle 1.

In practice, frictions to the allocation of control are created by legal, regulatory, political, and social factors. In particular, there will be resistance to reallocations of control that affect distribution of power and wealth by those whose influence will diminish as a consequence. These parties will use their political and social influence over law and regulation to impede transfers of authority. This suggests the second principle of corporate governance relating to measures of performance defined in terms of total capital value:

Principle 2:   Total corporate value will deteriorate where law and regulation impede appropriate transfers of control.

Transfers of control are required to respond to external influences, such as changing technologies, social pressures, and environmental constraints that alter the nature of capital constraints. For example, the Internet has diminished constraints on hotels and taxis, by facilitating sharing of private properties and automobiles, and on hoteliers and taxi drivers, by employing part-time drivers and landlords, while increasing requirements for others, for example the skilled labour involved in designing the computer applications that manage the sharing economy. The transfers of control that these changes demand are inevitably resisted by the losing parties who seek political and social support for laws and regulations that impede them.

An interesting illustration of this was the event that caused the suppression of dual-class shares in Britain described in Chapter 4. Dual-class shares and takeover defences featured prominently for a brief period of time in Britain in the 1960s when companies attempted to defend themselves against the newly emerging market for corporate control—hostile takeovers:

> These takeover defences met with stiff opposition from an influential quarter—the institutional investors and the London Stock Exchange. They were concerned about the interference with the takeover process, the ability of management to entrench itself behind takeover defences and the withdrawal of their voting rights. Under pressure from the institutions, the Stock Exchange made it known that it disapproved of the use of dual class shares and would not permit their use in new equity issues. The intervention of the institutions and the Stock Exchange proved decisive and during the 1970s and 1980s companies steadily withdrew dual class shares.[29]

Unconstrained transfers of control can indeed be total value diminishing if the gainers cannot compensate the losers. In other words, they risk value diversion, i.e. making one party better off at the expense of another, rather than value creation, i.e. increasing the total size of the pie. To avoid this, profit should only be recorded after all the costs associated with compensating losers have been accounted for. So, for example, there is only a total surplus resulting from the sharing economy if there is a profit after compensating for the losses sustained by taxi drivers and hoteliers. This suggests a notion of capital maintenance by which provision has to be made for the costs of maintaining all forms of capital (human, natural, and social) as well as that of existing controlling capitals (financial and material):

> Principle 3: Profit should be measured net of total capital maintenance associated with sustaining all forms of affected capital.

We return to illustrate the application of this third principle in Chapter 6. It suggests that there are limitations to the degree to which the controlling party can exploit their positions. This is reinforced by the observation that throughout the six ages of the corporation, more than one type of capital is scarce. This has been particularly pronounced recently with all of human, intellectual, natural, and social capital being arguably scarce to varying degrees in different corporations.

Together, the above principles have several implications. First, existing studies are deficient in focusing exclusively on financial performance for shareholders. In an era of diminishing financial constraints and increasing financial abundance, such studies are of limited relevance and, until a wider set of measures beyond financial returns is available, it will be difficult to undertake reliable tests of performance. This emphasizes the importance of being able to extend measures of capital beyond financial capital to include human, intellectual, natural, and social capital.

The second implication is that in light of the co-existence of multiple forms of scarce capital and the need to protect the interests of abundant as well as scarce capital, controlling parties have the responsibilities of trustees to act on behalf of multiple parties not just themselves. As noted in Chapter 1, corporations are commitment not control devices that are required to uphold the interests of multiple not single parties. That is why the institutions of trust were so important in the development of corporations during the twentieth century described in Chapter 4.

This conclusion is particularly relevant to natural capital. It is only over the last few decades that the constraint imposed by natural capital has become evident; before then it did not feature prominently at all. But we now recognize the problems created by consuming at the expense of nature and future generations. How do we allocate control to natural capital? Do we put the rhinoceros or the giraffe in charge of our multinational corporations? How do we give the unborn a voice at our annual general meetings?

In *Firm Commitment* I discuss the problem of what is termed 'the tragedy of the commons', which involves overgrazing of the commons by current generations at the expense of future generations. The solution I suggested there involves giving young generations the authority to allocate grazing rights to older generations. Realizing that (a) what they will inherit will depend on how much they allocate today but (b) they will be the next older generation and therefore dependent on the wisdom of the generation beyond them, they exploit neither the commons nor the older generation. In contrast, if control is allocated to the older generation then the younger generation is entirely at the mercy of the altruism of their seniors.

There are therefore two possible solutions to the protection of natural capital. The first is to allocate control rights predominantly to younger generations of owners and require them to relinquish control to their successors as they age. The second is to put natural capital ownership in trust of older generations whose concern about their reputation will make them take their role as custodians seriously with the proper interest of future as well as current generations in mind. A recent example of the latter is the Whanganui River in New Zealand, which in March 2017 became the first river to be granted legal status as a *Te Awa Tupua*, an indivisible, living whole, with two guardians, one from the Crown and one from the Whanganui River Maori community.

The three principles described above account for recent observations of corporate forms 'going private', seeking to be more adept at responding to new opportunities by removing the restrictions imposed on them by public equity markets. They provide an explanation for the observations made repeatedly throughout the book of the apparent success of corporate forms, such as cross-shareholdings, industrial foundations, and pyramid structures, which on conventional shareholder-value principles should have been unmitigated disasters. They are consistent with the persistence and continuing dominance of families employing control devices such as dual-class shares that allow idiosyncratic values to be sustained in the face of their apparent detriment to shareholder value. They explain the rise of the Middle East on the back of its commercial lead in adopting partnerships and then its decline in failing, for a mixture of political, religious, and social reasons, to adopt the corporate forms that were emerging elsewhere. They are associated with a country with historically one of the strongest levels of investor protection and shareholder primacy, the United Kingdom, declining progressively in economic status over the last hundred years relative to one with some of the weakest, Germany.

Above all they bring us to the heart of the problem with the Friedman doctrine. It is not the notion of making profits or even prioritizing profits that is at fault. It is the way it has morphed into an obligation on companies to maximize profits and achieve greater profits than other firms at all times that has been the source of corporate failure. It drives companies to extremes of seeking the pursuit of shareholder value at the expense of all and everyone else, resulting in abuses and erosion of trust. The rise of the market for corporate control in the form of takeovers and institutional activism is the reason why the problem has been most acute in the United Kingdom and the United States with their dispersed forms of ownership and absence of anchor shareholders to moderate its effect. And the inability of firms in the United Kingdom to adopt takeover defences has made the problem even more acute there than in the United States.

Recent ideas on conscious, inclusive, mutual, purposeful, shared business capitalism and economies all have their merits in promoting better practices and processes but none of them are inconsistent with the Friedman doctrine of pursuing profits and none get to the heart of the problem. It is the manifestation of the doctrine in the unrelenting drive to greater profits that is the source of its deficiencies and its consequential undermining of the ability of management to act 'reasonably'. It is not that directors are angels dancing at the heads of corporations, but that their vision has been clouded by the persistent pre-eminence of shareholder value.

Definitive support for the principles must await more specific testing of, for example, impacts of external influences such as technological, social, political, legal, and regulatory changes on allocations of corporate control in organizations. However, even without such evidence they appear to provide a coherent account of much of what history and experience from around the world has to tell us about the way in which corporate ownership, governance, and management affect the performance of firms.

The Governance of Purpose

The purpose of governance is the governance of purpose. Superficially doing well by doing good would appear to be a problem of management. There are unrecognized and unmeasured benefits from promoting human, social, and natural capital as well as financial capital, and there are problems of managing companies' supply and distribution chains to realize these benefits.

Complex though these are, there is more to doing well by doing good than just measurement and management. There are still greater challenges at the top of organizations in legitimizing and advocating these approaches to business. They demand a commitment of leadership that flies against conventional wisdom and frequently faces stiff resistance from lower down in the organization. For a business to do well by doing good it requires the board to take charge of creating a conducive corporate culture throughout the organization from the board to the shop floor, from the workplace to the fields and slums of the supply and distribution chains. And it is not just the board that needs to be committed, so too do the owners.

This is why what appears to be a matter of management is actually a challenge of corporate governance. Corporate governance is about the structure and conduct of the ownership and control of companies to fulfil corporate purpose. It lies at the heart (*cor*) of the body (*corpus*) and head (*caput*) of the corporation. It governs how the purpose and values of the business are translated into actions in the organization that are transmitted into value for investors. Along with ownership, law, and regulation, the absence of purpose from the centre of corporate governance is a primary reason why firms fail to deliver on purpose.

6

Performance

Many of the things that you can count don't count; many of the things that you can't count really count.

Albert Einstein

What Counts?

Accounting is not a topic that generally sets the world alight. But there is one area where it should, and that is where it literally could set our world alight by threatening our survival as well as prosperity. No less an issue is at stake in relation to accounting for our environment and natural capital.[1]

At present, for the most part we do not account for the environment and natural capital. We count our financial and material assets but not some of our most vital and basic assets that help us breathe and live. Why does this matter? How can accounts destroy or save our planet?

The answer is that we have become transfixed by accounts and base our lives around them. We assiduously record what we do as an asset and liability and then reward people on the basis of the profits and losses that they create. The cost entries of our accounts have become the compass of our existence. The problem is that those entries in accounts are often simply wrong. The compass is a source of inaccurate fascination that is steadily guiding us to a precipice that threatens our survival. The mistake we are making is in recording activities and transactions without taking proper account of their effect on our environment and natural capital. The consequence is that we are recording profits where there may be none and failing to report them where they may be substantial.

A simple example will illustrate the point. Consider a company that is considering building a manufacturing plant or drilling for oil in the middle of the Amazon rainforest. At present it records the cost of the land it purchases, the buildings, equipment, and other supplies it acquires and the people it employs. It then records the revenue that it earns from the production of the plant or the oil it extracts and the profits that result by subtracting the costs of the inputs. What it fails to recognize is the destruction of the rainforest. It incurs a cost in chopping down the trees and earns income from selling the timber but the impact of the destruction of the trees on the environment, the Amazon forest ecosystem, the carbon capture, or the water table remain unrecorded.

The reason it does not record these is that it is not paying for them or rewarded for them. Its balance sheets and income statements only incorporate items that affect the financial performance of the firm. If there is no effect on the company's earnings and expenditures then there is no entry. The company is not misleading anybody; it is doing what it is expected to do. It is just that in the process of doing what it is required to do, it is misleading everybody.

It is not only in relation to natural capital and the environment that these issues arise. Suppose that the company was not only cutting down the forests but also employing workers at below a living wage or, worse, below a subsistence level. If it is breaking the law then its profits are clearly being overstated because there is a possibility that it will be fined for its employment practices. If it is not, then there is no apparent cost to the firm in continuing what it is currently doing.

Or to take a third example, suppose that the firm's activities are destroying the existing communities within which it is operating, undermining the local infrastructure and endangering the health of the people in and around its plants. Again, if it is breaking the law then it may incur a cost but otherwise it will not.

In all these cases, so long as the firm is operating within the law, the firm's profits are not affected by its actions and the consequences of them for the environment, natural capital, human capital, or social capital are not reflected in its accounts. These are effects for which it is not being paid or penalized and should not therefore be reported in its measured performance. Put another way, accounts conventionally capture the legal liabilities and claims of what the firm does. They do not incorporate activities for which there is no legal liability or claim. These fall outside the boundaries of the firm and have no place in its financial reporting.

The nature of the accounting therefore naturally corresponds with the Friedman doctrine described in the Preface. Firms' sole objective is to maximize their profits subject to upholding the law and social norms. So its accounts should reflect what contributes to or detracts from that and exclude everything else. There is therefore an internal consistency in the way in which the firm is conventionally conceived and its performance is measured. It is not possible to alter one without altering the other. It is no good wishing we measured company profits differently so long as the purpose of the firm is to maximize profits, and there is no point in changing the purpose of the firm if we continue to measure its performance just in relation to profits. Moving one involves moving both.

Thrive and Survive

While internally coherent, the conventional approach is logically inconsistent. To see this, consider its long-run consequences. Consider a company that is profitable, growing, exploiting its natural capital, paying its workers below a subsistence wage, and destroying its local community and infrastructure. What will happen to it? The answer is it will thrive but not survive. According to its financial accounts, it will be doing splendidly and it may continue to do so for some time to come. But it will eventually run out of the natural, human, and social resources that it requires for its existence. That follows immediately from the observation that it is depleting finite resources necessary for its survival at a faster rate than they are being renewed.

The survival of firms depends as much as we do on the maintenance not only of physical and financial capital but also of natural, human, and social capital. The long-run growth of the firm requires the balanced growth of all of its capitals not just material and financial capital.

The significance of different capitals will vary depending on the activities in which firms are engaged. For some, material and financial capital are predominant. For others, in particular in the service sector, human capital is of greater significance. For those in the natural resource business, natural capital is a primary input. But in no firm can profits be sustained at the expense of finite capitals on which its survival depends.

What this points to is a notion of capital maintenance that goes beyond current concepts. At present, a firm's profits are measured after subtracting the cost of maintaining its physical capital, namely the depreciation of its buildings, equipment, plant, and machinery. No account is taken of the cost of maintaining its natural capital, upholding the health and well-being of its workforce, or preserving the local infrastructure and communities within which it is operating. In other words, at present a firm can be highly profitable at the same time as it is entirely unsustainable because while it makes proper provision for preserving its physical capital, it makes no provision for the cost of maintaining its natural, human, and social capital.

The implication of this is that what a sustainable firm needs to do is exactly the same as what a responsible firm should do. It should account for the cost of maintaining not just its physical capital but all of its capitals—its natural, human, and social capitals. It should measure the depreciation of all of these capitals and record its profits net of the cost of maintaining and restoring them. If it fails to do so then it is simply mismeasuring profits and in most cases overstating them.

The importance of this is twofold. First by misstating profits, companies are misallocating their resources. To see this, return to the company building a plant or drilling for oil in the Amazon rainforest. By failing to account for the cost of preserving the environment and natural capital, the firm is reporting profits that simply do not exist—what might legitimately be described as 'fake' profits to contrast them with the 'fair' profits that are associated with sustainable activities. It may no longer be profitable for the firm to be undertaking these operations if its profits were correctly reported. We are at present promoting activities that should not be taking place because, while they appear to be profitable, they are not—they are fake.

Second, and equally important, by restating profits correctly we are stopping companies distributing profits to their shareholders that they do not possess. According to company law, companies cannot distribute more than their accumulated capital. Their accumulated capital comes from their retained profits. Their measured profits are therefore important in setting a bar on the amount that the company can pay to their shareholders. At present, distributions are excessive in relation to companies' true profits because their profits are overstated. By correctly measuring depreciation and capital maintenance in relation to all relevant forms of capital then firms' profits are appropriately restated and permissible distributable profits correspondingly reduced.

So at the very least, what a correct system of accounting does is to report profits after a proper provision for the maintenance of all forms of capital. That in itself will have a dramatic impact on the conduct of firms. But it is only one half of the story.

A Man's Firm Is His Fiefdom

As noted in the preface, the determination of what is currently recorded in companies' accounts is determined by a property view of the firm:

What is the property of the firm gives rise to legal claims and liabilities. What falls within the legal boundaries of the firm is reported and what does not is excluded. Again it is an internally coherent concept but it is irrelevant.

It is irrelevant because the boundaries are not relevant. It is like defining the boundaries of a country as residing at its borders when it is a part of a union with neighbours that permits the free flow of people and goods across its borders without restriction. Its borders are a fiction, and so long as they are recognized as such they do no harm, but if they are not then they can be very damaging.

The legal borders of the firm are equally fictitious but are not recognized to be so and have thereby been extremely damaging. The reason that they are fictitious is that, regrettably, noise, smoke, polluted water, poverty, and personal distress do not recognize legal borders. They permeate where they wish with no consideration for where the law believes that they should not trespass.

The economic significance of this is that by defining the boundaries of the firm where they do not exist, we are excluding activities that should be included and including those that should not be. To go back to the example of the firm in the forest, we have already established that its profits should not be insulated from the havoc it inflicts on its environment, people, or communities. But nor should it be unrecognized for the good that it does.

At present, the firm gains no credit, or more seriously no reported asset, for improving the environment, for educating its workforce, or for contributing to the education and health of its local communities. It gets no credit because they are external to the firm and fall outside the legal boundaries of the firm where they would be recognized in its accounts.

This is nonsensical. If these assets contribute to the corporate purpose then they should be recognized as such. Their costs should be reported as human, natural, and social capital assets alongside material assets on which the company may or may not earn financial returns in the future. If it is not expected to earn a financial benefit of a value equal to the cost of the investment then it should write down the asset in the normal way, as it would do for a material asset. If on the other hand it can find imaginative methods of commercializing the asset employing the innovative management practices described in Chapter 5 then it will in due course earn a financial return that will further justify the expenditure.

Furthermore, if the purpose of the company involves furthering human, natural, or social capital then the attainment of those objectives will be benefits in their own regard, compensating for lower financial returns. In other words, recognition of non-material assets should reflect their contribution to both financial performance and the achievement of corporate purposes more generally.

No wonder economics depicts *homo economicus* as unremittingly self-centred and selfish when all it records is his contributions to being so. At the moment we do not recognize that which is good but unrewarded and acknowledge that which is rewarded but bad. There are therefore two failures of existing systems of accounting. First they attribute profits where they do not exist and destroy value; second, they fail to acknowledge assets where they exist and create value. As a result, they are both an overstatement and understatement of performance, and therefore wrong.

Natural Income

Thus far we have discussed accounting in the context of firms and corporate accounts. But these problems are as important and potentially even more so at a national and international level. National accounts are a record of the economic activity of a nation. They report its output, income, and expenditure and are key to macroeconomic policy. In particular, they were integral to the emergence of demand management as a tool of macroeconomic policy in the second half of the twentieth century.

The basis on which national accounts are constructed is the goods and services that a country produces, the income that its inhabitants earn, and the expenditures they make. They therefore report what is produced, earned, and spent. As in the case of corporate accounts they record earnings net of the cost of maintaining the physical capital of the nation but, as in the case of corporate accounts, they do not record the cost of maintaining other forms of capital—natural, human, and social capital. As a result, growing national income can be associated with declining natural, human, and social capital. It is as if the landlord of a property records her rental income without acknowledging the deterioration in her properties and thereby misperceives both her true wealth and disposable income.

There is a second and potentially even more serious consequence of the preoccupation of national accounts with flows and not stocks and that is a failure to measure public-sector debt and borrowing requirement correctly. Companies do not talk about their debt or borrowing requirement, at least not in the way in which the public sector does. They refer to their net assets—net of their liabilities—and their net income or profit as the changes in their net assets.

The public sector cannot do the same because it does not systematically measure its stock of public assets and investments. It should but currently does not record natural capital as a national asset and expenditure on it as a national investment. It should but at present does not measure public-sector net wealth as the difference between the stock of public assets and liabilities, and the public-sector net surplus as the change in public-sector net wealth.

The consequences of this are twofold. First, national accounts mismeasure national income and output. They overstate it by failing to make provision for the cost of maintaining natural capital. Second, they fail to record natural capital assets and therefore understate net national wealth, the accumulation of net national assets, national saving, and public-sector net surpluses.

The problem is not by any means restricted to natural capital. The same is true of human and social capital because neither they nor public-sector investments in them are recorded as national wealth or contributions to its enhancement. In fact, as Chapter 10 will describe, the absence of national balance sheets has still wider repercussions because the public sector does not even record its stock of material capital—its infrastructure—comprehensively.

As a result, resources are allocated inappropriately. Too few are devoted to public-sector investments that enhance our national wealth in human, social, natural, and infrastructure assets, and too many to restraining public-sector borrowings that give false impressions of the deterioration of our national wealth.

Precisely how large the mismeasurement and overstatement have been is difficult to say because until recently there have been few attempts at measuring natural, human, and social capital. This deficiency has increasingly been recognized and more comprehensive forms of accounting have been developed to measure national wellbeing, i.e. human, social, and natural capital, as well as material and financial capital. In particular, accounting for our natural capital (our environment and ecosystems) has risen to prominence and become the subject of national and international initiatives. For example, a System of Environmental-Economic Accounting (SEEA), a joint initiative between several international agencies, has created a common framework for the adoption of natural capital national accounting by national governments.

It is early days in the production of reliable estimates but the 2012 *Inclusive Wealth Report*[2] has produced a set of estimates of measures of natural capital in twenty countries over the period 1990 to 2008. It tells a sobering story in relation to natural capital. In nineteen out of the twenty countries there has been a decline in natural capital—the only country to report an increase was Japan because of a rise in its forest cover. Separate estimates by the UK Office of National Statistics for the United Kingdom report a decline of natural capital of 4 per cent in just four years over the period 2007 to 2011.[3]

Failure to account for the cost of maintaining natural capital is resulting in both over- and understatements of countries' true income and wealth. The *Inclusive Wealth Report* records that in six of the twenty countries in its analysis, declines in natural capital led to a decrease in overall wealth that includes human and natural as well as material capital.

No Gain with Pain

So how should we put this right? The proper way to account for both corporate and national accounts is to do two things. The first is to recognize the liabilities associated with eroding human, natural, and social capital—a 'do no harm' principle. The second is to record the costs associated with enhancing human, natural, and social as well as material and financial capital as assets—a 'do good' principle.

Put very simply the first implies that if you earn 100 and have to spend 20 on restoring the fabric of your properties, your income is 80, not 100. Correspondingly, if national income is 100 and the cost of restoring natural capital to its condition at the start of the period in question is 20 then net national income is 80 not 100 as currently reported.

The second principle implies that if the 20 you spend actually improves the quality of your properties then the value of your property has appreciated by 20. Correspondingly, if 20 is spent on enhancing the quality of natural capital, for example cleaning up rivers and lakes, then that should be reflected in a higher value of natural capital assets. Get credit where credit is due but not where it comes from the damage you do.

What Makes Natural Capital So Valuable?

Natural capital is very special because nature is very special. The hand of man has touched many if not all forms of natural capital but nevertheless what distinguishes natural capital from its material counterparts is that it also largely comprises nature. Where that nature is living it gives natural capital a unique and important feature in relation to its material counterparts—its ability to regenerate and sustain itself. When we consume material capital we use it up. When we consume at least some natural capital, as if by magic, we have as much of it as when we started.

That is the power of renewables. Provided that we do not consume too much of them then their regeneration property means that we do not have to maintain them. They maintain themselves. That makes natural capital an incredibly valuable form of capital. There are few other forms of capital (knowledge and information perhaps being two) that have an infinite life and do not depreciate in value when consumed.

Furthermore, the enduring nature of some aspects of natural capital, such as the world's mountains and the prospect that the sun will continue to rise tomorrow, mean that there are many elements of natural capital that we do not have to depreciate. Our consumption of the rays of the sun does not impinge directly on its ability to continue to emit them, and the enjoyment that we derive from the existence of mountains does not affect their enduring presence.

The significance of this is that we do not have to set aside an amount for the maintenance of some forms of renewables. We do not have to determine a measure of capital consumption of these non-depleting assets. In contrast those forms of renewable that we are over-consuming, and in particular those that are at risk of potentially serious or catastrophic collapse, do need to be maintained and restored. It is those renewables that are at risk of deterioration or collapse that should be the focus of investment by companies and governments, and it is these that require a depreciation and maintenance charge in both corporate and national accounts.

How Should Natural Capital Maintenance Expenditures Be Determined?

The first stage of righting the wrongs is to determine which forms of natural capital are at risk because of overconsumption or exploitation. The second stage is to determine the cost of preserving and restoring those forms of natural capital back to a level at which they can regenerate themselves. That cost might be the expenditure needed to protect natural capital or it might be the value of productive activities forgone in the process of protecting the natural capital. So, for example, the company producing or prospecting for oil might plant additional trees or move its production elsewhere. That is the maintenance expenditure.

The restoration cost is the cost of not just putting the existing wrong right but going further in restoring the natural capital to a state in which it can regenerate itself. So the company may invest in the Amazon forest to restore ecosystems that are in decline. By bringing the condition of the ecosystem above its critical level, these larger expenditures now may avoid the need for repeated expenditures in the future to prevent further decline.

An important assumption underlying these maintenance or restoration costs is that existing natural capital has to be protected. There is no room for substitution of one form of capital for another or the offset of deterioration of natural capital in one location by investment elsewhere (for example, in nature reserves in place of natural habitats). No substitution sounds like a restrictive and extreme requirement. Its justification comes from the fact that the party most affected by today's decisions about natural capital—future generations—is the one with no voice on the matter. The only way in which they can be given a say is by preserving natural capital as it is today, leaving them to determine what to do with it when they inherit it. We are in essence trustees of natural capital for future generations.

The importance of this is reinforced by the fact that the purposes to which we believe that natural capital can be best put today may be quite different from what future generations value the most. There is an option value of deferring decisions about the deployment of natural capital to future generations. For example, forests may at one time have been most valued for the fuel that they could provide, whereas today their recreational and carbon sequestration benefits may be more highly prized. Furthermore, the complexities of understanding the nature of ecosystems and the environment suggest that we should err in the direction of caution, imposing restrictive rather than lax rules on preserving them as they are.

A less restrictive approach is to consider categories of similar forms of natural capital that together should be conserved but which individually need not be. So, for example, the total stock of a particular species might be critical to its survival while its prevalence in a certain location is not. Or access to recreational land within a specified radius of an urban conurbation may be important while its situation in an existing locality is not. In other words, it may be possible to 'offset' detriments of one form by enhancements of another. While vulnerable to abuse, properly administered offsets offer a pragmatic resolution to purist restoration.

Avoiding Valuing the Invaluable

An important aspect of the approach described here is that it does not involve valuing natural capital. It involves identifying where natural capital is deteriorating or in danger of deteriorating but it does not put a price or value on that deterioration. It simply states that it is the responsibility of companies, landowners, and nations to put that deterioration right and not record a profit or income without having incurred the cost of putting it right.

This is about measuring profit and income correctly and it is as applicable to human and social capital as it is to natural capital. There should be no gain where it inflicts pain on employees, communities, or future generations—the pain should be borne by the perpetrator not the victim. Profit should only be acknowledged once it has been corrected for the cost of remedying the pain it has inflicted on others, be they employees, suppliers, customers, communities, nations, or the unborn.

There is no attempt at evaluating the value of these different types of capital. Neither a company's nor a nation's balance sheet includes the value of its human, natural, or social capital. These are important exercises that the *Inclusive Wealth* analysis attempts to undertake. They are important in establishing the scale, location, and distribution of different forms of capital. How large are human, natural, and social relative to financial and material capital? Where are they most prevalent and deficient? How are they changing over time?

These are important but difficult questions. They are difficult because of the scale of the exercises. For example, they involve identifying not just natural capital at risk of deterioration but all forms of natural capital, in principle sunlight and mountains as well as fish stocks and forests that are being exploited. They require prices to be attached to almost immeasurable concepts, such as the value of a particular species in the valuation of natural capital or social cohesion in social capital.

The scale and complexity of these exercises lead to scepticism and cynicism about their relevance and reliability. In particular, they raise concerns about economists' preoccupation about knowing, in Oscar Wilde's words, 'the price of everything and the value of nothing'. They arouse fear that attaching a price to natural capital is the first stage in creating a market in it, which leads to it being traded for financial gain—and with much justification.

Economic principles have led to a preoccupation with the application of economic valuations to accounting. These are often described in terms of 'marking to market'. The problem is that markets only exist for a small proportion of the activities in which companies and countries engage. Most are not priced, and, as a consequence, resources are erroneously allocated to activities, such as takeovers and sales of public assets, that augment market values at the expense of other parties whose capital losses are not equivalently reflected in market valuations.

That is not what is being suggested here. Instead, income and profit should be measured correctly to preserve and protect human, natural, and social capital against exploitation for illusory profit. The scale of the task is much more manageable because it only requires capital at risk to be identified and costs of remedying deterioration, not prices and values, to be determined.

This is not to diminish the significance of market values. They play an important role in the identification of value creation and the allocation of resources. But market values do not equate to firm values. The values of the firm encompass more than their market values and reflect the interests and non-observable valuations of other parties as well. That is why unrestrained markets in corporate control can be so damaging and why the contemporaneous existence of both liquid stock markets and block holders provide such a powerful means of combining the information content of markets with the promotion of the long-term success of the corporation as a whole.

Lie of the Land or the Land of Lies

Once we have measured profit correctly after the cost of putting wrongs right and alleviating the pain inflicted on others—fair profit—it provides an appropriate basis on which to measure gains from improvement. The reason is simple. Profits are not fair where they come at the expense of others (fake profits) so where they are fair, they have been earned without detriment to others.

One person and one company illustrate this particularly poignantly. Thomas Midgley was an American mechanical engineer and chemist who was the recipient of a glittering array of prestigious awards and prizes including the Nichols Medal in 1923, the Longstreth Medal in 1925, the Perkin Medal in 1937, the Priestley Medal in 1941, and the Willard Gibbs Award in 1942, and he was elected President of the American Chemical Society. These awards were in recognition for the work that he did leading teams of researchers at General Motors that made two major and highly profitable inventions. The first was ethyl, which used lead in petrol to avoid 'knocking' in internal combustion engines, and the second was chlorofluorocarbons (CFCs) to replace toxic and explosive substances previously used in air conditioning and refrigeration systems. He was therefore responsible for the adoption of new technologies that radically improved the functioning of combustion engines, air conditioning, and refrigeration. But those very same inventions were also the cause of the release of large quantities of brain-damaging lead and ozone-depleting CFCs into the atmosphere that have afflicted the lives of generations of people around the world ever since.

Thomas Midgley did not live to witness the full effect of his inventions because in 1940 at the age of 51 he contracted paralysing polio and died tragically when he became entangled and strangled by an elaborate system of strings and pulleys that he designed to help others lift him from his bed. However, his employer General Motors not only survived but thrived on the back of profits from inventions that arguably, once account is taken of the cost of cleaning up the mess, generated none.

Profiting on Purpose

One of the most important benefits of distinguishing between fake and fair profits is its promotion of purpose. This might sound odd given previous assertions in the book that the purpose of business is not to produce profits. That is certainly true so long as profits are fake in being earned at the expense of another party. But if they are fair in being measured net of the cost of cleaning up any mess associated with them then they reflect a true social benefit.

The purpose of the company determines the allocation of expenditures between different activities and capitals and in particular between material, human, natural, and social capital. A firm that regards human, natural, and social capital as critical to its activities should record these assets as equivalent to the material capital that is currently reported. It should record the cost of maintaining these assets alongside its material capital and it should augment the value of these assets as it invests in them. The degree to which it can convert them into financial returns depends on the extent to which it is able to internalize the external benefits through the innovative business practices of Chapter 5, forming partnerships with relevant parties including the public sector.

Likewise, an increase in net wealth of a country with at least the maintenance of all forms of capital—human, natural, social, as well as material—represents a welfare enhancement without detriment to any party. The criteria for evaluating maintenance and enhancement of capitals depend on a country's prioritization of public policies and determinants of human and natural rights. These might, for example, include rights to a living wage, access to clean water, free education, free health care, and preservation of forests and species. These fundamental requirements determine maintenance expenditures needed to sustain net wealth before enhancements are acknowledged.

In exactly, the same way as a company should not be credited with a profit before it has provided for the maintenance of the capitals required for the achievement of its purposes, so too a nation state should not record a net income before it has provided for the maintenance of the capitals fundamental to its citizens' well-being. Conversely, just as a company should be credited for the expenditures it makes to enhance the capitals associated with the fulfilment of its purposes, so too a nation should be credited in its public-sector accounts for investments that augment the capitals it values. A failure to do both of these results in an overstatement of corporate and national profits and income, and an understatement of private- and public-sector net accumulation of assets that contribute to the realization of their respective purposes.

Chapter 10 will describe in the context of infrastructure investments how the corporate form provides a natural vehicle for coherent and consistent accounting across public and private sectors. In both cases, capital is recorded at cost not economic value. It is the cost of maintenance of capitals that is subtracted from corporate profits and national income, and expenditures on capital investments that are recognized in private- and public-sector balance sheets.

Creation Not Conservation

The relevance of this extends well beyond just conservation and preservation. It is about creation of benefits for man, nature, and society as well as investors and how the measurement of income and profit should reflect the benefits that employees, species, and communities as well as shareholders derive from it.

Unless there is recognition of the costs incurred in enhancing the education of employees, cleaning up rivers, or improving social cohesion and trust then there will be no incentive to undertake them. These are benefits that employees, future generations, and societies derive but which organizations and institutions cannot currently capture in their accounts.

They are what economists describe as externalities—benefits that accrue to one party from activities undertaken by another without the latter being rewarded for the former. We might reasonably expect or require companies and nations not to record profits or income where there are none but we cannot require them to show profits where they earn none. Costs of cleaning up the mess should legitimately be included; the benefits of beautifying it even more cannot be, at least not in existing financial statements.

We are at the limits of what accounting can do. It has achieved a lot if it can help avoid the destruction of what man and nature between them have created. But to go further, to enhance what man and Mother Nature have produced, brings us back to the governance and management issues of Chapter 5, and the legal, regulatory, financial, and investment questions of Chapters 7 to 10. How can firms and other organizations capture some of the benefits that they create for others? How can governments incentivize companies to produce them?

What is required are means of sharing the benefits to ensure that firms and other organizations have incentives to produce them—to internalize the externalities. Are there new innovative ways in which firms can create mutual benefits for themselves and their employees, societies, and future generations? Chapter 5 argued that there are through the building of partnerships between different parties in an ecosystem and that the focus of management and public policy should be on identifying those innovations that create profitable beneficial outcomes—good companies doing well by making things better. We will illustrate with one organization that is engaged in just such an endeavour.

The Natural Capital Committee is a UK government committee that is promoting the protection and enhancement of natural capital in the United Kingdom. As part of its remit, it has piloted the adoption of the above principles of natural capital accounting with several companies and landowners, including the UK National Trust, which is dedicated to the conservation of the United Kingdom's cultural heritage. One of its properties is Wimpole Hall situated in Cambridgeshire on an estate that covers 1,200 hectares of semi-ancient woodland, open parkland, semi-natural grassland, and enclosed farmland. This provides a habitat for twenty-five nationally scarce species, and the site attracts over 270,000 visitors a year.

Wimpole Hall farm, covering 400 hectares of the estate, is the largest lowland farm managed in-house by the National Trust. Prior to 2007, the management of the farm was contracted out and farmed at intensive levels. Informed by the results of a soil survey undertaken in 2008, which showed the soil to be in poor condition, the National Trust took the decision to take management of the farm in-house and convert it to organic farming. It was hoped that the change from conventional arable to organic, less-intensive farming would improve the quality of the soils, provide a richer habitat for biodiversity, and enhance the visitor experience. The farm now produces organic cereals, wheat, barley, and oats in rotation with other crops, such as beans, and rare native-breed livestock graze on the grassland. While the farm has to be financially sustainable, it is not managed to maximize profits, but rather to maintain and enhance the Estate's agricultural history and landscape.

In conjunction with the National Trust, the Natural Capital Committee created a partial account of the Wimpole Estate's natural capital assets, which include food provision, recreation, carbon storage, and wildlife. A natural capital balance sheet was constructed that reported changes in asset values and liabilities over the period of transition from traditional to organic farming. It showed that the natural capital assets annually provide a significant value both to the National Trust (£14.1m) and to society (£12.3m) against a relatively small annual input cost of £5.1m. Furthermore, the account reported that both private and external values were enhanced between 2008 and 2013 as a result of the change in land management with the value to society, in particular, increasing substantially (by £4.4m).

What this illustrated was both the practical applicability and significance of accounting for natural capital. In the absence of such accounts, the income of the National Trust was misstated (fake profits), and the private (fair profits) and societal benefits of sustainable farming were not recognized. Furthermore, the creation of natural capital accounts provided an inducement to cease activities that were detrimental to some and engage in activities that were mutually beneficial to all.

This example also illustrates another and broader point that, if profit maximization had been the sole purpose of the National Trust then a mutually social and profitable activity, namely putting the farm onto a sustainable basis, would not have been undertaken. Income was enhanced by converting to organic farming but not as much as it could have been, at least in the short term, had the National Trust instead harvested the farm for what it was worth and then sold it to the highest bidder. With a purpose that incorporated social and environmental as well as financial considerations, the full benefits of the redeployment of assets were recognized.

Implementation

The above suggests some fundamental principles of accounting that have not been fully recognized to date:

1. Companies should record their investments in human, natural, and social capital in exactly the same way as they do in material capital, where they contribute to the attainment of corporate purposes as well to the financial performance of the firm.

2. In line with conventional accounting principles, the investments should be recorded at cost not at economic value except where the combination of their financial benefits and contribution to corporate purposes fall short of their costs.

3. The costs of maintaining human, natural, and social capital should be subtracted from corporate profits as a maintenance charge equivalent to that on material capital.

4. The valuation of human, natural, and social capital investments on corporate balance sheets of companies should be recorded net of their maintenance charges.

5. Equivalent procedures should apply to national as to corporate accounting in the form of net national income and the recognition of human, natural, and social assets at national as well as corporate levels.

In sum, there should be recognition of human, natural, and social capital exactly in conformity with existing accounting standards. In contradiction to this being in conflict with conventional accounting practices, it is a reflection of the deficiency of existing procedures in failing to apply standards consistently across different types of capital.

There is an urgent need to remedy the serious misrepresentation of company and country performance created by existing accounting conventions in reporting profits and income where there are none and failing to record investments and assets where there are some. These misstatements have resulted in a fundamental misallocation of resources in companies and nations towards material at the expense of human, natural, and social capital, and promoted purposes that have produced neither profits nor prosperity.

Part 4
Policy

Commit: to give to someone to take care of, keep, or deal with; to give in charge or trust, entrust, consign to (a person, his care, judgement, etc.) from Latin committĕre to put together, join, also (com- intensive) to put for safety, give in charge, entrust, deliver.

Oxford English Dictionary Online

There are a number of striking features of the above definition of commit. First, it encapsulates the notion of giving or entrusting something or someone to the care of others. Second, there are no contracts or incentives associated with the act of giving but there are obligations and responsibilities thereby arising. Third, the recipient is obliged to look after that which is entrusted to them and to ensure it is held and employed wisely in the interests of the other party.

It is not a concept with which economists feel comfortable. There are no contracts or incentives to ensure good performance. There are not even repeat relations to discourage default. There is just trust that the recipient will not abuse their position. But this and the next part of the book will argue that commitment lies at the heart of the formulation of public policy towards the firm. The success of policy hinges critically on its ability to be able to promote commitment towards the fulfilment of corporate purpose. To achieve this, policy itself, in the guise of the law, regulation, taxation, finance, and investment, has to be considerably more purposeful than it has been to date and to demonstrate the degree of commitment to purpose that it should legitimately expect of others.

7

Law

The law giveth,
And the law taketh away.
Debt to debt,
Assets to assets.

Context

Law is in general important but in the case of the corporation it is defining. Corporate law creates the corporation. It would not exist without corporate law because the corporation is a product of the law. It is a legal fiction whose presence is defined, determined, and dependent on the law. Few other parts of the law have such powers of creation.[1]

That power of creation makes corporate law a remarkable tool of influence. Since, as has been described previously, the corporation is one of the most important institutions in our lives, touching on virtually every aspect of them, the way in which the law influences this creature, which is of its own making, is of profound significance. It has the power to let a genie out of the bottle that can be our guardian angel or our malevolent destructor. As described in Chapter 1, it is currently poised somewhere between the two. To ensure that it delivers us from evil into ecstasy, we need to understand its basic function.

Company law is regarded as being the source of rights and rules imposed on its constituent members. It defines the basis on which the legal entity is established and the obligations on those who comprise it. It is a set of rules that define how the corporation is structured and conducts its affairs. As such it is like a toolkit that defines the framework around which the corporation is constructed.

The traditional view of corporate governance described in Chapter 5 mirrored this notion of corporate law. It saw the governance of the company as delivering on the framework established by law in promoting the interests of the company for the benefit of its members. The law defines the rules, and corporate governance adopts them. It is the basis of the plethora of regulatory rules that will be discussed in Chapter 8 and the conventional delineation between the state and business—the former sets the rules by which the latter plays for gains.

This book argues that this conception of the corporation and its relation with society is incorrect and that the conventional separation between state and firm has been damaging and unrealistic. This is reflected in a misconception of the nature and role of corporate law. It should not simply be considered as a set of rules that define rights and responsibilities and what firms can and should do, but instead as a way of allowing different parties to commit to the common purposes that the corporation promotes. The remarkable contribution of corporate law has been to provide commitment devices that bind people and organizations together in such a way that they fulfil purposes that would otherwise be infeasible.

Commitment is a complex concept in regard to individuals but it is largely absent from a corporate context. Contracts, control, incentives, and fiduciary duties feature prominently, but commitment does not. The reason is straightforward: it is not thought to be credible. It is not credible to think of commercially oriented institutions sustaining relations of trust. We would be remarkably foolish to commit something or someone to the care of an individual let alone a corporation whose sole interest is focused on enhancing its own well-being. We would be naïve to entrust our property or possessions let alone ourselves without watertight contracts or strong incentives that aligned the interests of the corporation with our own.[2] But that is precisely what nearly all commercial transactions and relations rely on, and until we have conceived, created, and confirmed the concept of corporate commitment we will not understand the functioning of corporations or the economies within which they operate.

Corporations are not first and foremost mechanisms for enforcing contracts or imposing incentives but vehicles for upholding commitments.[3] The law plays a critical role in this by allowing companies to make and sustain commitments through the types of ownership and governance arrangements that were described in Chapters 4 and 5. This chapter will describe how the law does this by conceptualizing what is meant by corporate commitments, and considering how corporations create and consolidate them through their ownership and governance arrangements. It will distinguish between laws that enable, empower, and enforce conduct that is consistent with commitment and those that require, restrain, and restore it. It will contrast forms of commitment that are self-regarding in furthering the success of the company itself[4] and those that have a wider social purpose in promoting the interests of communities and societies beyond the firm.

Concept

Consider these statements by some US corporations of their 'corporate commitments':

> As a responsible global citizen, Formica Group has established numerous programmes of environmental management reflecting our belief that significant action must follow good intentions and ambitious goals.
>
> We continually develop strategies that enable us to move toward sustainability with efforts to:
> - reduce energy use throughout the life of our products;
> - reduce carbon emissions by developing renewable energy sources, waste-to-energy technologies and fuel-efficient freight activities;
> - work with suppliers to increase recycled and eco-friendly content in our raw materials, making mandatory the use of fibres from sustainable forests.
>
> Formica Group

> At Columbia Group our customers' success drives our success. We promise to provide the right resources with unrivalled expertise and the personal commitment to deliver superior solutions and facilitate your mission.
>
> Columbia Group

> By building an inclusive work environment, we help ensure that Lockheed Martin is able to attract, develop, and retain a diverse workforce that has the opportunity to showcase and develop their skills and abilities. We believe that all employees should have a safe and inclusive work environment—one in which everyone is treated fairly, with the highest standards of professionalism, ethical conduct, and full compliance with the law. From the CEO down, we are actively committed to promoting diversity and inclusion throughout our Corporation. Lockheed Martin

> At Northrop Grumman, we look at diversity and inclusion as being integrated into all our business practices. We take pride in creating a working environment where diversity and inclusion is valued and leveraged to foster creativity and innovation, thereby allowing us to meet the business challenges of tomorrow. Northrop Grumman

Happy? Reassured? Our corporations are committed to looking after our environment, customers, and employees. Others are committed to looking after communities, suppliers, investors, the elderly, and the vulnerable. 'From the CEO down', they are committed to you, your families, and your descendants because we live in a world of committed caring corporations.

Well, we would be happy, if we had one iota of confidence in these statements. Our scepticism derives from the fact that we know full well that 'from the CEO down' what they are really committed to is their own and their owners' interests, and ours and our societies' only feature to the extent that they are consistent with theirs. Where they diverge then we know who will come off the better, and we do not expect it to be us.

Our scepticism derives from the fact that these are not in practice commitments in the conventional sense. Contracts are obligations to abide by statements, written or verbal, which are enforceable by law. Commitment is an obligation to abide by statements, principles, or values stated or presumed that are not enforceable by law. Corporate commitment is an obligation on the part of the corporation so to abide.

Commitment can be self-regarding, communal, and social. *Self-regarding commitment* benefits the provider by giving the recipient sufficient assurance of its irreversibility to encourage them to do things and in particular make investments that otherwise they would be reluctant to undertake. For example, they encourage employees to make firm specific human-capital investments in education and training that they cannot readily transfer to another corporation. They induce customers to make purchases from suppliers on whom they are then dependent for after-sales service. They are self-regarding in so far as they are reflected in the benefits, either priced or reciprocal, that the provider derives. In other words, they are consistent with, not divergent from profit maximization in improving the terms on which the corporation can trade by lowering its cost of employment, purchases, and capital and raising the prices it charges its customers.

Communal commitments confer benefits on the communities of which the provider is a part, the employees who work for it, the suppliers to and purchasers from it, and the locality in which it operates. Communal commitments may not confer direct pecuniary benefits on the corporation but they may derive non-pecuniary benefits of status and prestige, which at least in part convert them into being self-regarding. A corporation that is committed to socially responsible investing cares for its employees and protects the environment and is a respected organization for which employees are proud to work, with which customers and suppliers are keen to be associated, and which governments and nations respect. This may in part be reflected in a willingness of employees to work for lower wages, of customers to pay higher prices, and of governments to engage in greater procurement, but not all of the benefits will necessarily be reflected in enhanced profitability; some will remain external.

Social commitments extend beyond the provider's community to society and nations more generally. There may not be any benefit that a corporation derives from adopting a policy of no corruption throughout the organization. On the contrary, it might forgo many commercial opportunities from so doing and derive little non-pecuniary benefit because its adoption is not widely appreciated. Its reason for implementing such a policy beyond its legal obligations may be because it believes it to be right or proper and for it to be inappropriate to do otherwise. Alternatively, social norms may encourage it to act in this way or there may be inducements that come from the provision of subsidies and taxes.

Commitments therefore relate to those components of obligations that are not enforceable by contract. Some of them are promoted by an alignment of incentives between the recipient and provider and some by more general forms of well-being that the provider might derive. In some cases, they reflect broader principles for which there may not be a direct profit motive.

Why are they needed? The significance of commitments derives from the fact that they are opportunity enhancing. In their absence the range of relations that can be sustained is constrained by those that are enforceable by contract or promoted by incentives. Most relations cannot be sustained in this way because they are dependent on the trustworthiness of the individuals and institutions involved and the trust that others have in them.

Many of the limitations on contracts and incentives come from conventional explanations—costs of writing and enforcing contracts, the impossibility of identifying all possible contingencies, and problems of what are termed the 'observability and verifiability' of outcomes by third parties, by which is meant the ability of disputes to be resolved in courts of law.[5] Some of the limitations of contracts are more fundamental, for example, the inability of future generations to negotiate on contractual terms about activities that impinge on them.

The result is that contractual protection is imperfect, incomplete, and often altogether absent, leaving exposed those who do not have rights of contract or ownership. Instead, those parties depend on the trustworthiness of corporations acting with integrity, principles, and compassion in upholding their interests as well as those of the corporation. But what justifies that conviction?

This goes to the central proposition of this chapter that a combination of the ownership and governance of the corporation and the legal environment within which it operates determines both the ability of the corporation to commit to its stated purposes and the degree to which it credibly can do so. Furthermore, the combination of ownership, governance, and law allows the corporation to provide degrees of commitment beyond those of which individuals are capable.

At a personal level, the ability of individuals to commit derives from a combination of aretaic (virtue), deontic (obligations), and consequential considerations.[6] It reflects character, rules, and outcomes. We infer the credibility of the commitments of others from their personality, family, upbringing, education, social background, and conduct. The problem this presents is that it is frequently difficult to evaluate these criteria and it takes a long time to do so. Only immediate family members may feel able to evaluate the character of their relations and the obligations that derive from being a part of the family. Even they may find it hard and slow to do so and still harder to establish how resilient their assessments are to adverse circumstances, such as the financial or personal stress of their relations.

As a consequence, the reliance that they or anyone else can place on their ability to evaluate the trustworthiness and commitment of others is very limited and they in turn respond by limiting the extent to which they are willing to trust and commit. To express this in more conventional terms, reputations take years to establish and seconds to destroy, and our inherent reluctance to engage in relationships therefore takes years to overcome and seconds to justify.[7]

The commitment capability of the corporation derives from the fusion of finance and administration that was the innovation in the evolution of the corporation from the guilds in Britain and the partnerships (*societas*) in Continental Europe described in Chapter 3.[8] The presence of the owners provides a constraint on the administration—the management—and the management limits the latitude of the owners. What this does is to allow the corporation to provide checks on the conduct of individuals to ensure that they abide by their statements, principles, and values. That is what ownership and corporate governance are concerned with or rather should be concerned with but that is not how they are currently conceived.

At present, ownership and corporate governance are perceived as being about aligning the interests of management with those of shareholders and the exercise of control by shareholders to do so.[9] Shareholders are the owners of the corporation and those entrusted with running it therefore owe the shareholders a duty to act in their interests and maximize the returns on their investments. They have a fiduciary responsibility to act with care, diligence, honesty, and loyalty at all times to their shareholders. Corporate governance is about ensuring that they do so through the accountability of management to shareholders, the information that is provided to shareholders for them to monitor the performance of the firm, the incentives that align the interests of management with those of shareholders, and the control that shareholders can exert to ensure that their interests are upheld.

What is wrong with this is the premise. As discussed in Chapter 5, corporate governance is not about aligning the interests of management with shareholders. It is about ensuring that the corporation abides by its stated purposes, values, and principles at all times. It is about confirming the basis on which the corporation can credibly commit to other parties in the delivery of its purpose.

It might be thought that promoting shareholder interests and establishing corporate commitments are equivalent if the commitments of the corporation are solely designed to enhance shareholder value, i.e. they are purely self-regarding. But even this would be incorrect for several reasons. First, corporate governance as currently conceived is not about the creation of commitments. It is about the rights of shareholders and the responsibilities of directors to act in their interests, not about the self-imposed restraint that both may have to demonstrate to create credible commitments to each other. In particular, restraints on the activities of shareholders have not been a focus of the corporate governance literature to date. Second, theories of corporate governance that emphasize shareholder interests fail to recognize the diversity of shareholders reported in Chapter 4. It is only comparatively recently that the divergence of interests between block holders and minority shareholders has been appreciated and still more recently that the potential conflicts between short- and long-term shareholders have been acknowledged.

Self-regarding commitments raise questions about whose self we are regarding—block holders or minority, short-term or long-term shareholders? More generally, they suggest the inclusion of other parties, such as employees, suppliers, distributors, and customers. The justification for this is not some normative argument about enhancing the welfare of others but a pure economic efficiency one that, in the absence of broader commitments, the relations that the corporation can sustain are restricted and its efficiency constrained. For example, employees that do not trust their employers, suppliers who do not trust their customers, and customers who do not trust their suppliers withhold their labour, supplies, and custom. In the absence of credible commitments to protect them, they restrict their participation in commercial transactions below the level at which they would be willing to engage with trustworthy firms.

Companies that are incapable of sustaining credible commitments to their vulnerable counterparties are impoverished in relation to those that can. Put simply, in a world in which contracts are incomplete, unenforceable, or infeasible, then the ability to commit and sustain relations of trust is critical to the scope of economic activity. We should encourage commitments to engagements that extend beyond the purely self-regarding because they are enriching in every sense of the word.

Creation

The corporation's existence derives from the law. The law establishes the corporation as an entity that is distinct from its individuals. It defines the various manifestations of the corporation and the boundaries within which it operates.[10] Corporate, securities, competition, commercial, and public law all contribute to the identification of the corporation.[11]

In creating the corporation, the law determines its characteristics. It does this by defining the permissible forms it can take: who owns, who controls, the responsibilities of different parties to each other, the information that they have to provide, and the powers that they can exert. Together these determine the nature of the corporation. They are the corporate genome from which the genetic make-up of a particular corporation, as reflected in its ownership and governance, is derived. One of the characteristics of the corporation that the law, ownership, and governance determine is its ability to commit to its corporate purpose. To date, corporate law and governance have failed to recognize their significance in this regard, and the next section attempts to rectify this by describing how they achieve it.

The way in which the law impinges on commitment is in establishing the range of relations a corporation can sustain. If the law states that the only obligations of class X of individuals can be to class Y of individuals then the range of relations that can be sustained is restricted to these two sets of individuals. It makes precise the nature of permissible relations of the corporation. Another society that permits the relations of class X of individuals to be with class Z as well as Y is potentially a richer one in a literal as well as metaphorical sense of sustaining a broader set of relations than that of the first society. However, by restricting permissible relations to a more narrowly defined class, the first society might assist its corporations in committing to a more restricted set of relations and, in so doing, may enhance not diminish its economic efficiency relative to the second society.

For example, if corporate law states that the responsibilities of the directors is solely to their shareholders then this prevents a broader range of stakeholders from exerting influence over them. This might be deleterious in preventing the executives from being accountable to their creditors, customers, employees, or suppliers, but it might be advantageous in making precise their obligations and preventing the executives from switching their allegiance at a future date from one party, such as the shareholders, to another, such as the employees. It is not therefore possible to determine a priori whether an exclusive or inclusive corporate form is preferred.

Enabling legislation is permissive in allowing corporations to adopt a range of different forms. It provides a broad framework within which corporations are free to select a particular structure that is suited to their activities. In particular, it allows corporations to define the ownership and governance arrangements that establish the degrees of commitment that they provide to different parties. The recent introduction of the benefit corporation is an illustration of a legislative innovation that permits of a greater variation in corporate form than previously existed.[12] The creation of limited liability partnerships at the beginning of the 1990s is another example.[13]

Chapter 5 described how the UK Companies Act privileges shareholders over other parties to the firm notwithstanding its reference in s.172 to the obligations on directors to take other party and long-term interests of the company into account. In practice, directors to date have paid scant attention to those other interests on the presumption that the force of the law favoured shareholders. The existing law could encompass more diverse forms by describing alternative models, for example, stakeholder participation models that grant rights of information and representation to employees and other stakeholders, or shareholder privilege models that confer greater control rights on long-term and engaged owners.[14]

Legislation enables corporations to *empower* different parties. Traditionally the two groups who are empowered are the shareholders and the directors of a corporation. Their spheres of influence are different, relating respectively to the property rights that are associated with the ownership of shares and the duties of administration of the employment of that property. However, entitlement need not be restricted to shareholders and directors, and could be extended to other parties such as employees, customers, and communities. They too could be granted access to information about the performance of the corporation in regard to their interests and rights of representation in relevant decision-making processes.

Associated with the allocation of rights are the liabilities arising out of them. The responsibility of the corporation to different parties creates obligations that in turn establish liabilities for actions taken or intended.[15] With the attribution of claims comes access to information about the status of the claims and the liabilities arising out of those claims. For example, if employees are empowered to have influence over corporate decisions then they should be party to relevant information on the performance of the corporation and their claims on the organization arising out of it.

As described in Chapter 6, accounting conventions and measures of performance should reflect the stated objectives of the corporation, and the commitments to employees, customers, or communities should be reflected in associated liabilities in income and balance-sheet statements. Different parties to the corporation should therefore have the information on which to judge whether it is abiding by its stated purposes and values. For example, benefit corporations are required to provide precise information on how they contribute to their social as well as private purpose.

Once endowed with rights, the relevant parties should have powers to *enforce* them. These powers may derive from voting within their particular class, voting corporately in conjunction with other classes, initiating class actions, or publicizing the opinions of members of the class in social media. Where the directors of a corporation fail to uphold the interests of the relevant party then it should have the right to have the deficiency remedied and compensated. Such remedies may result from enforcement through the courts, the ballot box, and the media.

In sum, there are three forms of legislation that facilitate the provision of corporate commitments: *enabling*, *empowering*, and *enforcing* legislation. Together these define available corporate arrangements and forms of corporate commitment. However, legislation may not only be permissive in facilitating the establishment of different corporate structures, but also prescriptive or restrictive in requiring corporations to abide by particular conventions.[16]

To date we have presumed that commitments are voluntarily entered into to enhance the value of the corporation for self-regarding reasons. The question is whether there should be obligations beyond those to which parties voluntarily agree to abide. The answer is yes if corporations do not address communal and social commitments adequately and thereby fail to internalize externalities that more socially oriented corporations would internalize.

In particular, the *requirements* of corporations will relate to their provision of human, intellectual, natural, and social as well as financial and material capital. There may be obligations to enhance human, intellectual, natural, and social capital beyond the levels that organizations would voluntarily choose. Corporations should be required to *refrain* from pursuing purposes and engaging in activities that could be detrimental to the maintenance of these forms of capital and to invest in those that would benefit from enhancement. There should be a requirement to make good failures and *restore* detriments where damage has been done.

In other words, there are three forms of legislation that regulate corporations: *requiring*, *refraining*, and *restoring* legislation. Together with those that establish corporations—enabling, empowering, and enforcing legislation—they provide the legislative framework within which corporations can determine their particular structures and processes. Legislation and governance together, then, define the nature of the corporation and its ability to commit.

Confirmation

The transformation of what is possible into what is realized is achieved through the ownership and governance of the corporation as described in Chapters 4 and 5.[17] The ability of the corporation to display self-regarding commitment derives from its ownership. Long-term owners endure the consequences of their actions; short-term owners may not, particularly if the consequences of them are not fully evident before the disposal of their shares. Long-term owners are therefore able to provide a menu of credible commitments that short-term owners cannot.

Neither is capable of offering commitments that extend beyond self-regarding ones without further assistance. That assistance comes from the governance of the corporation. There are three components to corporate governance: the *articulation* of values and principles; *accountability* and accounting for liabilities attributable to the values and principles; and *attribution* of responsibility for attainment of the values and principles and adjudication over their allocation between different parties. The combination of articulation, accountability, and attribution allows for communal as well as self-regarding commitments. This can be illustrated in the context of the corporate commitment statements quoted at the start of this chapter.

This was Formica Group's statement about sustainability:

- reduce energy use throughout the life of our products;
- reduce carbon emissions by developing renewable energy sources, waste-to-energy technologies and fuel-efficient freight activities;

- work with suppliers to increase recycled and eco-friendly content in our raw materials, making mandatory the use of fibres from sustainable forests.

These statements raise three questions. Question 1: does this statement by Formica mean continuously reducing the use of the volume of all forms of energy used in all of its products? Question 2: what has been the substitution between conventional and renewable energy sources and the overall level of carbon emissions? Question 3: what are the target levels of increase of recycled content in raw materials and what precisely is meant by eco-friendly content? In other words, values and principles need to be specific and have measurable goals and targets for them to carry conviction and content. The values and principles by which the corporation will abide need to be clearly and precisely stated. By their articulation and specification they should create obligations and responsibilities on corporations that are persuasive and precise.

To illustrate accountability, consider the statement by Lockheed Martin: 'Lockheed Martin is able to attract, develop, and retain a diverse workforce that has the opportunity to showcase and develop their skills and abilities.' Northrop Grumman made a similar statement about diversity. How should diversity be measured and what are its target levels in regard to new recruitment and retention of existing employees? What are the financial liabilities associated with these diversity targets and how are they reflected in Lockheed Martin and Northrop Grumman's accounts? Arising from the stated purposes and values, there should be associated liabilities that are reflected in corporate accounts. As suggested in Chapter 6, the content of corporate accounts should correspond with the purposes of corporations and be tailored to their particular needs. Accounting statements should be consistent with corporate purpose statements.

Finally on attribution, consider the next part of Lockheed Martin's statement: 'We believe that all employees should have a safe and inclusive work environment—one in which everyone is treated fairly, with the highest standards of professionalism, ethical conduct, and full compliance with the law.' Who is responsible for ensuring safety? Who adjudicates on the fair treatment of employees and the resolution of disputes between employees and between employees and their employers? There should be a group of individuals in Lockheed Martin who take responsibility for these statements, bear the consequence for upholding them, and arbitrate disputes between different interested parties.

In other words, what converts these assertions, to which at present we attribute little significance or credibility, into credible commitments of

substance is precision in their articulation, accounting for their implementation, and allocation of responsibility for upholding them and
bearing the consequences of a failure to do so. Without that precision,
measurement, and responsibility, the statements are vacuous; with them,
they are powerful assertions of binding commitments that have consequences for the corporation in terms of its profitability and for individuals
within it in relation to their careers and reputation for a failure to deliver.

By articulating clearly in whose interest the corporation is run, making the corporation explicitly liable to those parties, accounting for
those liabilities in a transparent way, and making someone specifically
responsible for ensuring that the corporation does not deviate from its
stated purposes, it is able to offer credible commitments to other parties.
By empowering other parties, allowing them to enforce their rights, and
making individuals within the organization accountable for this, the
corporation can extend its commitments beyond the self-regarding
interests of its owners to those of other members of its community.
The scope of self-regarding commitment has been broadened by making
other groups parties to the corporation and conferring rights on them
that are analogous to those of shareholders. In other words it has
converted them into meaningful 'stakeholders'. The mere act of requiring companies to articulate their purposes and demonstrate a credible
commitment to their delivery will, in and of itself, be transformational
in reforming the corporate landscape.

Nevertheless, the domain of commitment remains within the confines of those that the corporation embraces as part of its community
through empowering them with rights as stakeholders. It does not
extend to society at large whose members do not have a specific claim
or right of enforcement on the corporation. To protect them, the corporation will have to act in trust in promising to uphold their interests.
In so doing, the owners of the corporation will have to relinquish
control rights to others, such as a board of trustees, whose responsibility
is to third-party members of society.[18] So while Lockheed Martin and
Northrop Grumman can credibly uphold the commitments to their
employees by empowering and conferring appropriate rights of enforcement on them, the Formica Group can only deliver on its promised
environmental protection by holding those promises in trust for society
at large. To be able to do that then there will have to be individuals in
the corporation endowed with the necessary authority to act as trustees
for society at large.

This is an effective way in which corporations can commit. By creating a board of trustees, the owners of a corporation relinquish control

and confer it on a board of directors responsible for upholding the values of the corporation. It is the responsibility of the trustees to ensure that the interests of those parties for whose benefit the corporation is run are respected.[19] On appointment, the trustees become the guardians of the values of the corporation. It is so powerful a form of commitment that it should be applied with caution because in the process of disenfranchising the owners, it places immense reliance on a board of trustees to provide effective governance of a corporation with little or no accountability for their actions.

As described in Chapter 1, it is a technique that has been used very effectively in industrial foundations which some of the most successful European corporations, such as Bertelsmann, the media company, Robert Bosch, the automotive supply company, Carlsberg, the brewery, Ikea, the furniture retailer, and Velux, the window manufacturer, have adopted.[20] It is also the organizational form of the Indian conglomerate, Tata and the US chocolate manufacturer, Hershey. These corporations are controlled by boards of foundations that are responsible for ensuring that they abide by the principles and values of the foundations. In many cases, the foundations have a charitable purpose. They were often created by founders of the companies who were concerned about succession and sought to avoid problems of inheritance by transferring control from their heirs to a body with a philanthropic and public purpose. Below the boards of the foundations, the corporations have operating boards that are responsible for formulation of corporate strategy and below these are executive boards that oversee its implementation.

Notwithstanding the fact that the industrial foundations are in essence ownerless corporations with self-appointing boards that are not externally accountable, and that the corporations are insulated from the discipline of markets for corporate control, their performance has been strikingly good. There are many possible explanations for this but the most compelling is the value that all employees from the board of directors downwards place on contributing to an organization that has public and social as well as private purposes. In other words, industrial foundations are able to command the trust and respect of their stakeholders through abiding by social as well as self-regarding and communal commitments.

The power of the corporation to commit therefore derives from its ownership and governance and its ability to align these with its commitments. Short-term owners can avoid commitments of any form. There may be drawbacks as well as advantages associated with commitments in imposing obligations on corporations which they would wish to avoid, and short-term ownership allows the corporation to do that.

Long-term owners can sustain self-regarding commitments. Empowering stakeholders allows corporations to provide commitments to their broader communities. Separating ownership and control by creating a board of trustees allows the corporation to provide social as well as communal commitments.

The flexibility of the corporation to commit reflects two features of it. The first is its ability to assign responsibility to directors to act as agents of shareholders alone, as agents of stakeholders as well as shareholders, or as trustees of society at large as well as shareholders and stakeholders. The second is its ability to allocate property rights equally and proportionally to all shareholders or to concentrate them in the hands of certain classes of, for example, long-term shareowners as against short-term shareholders. The first feature of the corporation's governance determines the cross-sectional breadth of its commitment to different parties, namely whether it is self-regarding, communal, or social. The second feature of the corporation's ownership affects the inter-temporal length of its commitment horizon, namely whether it is of long or short duration. Together with the depth of capital committed, the product of the length, breadth, and depth establishes the volume of committed capital.

The degree of trust that the corporation's communities and societies place in it is a function of its volume of committed capital.[21] In the absence of full protection from complete and binding contracts, it determines the terms on which different parties (customers, employees, investors, and suppliers) are willing to trade and invest in it. The volume of committed capital therefore affects the prices the corporation can charge its customers and its cost of capital, labour, and material inputs. It therefore influences the corporation's capital structure, employment, and investment, and it bears critically on its performance measured in both conventional profitability and broader stakeholder and social terms.

In essence, what commitment and the structures associated with it do is to place the corporation in a social and political context. The corporation can be the narrow self-regarding instrument with which economics and finance traditionally associate it, concerned with the interests of its owners and its executives alone. Alternatively, through relevant legal, ownership, and governance forms it can extend its obligations to other parties in the corporation such as its employees, suppliers, and local communities, or it can go beyond that in creating responsibilities to societies and the public at large. The corporation should therefore be regarded in a system as well as an individual entity context, and sociology and politics bear on it not just through the duties that society and nations impose on it but through the commitments that it makes to them.

The structure of ownership and governance gives the corporation a 'personality'. As described in Chapter 2, this has normative virtues associated with it that derive from the purposes and values of the corporation. These in turn establish internal norms and rules, which together with those externally imposed by society through regulation create obligations that constrain the behaviour and conduct of the corporation.

What makes the ethical basis of the corporation and its power to commit potentially stronger than that of individuals is the juxtaposition of its ownership with the control exercised through its board of directors and the public manner in which its purposes and values are stated. These make the character of the corporation transparent in a way in which it remains opaque for individuals, and allows the corporation to provide commitments that are more credible than those of individuals. In the terms of Chapter 2, they allow our individual *mintegrity* to be converted into a corporate *maxtegrity*. Whereas economics typically places welfare analysis in a consequential framework, its basis in the corporation can equally be a reflection of virtues and obligations.

Consequence

Europe provides illustrations of all these forms of corporations and corporate commitments. The United Kingdom, in particular, with its dispersed ownership is dominated by short-term shareholders rather than long-term shareowners, and is therefore a low commitment economy. UK corporations can avoid the commitments that constrain their counterparts elsewhere and thereby demonstrate a greater degree of flexibility to changing circumstances. Nordic countries confer control on long-term owners, in particular families, who are actively engaged in the oversight of corporations. These long-term owners are able to uphold self-regarding commitments. Central European countries, such as Austria and Germany, confer control rights on stakeholders, in particular employees, as well as shareholders through workers councils and co-determination on supervisory boards. These allow Austrian and German corporations to offer credible communal commitments beyond those that are self-regarding. In the industrial foundations of, in particular, Denmark, founders of corporations relinquish control rights to a board that is responsible for ensuring that the corporations act in trust for the philanthropic benefit of other members of society. The foundations are therefore able to offer social as well as communal and self-regarding commitments.

The combination of enabling legislation, ownership, and corporate governance allows corporations to fulfil a range of communal and social as well as self-regarding functions. Where corporations do not or are unable to offer the level of commitments that society demands of them then it resorts to prescriptive regulation in place of permissive enabling legislation. In other words if corporations do not demonstrate the levels of commitment that society requires of them then they sacrifice their powers of self-determination to externally imposed restrictions on their activities. It may therefore be in the interests of corporations that they provide the forms of ownership and governance that allow them to offer the levels of commitment which communities and societies demand of them.

The attainment of particular levels of communal and social engagement would require high levels of regulation in the United Kingdom to compensate for its low levels of corporate commitment, modest levels of regulation associated with industrial foundations that sustain high levels of social commitment, and intermediate levels in Central European countries where corporations provide commitments to stakeholders but not society more generally. However, nations are constrained in terms of the regulations that they can impose to correct for deficient corporate commitment by the impact that these have on the efficiency and commercial performance of their corporations. So, marked variations in levels of trust across countries persist, with consequences for the nature of both corporations and the societies within which they operate.

Conclusion

Ownership and governance determine the balance between permissive, establishing and restrictive, regulating legislation. The longer the controlling ownership of the corporation, the broader the scope of corporate values and principles, the greater the accountability of the corporation to its stakeholders and the clearer the attribution of responsibilities for upholding values and principles, the less the need for regulation and the greater the potential diversity of corporate forms and commitments. The advantage of this is that it allows for a richer set of commercial arrangements that in turn promotes economic efficiency and well-being.

In contrast to the enriching nature of enabling legislation, the drawback of regulation is that it is essentially retrospective and restraining in limiting potential commercial arrangements. Therefore, if corporations can themselves demonstrate a credible ability to commit then legislation will be available to provide the framework within which corporations have the latitude to do this. If, on the other hand, the willingness of corporations to commit is weak then legislation will have to fill the gaps through the imposition of regulatory rules.

This chapter has pointed to the centrality of commitment in the functioning of corporations and economies. Why have we failed to recognize corporate commitment to date? The answer is that we have not always failed to recognize it. As described in Chapter 2, charters originally endowed corporations with public purposes. At that stage commitments were intrinsic to the corporation. With freedom of incorporation the intrinsic commitments were relinquished. Nonetheless, so long as the corporation remained in family ownership then commitments were synonymous with the values of the families. As ownership became more dispersed it was the board that could commit, safe in the knowledge that the degree of control that shareholders would in practice exercise was limited. However, in an attempt to address the resulting agency problem through markets for corporate control, discretion of management became progressively more constrained to a point at which it was subsumed in shareholder-value maximization. Furthermore, the horizon of shareholders diminished with the shortening duration of shareholdings and, in the process, the latitude to commit was extinguished.

The consequence has been a futile attempt to rectify this by seeking ever more extensive contractual arrangements and imposing tougher regulatory requirements that constrain the commercial potential of the corporation. We need to break out of this destructive spiral of declining commitment and intensifying regulation by conceiving what corporate commitment is capable of achieving and creating the context within which it can realize its full potential to perform communal and social as well as self-regarding purposes. Otherwise, as Chapter 8 will reveal, regulations that not only distort but also threaten greater financial instability than the crisis of 2008 will inevitably intensify.

8

Regulation

Our manufacturers must consent to regulations; our gentry must concern
themselves in the education as well as in the instruction of their national
clients and dependents, and must regard their estates as offices of trust,
with duties to be performed in the sight of God and their country.

Samuel Taylor Coleridge, 'A Lay Sermon
("Blessed are ye that sow beside all Waters!")'[1]

The Purpose of Regulation

The purpose of regulation is to set the rules of the game within which
the private sector plays. The purpose of the private sector is to pursue
profits while staying within the rules of the game.[2]

This conventional post-WW2 consensus on how economies operate
has guided the formulation of policy everywhere—in competition policy,
privatization, regulation of monopolies, investor protection, corporate
governance, and corporate law, to name a few. It is based on the premise
that regulation is there to stop people and organizations doing things—
driving too fast, polluting too much, pricing too high, and building too
precariously. It restrains where we fail to refrain. It is a response to our
innate irresponsibility, imposing rules of reason where reason fails to rule.

And reason has failed the most where it is most required—in finance.
Nowhere are we more dependent on our ability to trust than when we
hand over our money to others. Nowhere is there a worse alignment
between the provider and the purchaser. Making other people wealthy is
not an innate source of personal satisfaction. We do not in general relish
other people getting rich; better to prosper ourselves while others fester.

And nowhere is it easier to steal. Money is fungible, odourless, and
untraceable. Finance is complex, opaque, unfathomable, populated by

smart, ambitious specialists, who understand the incomprehensible. We part with our farthings on the promise of a fortune. No wonder we need regulation. Finance without regulation is a licence to steal.

The question is not then whether but how. How should we regulate finance to convert a cesspit of self-interest into a cockpit of high principles? It is not easy but we should start by asking, what is the purpose of finance?

The Purpose of Finance

The conventional answer is to enhance economic prosperity. The way it does it is through financial institutions and markets that intermediate between savers and borrowers and facilitate the allocation of capital to where it is most effectively employed. These institutions collect and process information that is otherwise unavailable or inadequately provided and reduce the costs of reallocating capital to its most productive uses.

There is a large amount of evidence of a relationship between financial development and economic growth. Several studies report an association of the size of financial systems at the start of a period and subsequent economic growth, and, controlling for other factors, financial development appears to contribute to growth. A variety of measures of financial development are relevant, for example, the volume of monetary assets, the size of banking systems, and the size of stock markets.[3]

The primary channel through which financial development contributes to growth and wealth creation is via the external financing of firms. Comparing the growth of different industries across countries reveals an inter-relationship between their growth rates, the degree to which they are dependent on external finance and the development of financial systems in which they operate.[4] Financial development therefore benefits industries and companies that depend on external finance.

These results suggest that a primary purpose of financial institutions is to improve allocation of funds within an economy. Institutions that direct financing to activities that are most dependent on external finance assist corporate, industrial, and economic growth. The studies therefore provide empirical confirmation at an aggregate or industry level for the theoretical underpinning of financial institutions.[5]

However, in 1995 two US economists made an interesting observation that 'in the United States, the importance of commercial banks as a source of funds to nonfinancial borrowers has shrunk dramatically. In 1974 banks provided 35 percent of these funds; today they provide around 22 percent.'[6] They went on to consider the implications of what was termed 'financial disintermediation' for the stability and regulation of the US banking system. They were not alone in documenting this phenomenon and perceiving significant implications for the conduct of financial and regulatory policy.

Disintermediation is a reversal of the cost and information advantages of banks and other intermediaries. With the growth of electronic trading, communication, and information, the benefits of employing middlemen between the suppliers and purchasers of financial securities diminished. Instead of economizing on distributing securities, collecting information, and monitoring performance, intermediaries just introduced a layer of costs that added little to what investors and firms could do directly themselves. In fact one study shows that over the last 130 years of massive investments in the financial sector, in its people, buildings, and technology, there has been no, literally no, improvement in the productivity of the financial sector whatsoever.[7]

With the growth of 'fintech'—computer-driven finance—the process of disintermediating traditional providers of financial services has accelerated. However, the limitations to this process have also become more evident. Electronic systems facilitate direct communication, information, and transactions between parties but do not of themselves overcome problems which afflict goods and services markets in general but are especially prevalent in financial markets, namely deficiencies of information about uncertain and frequently distant prospects. Evaluating the quality of information that is available to market participants is complex, and while electronic systems increase the volume of information, they do not necessarily improve its reliability. Reputations, relations, and trustworthiness remain critical components of financial markets, and although technological advances might have altered the way in which these are established, they have not eliminated or diminished their significance.

Therefore, while the 1980s and 1990s saw a shift from funding from banks and other intermediaries to securities markets, the 2000s and 2010s are seeing the re-emergence of market-facilitating intermediaries. Essentially these span the functions traditionally performed by financial intermediaries and markets, and complement their respective activities. The most significant example of this is the growth of financial institutions as intermediary investors.

Individuals and institutions frequently employ investment managers (asset or fund managers) to manage portfolios of shares on their behalf. Investment management has been one of the fastest growing areas of the financial industry. It includes wealth management on behalf of wealthy private clients and hedge funds investing predominantly on behalf of institutional investors. Alongside institutional investors that hold securities, investment banks that issue them, and investment managers who manage them are advisors, analysts, consultants, and credit-rating agencies which collect and process information on behalf of investors and firms. They facilitate financial investments by improving information flows in markets.

So in short succession we have observed intermediation, disintermediation, and reintermediation in the financial sector. In addition to technology, one key influence on this process has been regulation. Whereas regulation is traditionally viewed as a response to conduct in financial markets, it is equally a cause. The way in which financial transactions are structured and the conduct of participants in financial markets are also responses to regulation. The directions of causation between financial conduct and regulation therefore run both ways.

The most significant response to regulation is to encourage the emergence of financial institutions and practices that replicate those of banks but are not classified and therefore regulated as banks. These institutions are frequently categorized under the general heading of 'shadow banks' or 'non-bank financial intermediaries'. Shadow banks have similar purposes to banks and perform their traditional functions of liquidity, maturity, and credit transformation. What distinguishes shadow from formal banks is that they are not deposit-taking institutions and do not have access to lender of last resort or deposit insurance schemes. They are institutions that perform similar functions to banks in regard to payments, liquidity, savings, and lending but they are not banks and not regulated as banks.

Herein lies the cause of the emergence of this shadow system and the seeds of its own destruction. Similar activities are being regulated in different ways, thereby creating strong incentives to take activities out of the formal regulated sector and put them in the informal unregulated one. Along with technology, regulation is driving financial innovation. Still more seriously, a regulatory system that is based on institutional form rather than purpose and function is not well placed to respond to the resulting financial failures. It does not matter whether an activity is performed in a bank and therefore subject to banking regulation or in a market intermediary and therefore subject to securities regulation, but it does matter a great deal if there is a lack of equivalence between the two. The way in which regulation is structured by institutions, not purpose and function, means that it is both a distortion to financial innovation and an impediment to the avoidance of the failures that are thereby created. As we will see, this will potentially be a cause of a systems-wide financial failure that will be more serious than the financial crisis of 2008.

There are four functions of a financial system: to undertake intermediation between savers lending their financial assets and borrowers using them; to provide safe-keeping of financial assets; to operate a payments system of transferring monies in the settlement of transactions; and to manage risks. Technology and regulation are causing profound changes in all four of them. We begin by describing the changing nature of intermediation and the emergence of a parallel system of shadow banking.

Disintermediation

The drive to disintermediation that occurred from the 1980s was in part a reflection of technological advances that allowed individual and institutional investors to undertake transactions themselves electronically without relying on banks to do it for them. These reduced the costs of transacting and encouraged a shift from organizing transactions within to outside banks. Examples of such developments are peer-to-peer lending and crowd sourcing which provide direct access of borrowers to lenders and savers to speculative investments via the web.

There was in addition a second factor that played an important role in promoting this shift and that was regulation. The regulation of banks is extensive and relates to their structure, personnel, conduct, and products. It impedes the activities in which banks can engage and in the process it raises the costs of undertaking transactions. Regulation therefore encourages a search for lower cost, unregulated activities and ways of doing business, and the emergence of market processes was therefore a natural reaction to the costs of bank regulation.

An early example of this was Regulation Q, which prohibited US banks from paying interest on demand deposits from 1933 onwards. One of its effects was to encourage the emergence of money-market funds as substitutes for demand deposits. Another was the stimulus it gave to the growth of the Eurobond market, which allowed issuers to circumvent domestic regulation of bond markets by issuing foreign-currency-denominated bonds. US investors could thereby earn significantly higher returns on US-dollar-denominated bonds issued in Europe than on US bank accounts. A more recent example is the imposition of increased capital requirements as part of Basel III to correct the failures of the financial crisis. These raise the cost of bank capital and encourage the diversion of banking activities to non-bank intermediaries.

The influence of regulation on the growth of market-based finance is illustrative of a general principle that regulation encourages substitution of lower cost activities that are subject to less onerous forms of regulation. It suggests that, first, one should not regard the structure of financial systems as independent of regulation or regulation as just a product of the financial system but recognize that, in addition, there is a reversed causation running from regulation to the financial system which makes the structure of financial institutions a product of regulation. Second, since there is a range of institutions that undertake similar activities, the imposition of regulation on some but not all of these institutions distorts competition and artificially diverts activities to the less regulated. One should not therefore think about regulation on an institutional basis but rather in relation to the financial purposes it is seeking to promote, for example, not focusing on the regulation of banks per se but on institutions that perform equivalent lending and savings functions.

Market intermediaries illustrate this principle very well because in many cases they have similar purposes and perform similar functions to equivalent bank-based institutions. The shift to market finance has created a need for a new type of intermediary associated with market activities. There are three fundamental drivers of such market-based intermediation—transaction and portfolio diversification economies, information collection, and governance and control.

A primary function that market intermediaries are supposed to perform is economizing on transaction costs—the costs of buying and selling securities that reflect fees and the spread between bid and ask prices. These are particularly significant in relation to small transactions as a consequence of the fixed as well as variable costs incurred. As a result, there are economies of scale in transacting in large amounts. A justification for financial intermediaries is therefore the costs that they can save by aggregating together the transactions of a large number of investors.

A related source of economy in investing comes from portfolio diversification. By spreading their risks across a large number of securities, investors are able to take advantage of the reduced risks that are associated with the uncorrelated, 'idiosyncratic' components of risk. So, for example, when investors hold the stock of one particular corporation, e.g. Apple, they incur the idiosyncratic risk of the performance of Apple being worse than expected, as well as the market risks that affect all shares on a stock market. When an investor holds a large number of shares then they still bear the market risk of the correlated movements in share prices across a large number of firms, but they extinguish the idiosyncratic risks of Apple's own performance.

There are therefore substantial portfolio diversification benefits of holding a large number of shares in a portfolio and costs associated with purchasing and managing the portfolio of shares. There are therefore diversification economies of pooling together the investments of a large number of investors.

Theories of banking place a great deal of emphasis on the role of banks in collecting information on borrowers. There are similarly substantial economies in collecting and processing information on market transactions. Much market intermediation is therefore associated with economizing on the collection of market information. In addition, to ensure that their investments are properly managed, investors will have to monitor them. They will need to establish that executive remuneration reflects the performance of their investments and that it properly incentivizes management to act on their behalf. They will have to intervene where management is failing and seek to replace them if necessary. In other words, investors will be responsible for the governance of firms in which they invest. There are significant free-rider problems of monitoring and governance reflecting the fact that the benefits of any such activities accrue to all investors not just to the particular investor undertaking them. There will therefore be under-provision of monitoring and governance and benefits from coordinated actions by financial intermediaries acting on investors' behalf.

Transaction costs, portfolio diversification, information gathering, monitoring, and corporate governance all have substantial economies of scale associated with them and justify intermediation by institutions between investors and the companies in which they invest. Disintermediation of banks by markets does not therefore obviate the need for financial intermediaries so much as change the nature of the intermediation that is required. Instead of banks managing their own portfolios of investments, market intermediation involves a range of institutions assisting with the process of gathering information, monitoring, portfolio diversification, and transacting in securities. That is what has driven banking into the shade.

Shady Banking

Traditionally the functions of liquidity, maturity, and credit transformation were performed in one institution, a bank. Shadow banking disaggregates these functions into component parts and engages different institutions in the process. It relies on market sources of finance rather than deposits to provide funding and enhances the credit worthiness of loans by providing a variety of forms of insurance and risk spreading. In particular, since it does not raise funds from deposits, the institutions involved are not classified as banks, they are not regulated as banks, and they do not enjoy access to lender-of-last-resort facilities.

The total value of liabilities associated with shadow banking is estimated to have reached a peak of over $20 trillion in the United States alone in the immediate pre-financial crisis period in 2007. It subsequently shrank to around $15 trillion in 2011. To put this in context, total bank liabilities in the United States amounted to around $10 trillion in 2007; so the size of the shadow banking system was at one stage double that of the formal banking system. By 2011 bank liabilities had risen to almost the same amount as shadow banking liabilities.

Shadow banking originated approximately eighty years ago in the US institution Fannie Mae, which was founded in 1938 after the Great Depression as part of the New Deal. The Federal Home Loan Mortgage Corporation, Freddie Mac, then joined Fannie Mae in 1970. The purpose of Fannie Mae was to securitize the mortgages of banks freeing them up to extend further loans to the housing market. It did this by buying mortgages in the secondary market, pooling them, and selling them as mortgaged-backed securities in the open market. Its source of funding was not therefore deposits but the capital markets and in particular the mutual funds. Fannie Mae was privatized in 1968 to remove it from the government's balance sheet but Fannie Mae and Freddie Mac both enjoyed implicit government guarantees.

Shadow banks perform the functions of pooling and securitizing assets but in addition originate loans and structure them in such a way that they can be packaged to different classes of investors, reflecting their risk appetite. A traditional bank originates, funds, and risk-manages loans while a shadow bank uses special-purpose vehicles to sell the loans on to investors in the securities markets. As a consequence, shadow banking involves a range of institutions, namely banks, broker-dealers, and asset managers, and is funded through global capital markets.

In particular, the purpose of shadow banks is to perform the three functions of credit, maturity, and liquidity transformation. Credit transformation is performed through packaging together individual loans and then selling them in tranches of different credit ratings. The best quality loans are put together and sold as, for example, AAA bonds, the worst as low-grade, investment, or below-investment-grade bonds. Maturity transformation occurs by loan origination of, for example, auto loans, leases, and mortgages being transformed into asset-backed securities and collateralized loans that are funded through wholesale markets by money-market funds. Liquidity transformation occurs through illiquid loans being backed by asset-backed commercial paper and repurchase agreements (what are termed repos), which are sales of securities together with agreements for the seller to buy back the securities at a later date. Through the intermediation process, shadow banking transforms long-term loans in, for example, the subprime mortgage market into risk-free, short-term, liquid money-market instruments.

The advantage of shadow banking over traditional banking is that it spreads risks across a large number of investors and engages investors beyond depositors in securities markets. Second, it segments risks into component parts allowing investors to specialize in particular parts of the risk chain. Third, it takes risks out of the formal banking system in which there are government guarantees to a part of the financial system where there is no formal government underwriting. Fourth, by disaggregating activities that are internal to banks it augments the amount of information in capital markets and provides price signals that were previously absent.

While these are supposed advantages of shadow banking, the financial crisis revealed many of them to be either spurious or over-stated. First, the notion of risk-spreading does not apply if the investors are interconnected in such a way that the failure of one or more investing institution impacts on others through an indirect chain. Second, the segmentation of risks is only advantageous if risks are properly priced. A significant problem that was revealed by the financial crisis is the difficulty of determining the true risks and therefore appropriate pricing of different bundles of securities. Third, far from removing risks from the banking system and taking them off balance sheets, residual or implied risks often remain within banks. Furthermore, to the extent that banks themselves purchase the assets that have been securitized then the shadow banking system can intensify the risks borne by banks.

The most serious problems relate to government guarantees and information flows. The creation of markets in place of intermediaries in principle places greater reliance on price signals and less on government underwriting. However, information in fragmented markets often only allows participants in the market to see a small part of the total picture. It is therefore difficult for investors to look through the web of complex interactions to gauge an understanding of the broader risks that prevail in a market. So while in principle governments can stand back and allow such informal market-based processes to operate, in practice it is difficult and potentially inefficient for them to do so. It is difficult because the repercussions of widespread failures amongst financial institutions has significant ramifications for a broad class of investors and threatens to impact on formal as well as informal banks.

It is inefficient because the failures are of a systemic nature reflecting the inability of markets to price the system-wide risks appropriately. A central regulatory or public body is in a better position to provide that system-wide oversight than individual institutions.

There is, in addition, a reversed causation between shadow banking and regulation. Not only does the emergence and growth of shadow banking create a need for government intervention in the face of failure but the emergence of shadow banking is itself a response to regulation in the formal banking system. The regulation of banks in, for example, the imposition of capital and liquidity requirements raises their cost of capital and their cost of doing business. As a consequence, there is an incentive on financial intermediaries to organize their activities in a shadow-banking form that is not subject to the same regulatory requirements and undercut the formal banking system. The emergence of shadow banking may therefore itself be a response to the costs of regulation rather than just a more efficient way of disaggregating, packaging, and selling financial products to investors.

As shadow banking grows in significance and economies become increasingly dependent on their shadow-banking sectors, it becomes difficult to argue with conviction that it can remain unsupported by government guarantees. In the event of a widespread failure of shadow banks, the economic consequences of a failure of shadow banking would not be dissimilar to that of the formal banking system—the consequences for the financing of the corporate sector, for the savings of investors, and for the operation of money-market funds would be on a par with those associated with failures of formal banks. Just as banks appreciate that as they grow they become too big to fail and come under the umbrella of an implicit government guarantee to bail them out in the event of failure, so too the implicit guarantee of the shadow-banking system strengthens as it grows in scale. Placing shadow banking outside of the formal regulatory system therefore risks creating a parallel financial system that overtime has come to dwarf the formal banking system as it enjoys similar privileges to banks but without the regulatory structure to which they are subjected.

This leads to the first principle of financial regulation—*functional equivalence*: financial institutions that have similar purposes and perform equivalent functions should be regulated in similar ways. Failure to do so results in 'regulatory arbitrage', by which institutions avoid regulatory costs through engaging in similar activities in the least regulated way, and the emergence of parallel systems of finance, with potentially catastrophic consequences. The next major financial failure will happen in the shades of the banking system, and, in the absence of formal mechanisms of regulating, providing emergency lender-of-last-resort facilities, or bailing it out, its repercussions will be far more widespread and difficult to control than the last.[8]

Key components of shadow banking are the other three functions of a financial system mentioned above—storage, payments, and risk management. We discuss the first two of these in relation to one of the most striking and significant examples of how technology is changing the nature of financial services.

Mobile Money

Mobile money is the use of mobile phones to make financial transactions. It is most in evidence in Africa and originated in Kenya in 2007 when the telecommunications company, Safaricom, working in conjunction with the Department of International Development in the United Kingdom and Vodafone, launched a new service called MPesa. Mobile money allows users to store, send, or withdraw money on their mobile phones.[9]

The impact on Kenya has been extraordinary. In the ten years from 2006 to 2016, financial inclusion in Kenya in the formal financial sector has increased from 27 per cent to 75 per cent of the population. The speed of take-up of mobile money has been approximately twice as fast as mobile phones in Kenya and nearly ten times as fast as cell phones in the United States. The revenue from mobile money has increased by nearly twenty times since 2008.

Transformational as this is for developing and emerging economies in which access to banking was previously restricted to a small proportion of the population, mobile money also has important lessons for banking and regulation everywhere. Indeed, given the cheapness, speed, convenience, and transparency of payments transacted by mobile phones that bypass banks, it may transform payments in developed economies as well if it is not derailed by regulation or vested banking interests.

The real insight it provides comes from the way in which it unbundles banking into its core functions: exchange of money, storing money, transferring it, and investing it. MPesa provides two functions. It stores money with a custodian and it transfers it. People storing money with MPesa are rewarded in the same way as if they had stored the money in a safe-deposit box: they get no interest and the nominal value of the money is preserved. The system requires reliability and integrity enforced by normal standards of commercial law and consumer protection but no prudential regulation or capital requirements.

In essence, this is a form of narrow banking—no fractional banking and no investment of monetary deposits—just pure custodianship.

But perfect security and mobility of money come at a price because the predominant form in which most people hold their savings, namely cash deposits, is no longer available for investment. One of the most significant sources of capital, monetary assets that are used for transaction purposes, is removed from the savings net. That is the price of narrow banking, and what mobile money demonstrates is that a perfectly safe and efficient monetary system can be created but at the price of raising the cost of capital for those parts of the economy, such as small- and medium-sized enterprises, which traditionally benefit from banking.

In the case of MPesa the custodians are banks that can employ the monetary deposits in normal banking functions. This reintroduces an element of prudential risk into mobile money but to the benefit of those who are funded by the banks from the monetary deposits. What this demonstrates is that by allocating the cash deposits of mobile money between pure independent custodians and banks, the regulatory authorities can determine an appropriate point on the trade-off between creating a perfectly safe but comparatively unproductive payments system and a useful but riskier one that supports normal banking functions.

The case of mobile money raises questions about whether payments should, in fact, be regarded as a core function of banking. But it also demonstrates the potential distortions caused by regulation. The reason why mobile money first flourished in Kenya is that the authorities took an enlightened view of its regulation. Despite pressure from existing banks, MPesa was not regulated as a bank and was not subject to the same prudential requirements as banks. Had it been then it might have been strangled at birth. Elsewhere, where existing banks have exerted more influence on regulation, for example in India, mobile money has been much slower to develop.

Mobile money, therefore, illustrates the second principle of financial regulation and that is *purposeful regulation*—the importance of regulating for a clearly defined public purpose, how a failure to do so can lead to inappropriate regulation, and how changing technology is rapidly altering the regulation that is appropriate for a particular form of financial service. This is particularly important as banks morph from their traditional function as receptacles for depositing and dispersing money to their role in the information age as repositories for the safe-keeping of data on their savers as well as borrowers. It will require regulation to recognize its changing role from scrutinizing capital structure and depository security to certifying computer systems and data storage.

The risk management of a financial system illustrates how purposeful regulation requires a detailed understanding of the way in which different financial institutions perform similar functions.

Risk Management

Asset managers provide services to individuals, governments, public agencies, banks, pension funds, insurance companies, and charities, to name a few. They are the interface between investors on the one hand and financial markets and companies on the other. As securities markets, insurance companies, and funded pension schemes grew in significance relative to deposit-taking and bank-lending, asset management played an increasingly important role in economic activity around the world. It performed the functions described above of economizing on transaction costs, portfolio diversification, and governance.[10]

Traditionally, asset management has been primarily associated with the 'stock-market' economies of the United Kingdom and United States. It has been much less significant in Continental Europe, the Far East, and other 'bank-dependent' countries, where savings have been primarily through deposits and debt instruments, in particular pay-as-you-go pension schemes. Countries at similar stages of economic development have very different asset management businesses. This manifests itself in several different forms. The size of the business varies markedly across countries. One reason for these disparities is that Continental Europe has traditionally had less well-developed stock markets and therefore had less need for a substantial asset-management business.

A second aspect of this diversity is that the nature of the asset-management business differs appreciably across countries. While the United Kingdom dominates the European pension fund and insurance asset-management business, historically it has been a smaller player in mutual funds, though this has changed significantly in recent years with the growth of exchange-traded funds (ETFs) as well as mutual funds. Differences in the size of pension-managed funds reflect the greater emphasis on funded pension schemes in the United Kingdom than in other European countries, where state pensions, pay-as-you-go, and in-house corporate pension schemes predominate. The distinction in asset-management businesses is not simply an Anglo-American versus Continental European one; there are significant variations within Continental Europe. For example, insurance companies are dominant in Germany, while the amount of mutual funds and insurance company funds in France are similar.

One implication is that both the business that is being regulated and the type of investor differ significantly across countries. In some countries, clients of asset management firms are predominantly large institutional investors, and, in others, they are private clients. In some countries, most investments are through pooled funds and, in others, through defined mandates (for example in Germany, the Netherlands, and the United Kingdom). Regulation therefore has a potentially different impact on investor protection across countries because of differences in the nature as well as the size of asset-management businesses.

Third, countries differ in the ownership as well as the activities of asset-management firms. Outside the United Kingdom and the United States, asset-management firms have been predominantly owned by banks and insurance companies, many of which may be classified as parts of large financial conglomerates. While this is the case in some of the largest asset-management firms in the United Kingdom, there are also a large number of small independent firms, and in the United States there are many more asset-management firms than in the United Kingdom. Concentration of ownership is therefore higher in Continental Europe than in the United Kingdom and the United States. Furthermore, there are differences within Continental Europe, where France has seen a rapidly increasing number of small, independent asset-management firms.

The significance of this observation is that the organization and ownership of firms crucially affect investors' exposure to loss. Firms that are part of large groups have more financial resources upon which to draw than independent firms, and may have more incentive than independent firms to provide protection to investors in the event of failure. If parent firms believe that either the intrinsic value of their asset-management firms or the loss of their own reputations outweigh the cost of compensating investors then they will protect investors against loss. Where asset-management firms are large and part of larger groups, investor exposure to loss is reduced by the ability of one part of a group to bail out another.

However, this presumes that losses across different parts of groups are uncorrelated and insufficiently large to threaten the solvency of the entire group. The financial crisis revealed the extent to which correlated risks across the different activities of financial conglomerates can suddenly emerge. In sum, the design of regulation has to be sensitive to the fact that the size, the clients, the activities, and the ownership of asset-management businesses differ across countries, and that this affects the desired pattern of regulation.

The nature of asset management also varies appreciably in terms of their clienteles, from mutual fund businesses that are targeted primarily at relatively unsophisticated individual investors to hedge funds which are designed for sophisticated wealthy individuals and institutions. The degree of investor protection that might be expected to be required of the two classes of investors is very different. Investors in mutual funds might anticipate a high degree of regulatory protection whereas the clients of hedge funds should be expected to evaluate the risks of the investments for themselves.

The degree of systemic risks associated with asset-management firms will also be quite different from many other financial institutions. Some asset-management firms are essentially pass-through vehicles that pass on the risks of investments to their investors. They do not, therefore, for the most part take positions on their own account in the sense of leveraging up the investments they make on behalf of their clients. They are not, therefore, vulnerable to the same types of risks of failures as leveraged financial institutions and in particular banks. The case for imposing capital requirements on asset-management firms to provide protection against systemic risks is therefore weaker than in many other financial institutions.

Other asset-management firms, and in particular hedge funds, take significant positions on their own account and leverage their business. Their risks of financial failure are potentially much more significant than those of mutual funds which do not have equivalent financial obligations. Even unleveraged asset managers may have operational leverage arising from the fixed costs of running the business, such as the administrative overheads and their IT systems. Others may have contractual obligations in the form of guarantees that promise their clients particular profiles of returns, for example, limitations on the downside risks of losses to which they are exposed. In such cases, asset-management firms are not pure pass-through vehicles but institutions with financial risks, which justify the holding of capital to provide protection against the possibility of failure.

The other types of risks to which investors are exposed are first and foremost fraud and misrepresentation. Fraud of the type associated with the activities of Bernie Madoff is in general associated with individuals and institutions that promise returns to their investors which are or prove to be unattainable. Fraud therefore emerges as a way of trying to disguise the inability to generate anticipated returns. Beyond fraud and theft, investors are at risk from failures on the part of the management process—buying instead of selling securities, purchasing the wrong securities, violating the terms of an investment fund, acting beyond the authority delegated to asset managers by their investors, and a failure of computer systems.

A significant degree of protection can be provided to investors from a variety of structural arrangements. For example, the use of custodians to hold client funds establishes a degree of segregation between the funds of clients and those of the asset-management firm itself.

Designated client funds offer greater protection than the pooling together of the funds of many investors. Oversight of the activities of asset-management firms by trustees offers investors the protection of supervision by independent parties. The auditing of clients' accounts is an important part of record-keeping.

Regulators frequently impose conduct rules that specify how asset-management firms should undertake their business. These relate to segregation of client funds, the use of custodians, the operating and computer systems that the firm employs, the price at which securities are bought and sold, the extent to which firms are able to purchase securities on their own account as against those of their clients, and the timing of such purchases in relation to those of clients. All these rules are designed to limit the exposure of investors to the investment-management process as against risks to financial systems as a whole, which is the pre-occupation of regulatory authorities in relation to banks and other financial institutions.

The above issues are as relevant to the newly emerging technologies such as peer-to-peer lending and crowdfunding as they are to more traditional investment vehicles. The central questions that they pose are as follows. (a) Do the institutions bear risks of failure themselves or are they pure pass-through vehicles with investment risks being borne entirely by the ultimate investors? (b) Are they financially or operationally leveraged or simply equity funded? (c) Do they offer any forms of guarantees to their investors? (d) Are they standalone institutions or embedded in other institutions which could fail as a result of their failure? (e) Do systematically important institutions invest in them or are their investors individuals? And (f) are their investors sophisticated and informed or relatively uninformed?

Pure pass-through standalone lenders that are unleveraged, investing on behalf of well-informed individual investors without any forms of guarantees, pose relatively little risk of contagious failures and arguably can be expected to operate on a *caveat emptor* basis. Where the vehicles are independent and unconnected but leveraged or offer guaranteed products, or investors are uninformed, then various forms of investor protection as described earlier should be employed. Where they are also embedded in other institutions or other institutions invest in them then they also pose systemic risks.

What the above demonstrates is the third principle of financial regulation—a *focus on failure*. It is only once the precise failures of financial institutions, the nature of their investment processes, their financial liabilities, their degree of interconnectedness, and the nature of their investors have been identified that appropriate regulatory responses can be determined.

Regulating on Purpose

The emergence of new forms of financial activity that bypass traditional financial institutions, in particular banks, is altering the structure of financial markets in profound ways. It is superficially undermining the role of financial intermediaries but in practice it is changing rather than eliminating them.

This chapter has recorded how shadow banking is disaggregating the traditional roles of banks into their component parts and undertaking them in a variety of financial institutions that access securities markets rather than deposits as their sources of finance. Deposit-taking functions may remain of primary importance but payments outside of the traditional banking system and investing by non-bank financial intermediaries are of growing significance. The relevance of different activities to economic performance is changing rapidly.

It is reflected in the dramatic rise of mobile money in Africa, which demonstrates how a combination of technological innovation and well-conceived regulation can transform the lives of the poorest people in the world through financial inclusion. It is also captured in the growth of asset management, peer-to-peer lending, and crowdfunding to facilitate savings activities, which substitute for many of the functions performed by banking in economizing on transaction costs, portfolio diversification, and monitoring and control of investments.

In principle, the disaggregation of functions associated with these expanding forms of market intermediation has significant benefits of specialization and extends the range of potential participants in the intermediation process. In practice, it can create serious risk of failures that are not as transparent as they are in single institutions. It therefore requires a good understanding of the nature of risks that can arise, and the purposes and benefits of different parts of the financial system.

In particular, it raises questions about the validity of the traditional approach of regulating on the basis of institutional form rather than purpose and functional equivalence. Regulation can be a cause as well as a product of disintermediation. The regulation of banks is arguably a cause of the growth of disintermediation. This is especially so for shadow banks, in so far as it has increased the cost of raising capital and doing business of regulated banks. This distorts resource allocation by promoting the development of institutional forms that have little underlying economic rationale or benefit except in avoiding the costs of regulation.

The first principle of financial regulation is *functional equivalence.* Different institutions can have similar purposes, perform the same functions, and have identical effects on both the real and financial side of the economy. Regulation by institutional form rather than purpose and function encourages the emergence of new institutions with similar purposes, performing the same functions but subject to less onerous regulation than existing ones.

Where the post-WW2 consensus on regulation errs is in presuming that regulation is predominantly there to constrain particular types of activities—charging too-high prices in utilities, polluting the environment through burning fossil fuels, endangering financial stability by holding too little financial capital. It fails to recognize that regulation should have a more noble ambition: to encourage companies and institutions to commit to purposes that respect their public as well as private obligations. This is the second principle of financial regulation— *purposeful regulation.* In attempting to draw a ring-fence around particular parts of the financial system and seeking to limit the scale of government protection, careful consideration needs to be given to purposes of financial institutions and the contribution that they make to economic activity. It is a critical component in encouraging the good, not just stopping the bad.

Purposeful regulation requires a detailed understanding of the functions of institutions and the way in which different institutions perform similar functions. It risks creating both over- and under-inclusive regulation. It is over-inclusive in applying regulation to institutions to control particular types of risks that only form a part of their overall function. It is under-inclusive to the extent that institutions, such as shadow banks, which perform equivalent functions to deposit-taking banks, remain unregulated. The type of regulation that is appropriate to different activities within the same institution may be very different, while the regulation that is required of activities in different institutions may be very similar. This points to the third principle of financial regulation—a *focus on failure.*

The focus on failure has to be on the protection of systems—water supply, environment, or financial systems as a whole—as well as its individual parts to avoid the unaffordable costs of systemic collapse. Shadow banking creates significant risks of systemic failures through interactions between banks and non-bank financial institutions. The involvement of large parts of the financial sector, including commercial banks through their investments in relevant money-market instruments and lending to shadow banking entities, makes economies vulnerable to their shadow banks. They have grown to a point where, in the event of widespread failure, their bailing out by governments is inevitable, complex, and unsustainable in imposing unaffordable burdens on national states.

The above principles of functional equivalence, purposeful regulation, and a focus on failure require a fundamental reassessment of regulation which starts with a careful consideration of the purpose of an activity, its functions, its risks, its requirements for success, and its measures of performance—exactly the same analysis as Chapter 5 sought of responsible companies. Regulation is one but only one part of the armoury available to governments. More generally, governments should seek to promote much deeper and more enduring partnerships between public and private sectors than have existed to date through the range of instruments from taxation to ownership that are available to them. In the process the private sector needs to be able to demonstrate its good intentions in respecting its side of the social bargain—and there are strong grounds for us to be deeply suspicious of this.

Part 5
Partnership

As Chapter 5 described, key to the successful implementation of corporate purpose are relationships. There are two types of relationships that are particularly important to companies—relationships with their financial institutions and governments. These require real commitments on the part of all three parties to the establishment of durable partnerships. But the law, regulation, and taxation frequently stand in the way.

Unilever's corporate purpose and values illustrate this. 'Our corporate purpose states that to succeed requires "the highest standards of corporate behaviour towards everyone we work with, the communities we touch, and the environment on which we have an impact".'[1] 'Our values define how we do business and interact with our colleagues, partners, customers, and consumers. Our four core values are integrity, responsibility, respect, and pioneering. As we expand into new markets, recruit new talent, and face new challenges, these guide our people in the decisions and actions they take every day.'

Contrast these inspiring vision and values of a commonality of private and public purpose with the objects of Unilever's articles of association: 'The objects for which the Company is established are to acquire interests in companies and business enterprises and to manage and finance companies and business enterprises regardless of whether these are group companies and to do all things which, directly or indirectly, may be deemed to be incidental or conducive thereto in the widest sense.'[2]

What would you as a customer, employer, supplier, neighbour, or citizen, let alone corporate lawyer, make of these objects as assurance of Unilever's commitment to uphold its noble purpose and values? Not much I suspect. And therein lies the fundamental problem with the defining determinant of the nature of the corporation—corporate law. It provides no persuasive principle on which to promote public prosperity in partnership with private purpose. In other words, vacuous statements of values create a vacuum in social contracts that companies cannot credibly fill themselves.

The law is at fault, but law is not the only culprit. As Chapters 9 and 10 describe, regulation and taxation as well as the law frequently stand in the way of the formation of durable partnerships between companies, financial institutions, and the state. But, since the law, regulation, and taxation are all human constructs, there are remedies at hand to reform corporations to the benefit of both them and us.

9

Finance

> Neither a borrower nor a lender be;
> For loan oft loses both itself and friend,
> And borrowing dulls the edge of husbandry.
> This above all: to thine own self be true,
> And it must follow, as the night the day,
> Thou canst not then be false to any man.
> Farewell. My blessing season this in thee.
>
> William Shakespeare, Polonius in
> *Hamlet*, Act I, scene iii

Borrower's Remorse

Low growth, low investment, insufficient spend on infrastructure, weak bank lending to the corporate sector, and funding deficiencies of small and medium-sized enterprises are all causes of concern in Europe. To many, they point to fundamental problems in the financing of European companies and in Europe's financial systems. They have prompted a raft of policy measures, culminating in Jean-Claude Juncker's €300 billion infrastructure investment programme announced in 2014 and the launch of the Capital Markets Union project by the European Commission to overcome cross-border barriers to investment financing.[1]

There has been an unprecedented decline in fixed investment in proportion to assets since the financial crisis in France, Germany, Italy, Spain, and the United Kingdom, a decline that is only now beginning to be reversed in some countries. It was greatest in Italy and Spain and least in Germany and the United Kingdom, and it was particularly pronounced in the construction and pharmaceutical sectors.

In analysing the causes of this, economists have exploited the shocks to economies caused by the financial crisis in 2008 and the sovereign banking crisis three years later. What this reveals is that it was companies with high levels of leverage before the financial crisis that cut back their investment the most afterwards. This points to what is sometimes termed a 'debt overhang' problem, namely that companies with the largest proportion of debt on their balance sheets were the ones most exposed to the financial crisis that had to respond with draconian cutbacks in their investment and employment.

The problem was not just high levels of overall debt but certain types of debt: companies with the highest proportion of long- as against short-term debt on their balance sheets were the ones most adversely affected by the crisis. This is striking because access to debt finance in general and particularly to long-term debt is often taken to be critical to the financing of long-term investment. A dearth of long-term finance is normally considered to be a deficiency of a financial system in meeting the investment needs of business.

That may well be the case, but long-term debt might be a double-edged sword, as it may also create the most severe constraints on new investment when financial conditions worsen.[2] Once put in these terms, the reason is clear: the burden of debt overhang is greatest where the period for which debt endures after a financial crisis is longest. A one-year debt is a millstone around a borrower's neck; a ten-year debt is a noose.

This points to the need to give serious consideration to ways of constraining the build-up of high levels of corporate debt during periods of benign financial conditions, as well as tackling high levels of debt, most notably long-term debt, during periods of weak financial conditions. And the solution to this is to find means other than contracts to solve the provision of long-term debt to companies. It requires long-term relationships between providers and users of finance not just long-term contracts.

Outside of Europe, the conflict between the benefits of long-term debt and its potential costs is particularly in evidence in developing countries because of their dependence on debt to fund infrastructure investment.[3] In general, developing countries have less well-developed domestic bond markets than developed countries, which make them particularly dependent on bank finance. However, their inability to access domestic bond markets may have allowed them to avoid some of the worst effects of the financial crisis that afflicted the developed world.

Another source of funding for the corporate sector, in addition to banks and bond markets, is the corporate sector itself, recycling funds from companies that have surplus financial resources that they cannot profitably employ to firms that have inadequate resources to finance their profitable investments.[4] That is precisely what trade credit should offer and in general we might expect that small rapidly growing companies would be recipients of trade credit from large better-endowed suppliers of their inputs.

However, that is precisely what is not observed. In a very telling analysis of flows of trade credit during the Great Recession, it has been observed that far from being recipients of larger amounts of trade credit, small and medium-sized enterprises (SMEs) in Europe increased the net trade credit that they provided to other firms.[5] Trade credit did not create a buffer to contraction in bank loans; on the contrary, SMEs found themselves forced to grant more trade credit to large companies. This had real impacts on SMEs' investment, inventory building, employment, and wages. The perverse outcome reflected the relatively weak bargaining position of SMEs in their trade credit relationships with large firms.

In sum, debt and, in particular, long-term debt present companies with the double-edged sword of funding for investment during good times but the shackles of indebtedness during bad times. Small companies do not have the luxury of accessing markets for their funding and are instead dependent on more short-term and cyclical bank finance. Furthermore, far from being able to call on the resources of their larger and better-endowed big brothers, SMEs find themselves forced to use their scarce funds to support them. They therefore faced a double pincer of bank-lending constraints and increased pressures to extend trade credit to large firms, with adverse effects on their ability to fund investment and employment.

The dependence of SMEs on bank lending makes the role of domestic banks in funding SMEs particularly critical. As described in Chapter 4, it is a role that local banking performed in Britain at the end of the eighteenth and the beginning of the nineteenth centuries. It involved the close relationships between banks and the companies in which they invested that local banking can provide. However, it exposed the local banks to the local economies on which they were dependent and when they failed, so too did the banks. There were therefore repeated banking crises that resulted in the central bank, the Bank of England, promoting the consolidation of British banks through mergers. As they merged, banks shifted their headquarters to London, and the relationships between the banks and the companies in which they invested were severed forever.

Since then, despite repeated attempts to rectify the problem, there has been a persistent deficiency of funding for SMEs in Britain. It is an illustration of how policy intervention designed to solve one problem, namely bank instability, can have unpredicted and unintended consequences for another—deficient bank lending to SMEs. Recently, however, one bank has demonstrated how local banking in Britain is not necessarily reliant on local banks—only it is not a British bank.

A Swedish Model

One of the most successful banks in Europe is currently the Swedish bank, Handelsbanken. It needed no bail out in either the financial crisis or the Swedish banking crisis. It is one of the highest equity return banks in Europe, and it is one of the fastest expanding banks in the United Kingdom.[6] The reason is very clear—in almost every respect it behaves in precisely the opposite way to traditional British clearing banks.[7]

The first feature of the bank is that it pays its employees no bonuses. Recall that we are routinely told that banks have to pay their employees substantial bonuses for them to be able to compete and retain their best people. Well, here is one of the most successful banks in the world earning substantial returns for its shareholders, paying its bankers no bonuses except the share of profits that they receive on retirement at the age of sixty from the bank's profit-sharing foundation, Oktogonen—a truly long-term incentive plan.

The second feature of the bank is that it devolves all decision-taking down to the level of individual branch managers, including participation of branch managers in decisions about the largest loans. Branches make decisions about all aspects of their activities including which products they sell, how much they charge, and how they are advertised. Risk is not in general managed centrally but devolved down to the branches, just as used to be normal practice in local banks in which branch managers had real authority.

The third feature of Handelsbanken is its shareholding. Its main shareholders are its profit-sharing fund, Oktogonen, and Industrivärden, a Swedish investment fund, one of whose largest shareholders is Handelsbanken. So Handelsbanken is part of a cross-shareholding in which control resides within the corporation itself. What would traditionally be deemed to be disastrous corporate governance is associated with highly successful, long-term growth and prosperity of the bank.

The Risk of Risk Committees

This is not an isolated case. Evidence from the academic literature suggests that those banks with the best corporate governance arrangements according to conventional measures were the ones that failed the most during the financial crisis and those with the highest-powered incentives were the ones that took the greatest risks.[8] Conventional views about corporate governance simply do not apply in relation to either specific examples or evidence from empirical studies of large numbers of banks.

The reason is that in highly leveraged institutions such as banks there is a particularly serious conflict between the two main investors—shareholders and creditors, namely its bondholders and depositors. Shareholders benefit from upside gains but it is the creditors (and ultimately the taxpayers in systemically important institutions) who bear the downside losses that force banks into bankruptcy. Remuneration structures that reward management for pursing shareholder interests are in conflict with those of creditors.

The way in which regulation has sought to address the problem of excessive risk-taking by banks is by encouraging them to monitor and manage their risks through central risk committees. There is indeed evidence that banks with strong risk controls took fewer risks than other banks during the financial crisis.[9] However, whether it is desirable is highly questionable. The first point is that, while it can be done, it is difficult to do well. Anyone who has been involved in risk committees knows how difficult it is to monitor risks centrally, and risk committees are prone to failure because of the complexity of the management task that they are expected to undertake.

Second, central management of risk is a source of systemic risk itself, not a way of mitigating it. If risk is managed centrally then when a failure emerges in one part of the bank it will be indicative of an institutional failure throughout because everyone is following the same management practices. It is similar to the argument suggesting that systemic risk is created when central banks and regulators impose prescriptive management rules on banks.[10] As soon as one bank fails then the market should quite correctly infer that the whole applecart is rotten because everyone is managing risks in the same way.

Third, centralized risk committees discourage banks from doing what they should be doing. They start from the presumption that the purpose of a bank is to limit risk. That is as wrong as the argument that the purpose of a bank is to maximize its shareholders' value. The purpose of a bank is to do things: to lend money and to screen and monitor borrowers, in particular where financial markets cannot or do not perform these functions. Criticism of British banking's failure to support small and medium-sized companies is illustrative of the problem. It has become more vocal since the financial crisis of 2008 and that is exactly what one would expect. If risk control is regarded as a primary objective and banks are penalized for taking it by being required to hold capital in proportion to their risk-weighted assets then they stop taking risks.

The Swedish Way

So the starting point behind risk committees is wrong. But so too is its approach. The way that Handelsbanken became a highly prudent, safe bank was not through its risk committee. It was exactly the opposite. It was through delegating not centralizing decision-taking. How did it do that? Two things. First it devoted a great deal of effort and attention to selecting people—people it could trust to act intelligently, prudently, and according to the principles and values of the bank. Second, it instilled a strong common culture about the purpose and values of the bank so that everyone was aware of how they were supposed to behave and what was acceptable conduct.

That is the way in which every successful organization in the world works. It is the way in which we bring up our families and children. We do not employ a risk committee to manage them. We educate and instil a strong sense of purpose and then we leave them to get on and run their own lives. Successful organizations operate in exactly the same way.

There are two exceptions. The first is when those in whom we have placed trust fail us. That is what happened during the financial crisis. The result was the largest banks in Britain were effectively if not formally placed in administration. And because banks no longer trusted those working for them, they effectively in turn put their entire organizations into 'special measures' transferring oversight and control to central committees and boards. As a short-term expedient it may have been necessary but as a way of running a bank it was disastrous. It extinguishes innovation, it creates systemic risk within banks and across financial institutions, and it stops banks doing what they are supposed to be doing.

If risk committees and risk officers were the ways of avoiding bank failures, it is hard to imagine that they would not have been invented some 700 years ago when banks first became established in Europe. That is not to say they should never be observed anymore than it is correct to say that central banks should never be involved in overseeing bank risks. They have a vital role to play in relation to one specific type of risk—aggregate systemic risk. Those risks that individual banks or individual divisions or branches of banks cannot observe or control themselves need to be centrally monitored and managed. A failure to do so is a failure to internalize an important externality within and across institutions and an abrogation of responsibility on the part of both banks and central banks. That is what the board and risk committees of well-run banks like Handelsbanken do. They are embedded in the banks' strategy to avoid excessive concentrations of activity in particular areas, to provide early warning of where risk concentrations are becoming excessive, to insure that those aggregate risks are hedged, to be able to establish whether failures are due to idiosyncratic random losses or a failure of management, and, where it is the latter, to intervene and change management. That is precisely what central risk committees should be doing within organizations and what the central bank should be doing in relation to the financial system as a whole.

But that is a very different mindset from saying that the purpose of a risk committee is to control risk. The only thing that we know from evidence on corporate governance and boards is that we do not know. We do not know what is the right way of managing risks. And the reason we do not know is that there is not a right way or a single best form of corporate governance and we should stop behaving as if there was. We should start to learn from cases of success such as Handelsbanken that there is not a simple toolkit for managing bank risks and that many of the worldly wisdoms we take for granted—one has to pay bonuses, one should centralize authority, one should expose banks to the market for corporate control—are neither worldly nor wise.

In Equity

One of the reasons for Handelsbanken's success in the United Kingdom is its focus on the customers who are least well serviced by existing British banks, namely SMEs. It is a highly purposeful and committed bank, filling a gaping hole in the UK financial system left by the demise of local banks by essentially recreating them, albeit in the context of a multinational bank. But it is a lender and therefore does not fill another gap in the SME market and that is the equity gap.

Some aspects of this have already been addressed through the rise of private equity. Europe's problem in financing high tech firms is no longer so much at the start-up phase of providing venture capital finance and in many respects Europe has caught up with the United States in the early stages of funding through venture capital.[11] Rather, it is in the later stages of scale-up to 'unicorns', i.e. start-up companies valued at more than $1 billion, where Europe still lags behind the United States. That failure reflects a combination of insufficiently large amounts of funding at later rounds, less well-developed markets for both primary funding and secondary trading of SMEs equities, and a tendency for European firms instead to sell out to acquirers. It is in transitioning from start-up to scale-up where European firms fail.

New markets for trading equities of SMEs are beginning to emerge in a number of European countries. These are encouraging the use of equity finance by SMEs but they remain relatively underdeveloped. The reason why scale-up is underprovided is that it is at this stage that the combination of private control to preserve idiosyncratic value with access to public equity capital is required. Public markets without dominant shareholders exist in the United Kingdom and private family control is widespread in Continental Europe, but it is the combination of the two that is required to promote purposeful well-funded companies.

The attraction of a parallel system of block-holder control with public equity as described in the discussion of family ownership in Chapter 4 is that it does not require institutional and other investors in public equity to invest for the long term. Only the block holders, be they families or institutions, need to commit to the long term. Meanwhile, public markets can and should encourage trading to provide price information as well as liquidity for investors.

Public markets perform the further important function described in the previous chapter of managing risks. Growth of mutual funds and exchange-traded funds (ETFs)—marketable securities that track baskets of assets such as commodities, bonds, or stock market indices (like the FTSE 100 and S&P 500 indices) and trade like common securities—has allowed investors to diversify their risks of investing across the world at low costs of transacting. While block-holder control promotes the creation of idiosyncratic values, public equity markets dissipate their risks across large diversified portfolios of securities, thereby reducing their costs of funding to levels commensurate with low-risk investments. Public markets therefore allow idiosyncratic value of human, natural, and social as well as material capital to be created at low costs of financial capital.

Through their powers to tax, governments are often thought to have the ability to pool risks more widely than private capital markets. However, with the rise of mutual funds and ETFs, private markets have been able to achieve levels of international diversification that extend well beyond the jurisdiction of individual governments. This may have reduced costs of funding social and natural capital investments to levels that are now below those achievable by public sectors. However, there are two serious impediments to this parallel development of committed long-term ownership and liquid stock markets. The first is the corporate tax system.

A Taxing Problem

Corporate tax systems differ appreciably around the world; however, there is one feature of them that is universally observed and that is the encouragement they give companies to employ debt finance in preference to equity. This results from the feature of corporation tax that allows companies to deduct interest payments on their debt but not their payments of dividends on their equity from their taxable income in determining their corporate tax liabilities. In the process, they provide a powerful incentive to both banks and companies to fund their activities through debt rather than equity.

Like so many irreversible distortions to tax systems, full interest deductibility of interest payments had its origins in a temporary expedient, in this case in a response to the 1918 introduction of a WWI 'excess profits' tax in the United States.[12] Interest deductibility was accepted as a temporary measure to compensate for the exclusion of 'borrowed funds' from the definition of invested capital on which excess profits were computed. But when the excess profits tax was repealed in 1921, full interest deductibility was retained in the corporate income tax that replaced it.

It is nonsensical. It has resulted in debt addiction of the corporate sector and encouraged over-borrowing and over-lending in the financial sector, exposing it, as well as the corporate sector, to failure. We should look to equalize the tax treatment of equity and debt in the corporate tax system, firstly to encourage banks to hold more equity and secondly to encourage companies to hold less debt. This would promote better-capitalized banks and less-leveraged corporations.

In fact, the distortion is even greater than that of the tax deductibility of interest payments because it is often accompanied by a plethora of other policies and incentives that encourage companies to borrow even more. Take for example the loan guarantee schemes that exist in many countries by which the government bears at least some of the risks associated with bank-lending to SMEs. One study exploited the considerable variation both across firms and time in the availability of loan guarantees in the Netherlands after the financial crisis to examine the impact of loan guarantees on a large sample of individual firms.[13] It found evidence that the introduction and then subsequent withdrawal of the loan guarantee programme had a substantial effect on the number of loan applications from companies, and that firms eligible for loan guarantees applied for more loans than those that were not.

In that respect, the loan guarantee scheme operated as intended. However, the study also found that banks accepted less collateral from and made riskier loans to firms covered by the loan guarantee scheme, suggesting that loan guarantees reduced the incentive on banks to screen and monitor the quality of the loans they were making. In that regard loan guarantees further distorted the allocation of bank credit.

Evidence in support of at least eliminating existing distortions comes from studies that have examined the impact of tax reforms introduced to eliminate corporate tax discrimination between debt and equity. One study analysed tax reforms introduced in Italy and Belgium in 2000 and 2006 respectively that decreased the cost of equity to banks and firms.[14] The reforms allowed banks and companies to deduct a notional return on their equity as well as their debt capital in computing their taxable profits, thereby reducing the tax incentive to issue debt in preference to equity. The decrease in the cost of equity capital for banks in Belgium and Italy led them not only to raise the proportion of equity relative to debt on their own balance sheets but also to lend more to firms in another country. Conversely, when the reforms were reversed, there was a decrease in lending by these banks, suggesting that the elimination of the tax distortion is a powerful mechanism for addressing debt overhang.

Elimination of the deductibility of interest payment on corporate taxes, potentially offset by compensating reductions in corporate tax rates to avoid a corresponding increase in corporations' tax burdens, is an extremely straightforward way of correcting a major distortion in our financial systems.[15] But it is not just taxation that is undermining the use of equity finance by the corporate sector—so too is regulation.

In Neutral

Public policy to the corporation has been dominated by an overriding concern—the 'agency problem' of aligning the interests of managers with those of their shareholders to avoid unprofitable growth or undue complacency. The common response has been the strengthening of shareholder rights. There has been a marked increase and convergence in investor protection in all major industrialized countries over the past twenty years. In some countries, such as China, Germany, and the Netherlands, it has been very pronounced. In others, such as the United Kingdom and United States, shareholder protection was already well established at the beginning of the 1990s and has only experienced modest changes since then.[16]

The justification for the strengthening of shareholder rights is twofold. First, in the context of dispersed ownership systems, such as those in the United Kingdom and the United States, it provides a countervailing power to that of corporate executives and managers who control corporate assets. Second, in more concentrated ownership systems that are commonplace outside the United Kingdom and United States, it gives minority investors protection against the dominant shareholders, in particular families, who can exploit their power to the detriment of other shareholders.

If equity markets are to operate efficiently as allocators of resources and monitors of the use of capital, then minority shareholders as residual claimants need to have the means of protecting themselves against both management and dominant shareholders—a truth recognized in nearly all countries.[17] Their rights therefore ensure that the policies and practices of companies are consistent with value creation not value diversion for the benefits of vested interests.

However, an emphasis on minority-shareholder protection comes at a price. It curtails the ability of owners to exercise direct and effective governance, and it prevents management from freeing itself from the tyranny of control by the market. In particular, it limits the ability of companies to establish the type of dual-ownership structures described in Chapter 4 by which block holders provide anchor shareholding while the remaining shares are freely traded on stock markets. It discourages these arrangements by raising the cost of being a controlling shareholder. It therefore undermines companies' ability to structure their ownership and governance in a form that is best suited to their activities. While promoting the interests of minority shareholders, investor protection can therefore have unintended and seriously detrimental effects on corporate development.

Examples of such unintended consequences are insider-trading rules discouraging investors from active engagement for fear of making themselves insiders; rights issues requirements preventing companies from placing blocks of shares with committed long-term investors; pension-fund valuation and insurance-company solvency rules discouraging institutions from holding equity capital; removal rights of shareholders preventing companies from committing to the long-term employment of directors; stock-exchange-listing rules discriminating against the issuing of shares that confer disproportionate voting rights on committed shareholders; and takeover defence restrictions preventing companies from protecting themselves against short-term arbitrageurs during takeover bids.

This is not to say that there may not be a strong justification for each of these rules and that on balance they may have beneficial effects. However, it warns that regulation should not prescribe either in favour or against particular corporate arrangements. It should as far as possible adopt the same neutral position that is advocated for taxation, namely neither encouraging nor discouraging companies from adopting certain types of financial structure or investment policy. There should be functional equivalence and it should be for investors and stakeholders to determine their appropriate corporate forms, not for regulators to prescribe them.

Enabling

A principle of neutrality flushes out adverse consequences of existing regulations but it does not achieve the positive results of enabling legislation. While the United Kingdom and United States are frequently regarded as having similar, stock-market-oriented, capitalist systems, their differences are as pronounced as their similarities. One of the most important distinctions is the greater degree of diversity of legal structure and corporate form in the United States than the United Kingdom. This in large part derives from the fact that much corporate legislation in the United States is formulated at a state rather than a federal level.

In that regard, the diversity in corporate form and legislation that exists across Europe might be a more appropriate benchmark than that in the United Kingdom. Freedom of incorporation across EU member states in principle provides at least as great a degree of variation as exists in the United States. However, one of the consequences of a withdrawal of the United Kingdom from the European Union would be that this variety might no longer be available to UK firms. This emphasizes the importance of diversity at the national as well as the supranational level.

It is sometimes suggested that UK company law achieves this by its permissive nature, namely that S.172 of the 2006 Companies Act permits companies to adopt almost any structure that they choose. But this is incorrect on two scores. First, there are hidden elements of discrimination, regarding, for example, the election and removal rights of shareholders to appoint and replace their boards of directors, which render mechanisms such as staggered boards that are commonplace in the United States infeasible in the United Kingdom. This is illustrative of why the adoption of a principle of neutrality is potentially of considerable significance.

Second, and more significantly, the Companies Act fails to identify what should be the primary objective of every firm: to promote and achieve their purposes. It does not even require companies to articulate their purposes in any meaningful way, as illustrated by the case of

Unilever in the introduction to this part of the book. Instead, by promoting 'the success of the company for the benefit of its members', the Companies Act encourages a focus, albeit not an exclusive one, on the interests of shareholders. It is therefore constraining in discouraging other purposes.

Even if there were no such forms of discrimination intended or otherwise, a permissive law is not the same as a facilitating one. In particular, what the United States illustrates is how the adoption of laws at a state level has encouraged the development of the judicial expertise that is required for the enforcement of different types of corporate form. To place this in a European context, German courts know how to enforce German-style corporate laws and Swedish courts understand Swedish laws. Without the prod that comes from public law, certain types of arrangements would simply never get off the ground because they would remain unfamiliar to lawyers and courts.

As argued in Chapter 7, this points to the importance of public laws and regulations in promoting, not just permitting, different types of arrangements. For example, it is sometimes suggested that it is not necessary for the United Kingdom to adopt a 'Benefit Company'—a company that has a stated public or social as well as private purpose—because it can be achieved under the 2006 Companies Act. However, the Act may not achieve the same outcome as a Benefit Company because of the substantial costs and risks involved in being a first mover in its adoption. In other words, innovation in public law is required to achieve innovation in corporate form.

Policy should therefore seek to promote companies of varied legal structures. This is key to the successful development of purposeful companies and financial institutions because supportive legal structures are critical to their formation. It is not the structure of a corporation that is offensive, any more than it is the genetic make-up of an individual, but the potential actions that either may take. The combination of enabling corporate law that promotes company purposes and purposeful regulation that avoids those that are socially detrimental is the key to the creation of purposeful firms and financial systems.

The law cannot force good conduct, but it can prevent or promote it. It can be prescriptive and restrictive, or enabling and facilitating. When it is the former it should be focused on offending purposes and functions and when it is the latter it should identify and promote corporate commitments to purpose. And there is one straightforward way in which it can do this. It should require companies not only to articulate their corporate purposes but also to incorporate them in their articles of association and demonstrate how their ownership, governance, values, culture, leadership, measurement, incentives, and performance promote the achievement of and commitment to their corporate purposes.

The act of incorporating corporate purposes in articles of association and requiring firms to demonstrate how their corporate structures and conduct deliver on them could have a transformational effect on the corporate sector and financial system. It would shift the onus of director fiduciary duties to where they should be on corporate purposes. They would require not only directors and management of companies to demonstrate commitment to purpose but also all external parties related to the firm to do likewise. For example, it would encourage institutional investors to demonstrate a commitment to promoting the purposes of the companies in which they invest as well as to their investors.

Abundance

Repositioning equity at the centre of corporate finance through neutral and enabling taxation and regulation re-establishes the relation between corporate finance and governance. Equity is not just a source of finance but also of voting control and as such is the dominant influence on the governance of firms. Shareholders are the pipers who call the corporate tune and the reason why companies are required not just to earn profits but also to maximize them at all times. In determining whether they should do well by doing good, companies have to demonstrate that they not only do well but they always do the very best that is possible for their shareholders. It is this continuous emphasis on doing the best for shareholders that militates against doing good—the best is literally the enemy of the good.

In some circumstances it is perfectly appropriate for companies to be expected to maximize their return on equity. Where constraints on the availability of financial capital exist so that it has to be rationed then it is correct to suggest that capital should be allocated to those activities that yield the highest returns for investors. If that is not done then a scarce resource is being inefficiently employed and could be better reallocated elsewhere. But where such constraints do not exist then there is no need to ration capital and only finance the highest-return activities.

Financial capital was once the major constraint on investment. In particular during the third age of the corporation when it was associated with manufacturing there were large demands for financial capital to fund physical investments in buildings, plant, and machinery. This is why external finance from local banks and then local stock markets played such an important role in the industrial revolution and the subsequent emergence of Britain as 'the workshop of the world'. However, as corporations have since then progressed to their fourth age of service firms and in particular financial services, limitations on capital have been relaxed. As they have moved to their sixth and current age of mindful corporations, the capital requirements of businesses have dwindled further to insignificance.

So while financial capital was once in short supply, it is no longer. On the contrary, it is in abundance and the world is awash with financial capital in search of profitable activities to fund. That is one of the reasons for the very low rates of return that savers currently earn on their investments. It may also be a cause of a striking feature of finance: the amounts of finance that companies in aggregate raise from stock markets is less than the amounts that they hand back to their shareholders in repurchases of their own shares and acquisitions of shares in other companies.[18] This is true around the world but it is particularly true in the two countries with supposedly some of the best-developed stock markets—the United Kingdom and the United States—and it is intensifying with the growth of share repurchases. The adverse tax treatment of equity in relation to debt is one possible reason for this, regulation of equity markets may be a second, but declining financing requirements of corporations may be the most important.

It is no longer finance where companies' most acute shortages lie—it is the supply of skilled labour to provide the minds behind mindful corporations, trust and cohesion among their communities and customers, and clean environments and preservation of natural capital that present business with their most serious challenges. In other words, it is human, social, and natural capital that are the scarce resources of the twenty-first century, not financial capital.

While shareholders were therefore legitimately once the pipers who called the company tune and required companies to maximize their capital value, this is no longer the case. They should have relinquished their pipes to others, and it is an anachronism to affiliate control with equity. That is why it is important that the law does not presume it to be so and regulation does not impose it; instead, both should encourage recognition of the growing significance of other forms of capital.

Integrating Finance and Investment

Underlying this is recognition of the interdependence between finance and investment that contrasts with the conventional view of a separation between the two. The conventional notion stems from a highly influential and cited economic theory of the irrelevance of finance to investment—the Modigliani and Miller theorem.[19] It is based on simplifying assumptions of complete, costless, and taxless financial markets that both this and the first chapter have suggested clearly do not apply in practice. It has promulgated a belief that the functioning and regulation of the financial system can be considered separately from the 'real side' of the economy—the corporate sector.

This has created what might be termed 'left side of the balance sheet (asset) paralysis', namely everyone in the asset-management and corporate chain is beholden to their liabilities—asset owners (e.g. pension funds) to their beneficiaries (pensioners), asset managers (fund managers) to their asset owners, boards of companies to their asset managers, senior management to their boards of directors, and workers to their managers— ignoring assets lower down in the process. It has created an attitude of deference and subservience to those above that has converted what superficially resembles democratic participation in the rewards of share ownership by the population at large as investors and pensioners into an autocratic system of control by superiors.

As Chapter 8 reveals, this has resulted in regulation that considers the functioning of the financial system in Wall Street and the City of London as separate from the corporate sector in Main Street and Manchester. As a consequence, financial regulation has paid insufficient attention to how, in protecting the owners of corporate liabilities, it afflicts the managers of assets in which they invest.

Requiring companies and financial institutions to demonstrate how they fulfil their purposes by establishing durable relationships between each other is a powerful mechanism for addressing the problem. It builds the partnerships that are required to reverse the separation between finance and investment that economic theory and financial policy have encouraged. It addresses left side of the balance-sheet paralysis by encouraging a turn to the right.

Putting Financial Policy Right

In sum, policy has privileged debt over equity through corporate tax, minority over anchor shareholders through regulation, and shareholder over human, social, and natural capital through corporate law. It is no wonder we are in a mess with over-indebted corporations and financial institutions, an absence of committed long-term shareholders, and avaricious shareholders exploiting other stakeholders.

We need to restore taxation, regulation, and the law to neutrality through functional equivalence, away from privileging a small stratum of society, towards enabling companies to adopt corporate structures that are suited to the delivery of their purposes. We should require companies to incorporate their purposes in their articles of association and demonstrate how their corporate structures and conduct, and those of all parties with whom they are related including their investors, assist them in discharging their duties to deliver on their purposes.

Tax, regulatory, and legal reform are key to addressing financing and control of our corporations. However, the role of the state in fulfilling its part of the bargain does not stop at incentivizing, permitting, and enabling corporations to adopt structures that promote the public as well as the private interest. It extends to erecting the economic superstructures on which private companies depend. While economic theory and current policy view finance and investment, private and public, and commercial and social as separate domains accountable to different people and organizations, they are in fact intimately interrelated and intertwined in the creation of the core component of economies—their infrastructure.

10

Investment

The Problem

As the etymology of the word suggests, infrastructure is the sub-structure of an undertaking on which other structures, systems, and activities are built. Its foundational feature lends it three essential characteristics: it is a public good at both local and national levels; it spawns a large number of diverse activities; and it is of long duration and embedded in long-term economic expansion.[1]

All major innovations in infrastructure, such as the introduction of electricity, gas, Internet, telephones, water, sewerage, public health, and education, display these characteristics. They have laid the foundations for economic activity around the world in every sector in most places over several centuries. But 140 years after the word was first coined, we still do not know how to provide and manage infrastructure. There is a chronic under-provision of it around the world, and where it is available it is often poorly delivered. The most advanced country in the world—the United States—is repeatedly criticized for its weak infrastructure. The European Union has launched a major infrastructure programme of €300 billion—the Juncker plan—to rectify deficiencies in European infrastructure. One of the fastest-growing economies in the world—India—has failed to provide the massive infrastructure programme the country desperately needs. The repeated inability to implement infrastructure programmes in Africa is one of the continent's main impediments to economic growth. And China's performance is in many respects no better than that of developed countries.[2]

The failure of infrastructure is not for the most part one of intention but of delivery and achievement. Despite the expenditures, UK and US infrastructures remain poor. Africa relies on China to builds its infrastructure. And the history of infrastructure in the European Union is one of repeated wasteful expenditure.

Why is it so difficult to get infrastructure right and what can be done to rectify the problems? The reasons are not hard to find: a failure to recognize the systems nature of infrastructure; its scale; its duration; incorrect accounting for infrastructure and consequent failures to fund it appropriately; and inadequate governance and management of infrastructure programmes. Together these have resulted in a failure to identify the purpose and benefits of infrastructure investments, to measure their impact on public and national accounts, to fund them appropriately, and to manage and implement them efficiently and effectively.

Until these are resolved, infrastructure will continue to display the same characteristics that it has to date, namely inadequate, wasteful, over-budget, over-time, and frequently corrupt expenditures. So long as this is the case then cynicism about government's ability to manage public infrastructure budgets will prevail and excessive reliance will be placed on poorly specified methods of delivering the infrastructure programmes that the world desperately needs.

There are corresponding solutions. The first is to provide a proper framework for identifying what infrastructure is required and the costs and benefits associated with providing it in different ways. Though conventional cost–benefit analysis has a role to play, it fails to reflect and measure the full systems nature of infrastructure—its significance as a substructure of something much bigger and broader. Systems have to be conceived, designed, evaluated, and implemented not as increments considered in isolation but as integrated wholes.

Second, infrastructure needs to be financed. Whilst the private sector is familiar with provisioning for capital maintenance and enhancements, and has balance sheets to account for the state of the assets under their control, governments are driven by cash-based national accounts. Indeed governments typically have no accounting framework for addressing the creation of assets and liabilities for future generations, and no mechanism for closing the gap between future benefits and current liabilities.

Third, there needs to be a governance system that provides for political decision-making, without succumbing to corruption, short-termism, and what might be called 'the trophy project syndrome'. The cynicism surrounding infrastructure expenditure is justified by its track record of failure. But if we can send spacecraft to Mars and Venus with stunning success, surely we can build roads, bridges, and electricity systems closer to home. An institutional, regulatory, and governance framework is essential for this and required to prevent the problems that afflict infrastructure.

The Big Sink

Infrastructure investment is in general thought of as filling gaps in an economy. There is a deficiency in the provision of particular infrastructure in a specific location that needs to be fixed at minimum cost to the public accounts. It starts from the stock of existing assets and adds on bits here and there as tentacles entangling an ever-expanding economy and environment.

There are many advantages to this pragmatic approach, including avoidance of the converse risk of embracing large unworkable, unmanageable, and unaffordable programmes. However, it can easily descend into crisis management—waiting until the deficiency is so acute as to make new investment essential or in general long overdue—as in the case of US highways, European gas supplies, and UK airports—and systems have deteriorated to decrepit states.

An economic approach should start from a more considered position of what is the desired and needed infrastructure system. What type of airport system, energy transmission and distribution networks, broadband, water supply, and rail and road network does an economy need over the next ten, twenty, and fifty years? These systems are public goods, and are almost always underprovided by markets, except during periods of 'irrational exuberance' as, for example, in the early railway mania in mid-nineteenth-century Britain and the dotcom mania across the developed world in the late 1990s. It is not a question of whether governments have a role to play but what it should be.

Technology and economies change. There have been some infrastructure networks that have remained roughly the same over long periods. The water and sewerage systems in many major urban areas—for example in London, Paris, and Rome—were put in place in the nineteenth century, and many of the assets still function more than a century later. The canals were built in the eighteenth century, the railway networks in the nineteenth century, and some roads have been in existence for a millennium. Other networks are more recent. Broadband is a new infrastructure less than a couple of decades old.

In some systems the speed of technical change creates a paralysis of decision-making, but a notable feature of current programmes is that many are very long term. New nuclear power stations are planned with a life of sixty years; rail programmes and new airport capacity are likely to be in use in the twenty-second century.

There are therefore three key features of infrastructure programmes—their scale, their breadth, and their duration. The magnitude of expenditures dwarf those that single private entities on their own can finance or manage. The programmes, if not universal, encompass at least a broad segment of a country's population in the provision of a diverse range of services. And the relevant timescale of the programmes exceeds that of conventional private-sector investment programmes and capital investment appraisals.

All of these point to the problems involved in relying on private capital markets to elicit the right scale or form of infrastructure provision without public-sector coordination and planning. But they are also the source of public-sector failure. The conventional tool with which to evaluate infrastructure programmes is cost–benefit analysis. The total social benefits of infrastructure are evaluated, set against the total social costs, and discounted back to the present at a social discount rate. If the resulting number is positive then the programme progresses, and, if there is a funding restriction, those projects with the highest positive net present value per unit of expenditure are chosen until the available budget is exhausted.

There are numerous problems with this. The first and most obvious is that given the timescale of the programmes all three components of a cost–benefit analysis—costs, benefits, and discounting—are subject to substantial uncertainties. Second, the objective of large infrastructure programmes is to change the nature of the economy in terms of both its overall activity and spatial distribution across people, goods, and services, whereas cost–benefit analysis is a partial analysis that takes all other components of the infrastructure and the economy as given. The appropriate question is therefore not so much whether a particular piece of infrastructure should be built but rather what infrastructure system does an economy need to underpin its long-term development. Thus the specific investment decision should be viewed in a wider context as part of a broader set of decisions, combining the infrastructure for the core services of water, sewerage, rail, road, air transport, broadband, and energy.

Recognizing the system characteristics and the interrelationships between systems provides the basic architecture of infrastructure policy. But it is not just the scale and breadth of infrastructure programmes that mark them out from other investments. It is also their duration. They span not just one but multiple generations and have to reflect the interests of the unborn as well as the current voting population.

When the Victorians built the London sewers, it is unlikely that they had in mind the benefits Londoners a century and a half later would reap. They were concerned with the 'Great Stink' in London, and the very immediate needs to clean up the mess. The project was economic in the shorter term, without worrying about the long run, but there are many projects where time horizons make a considerable difference.

The combination of the interconnected-systems nature of infrastructure, the vast scale of required expenditures, and their long duration combine to make underinvestment a ubiquitous problem that afflicts the developing world even more than the developed. Together they render infrastructure particularly prone to the 'market failures' that make the private sector unable to provide it unaided by government. In particular, in the absence of public-sector funding, the private sector is prone to discount the future benefits of infrastructure more rapidly than society as a whole would wish.

However, the framework of this book provides a more insightful view of the problem and its potential solution. It points to the importance of commitment to the ability of both the private and public sectors to contribute to the provision of a country's infrastructure and the particular difficulties that both parties face in committing to programmes of the breadth, scale, and duration of infrastructure systems. It suggests a solution by emphasizing the similarities between private and public sectors rather than their differences. The conventional dichotomy between the state and the firm sees the same type of division between public rule-makers and private profit-makers in infrastructure as prevails elsewhere. This has erected damaging barriers between the two that have undermined the effective functioning of either. The removal of these barriers provides the means to address the global chronic underinvestment in infrastructure.

Not Accounting for Infrastructure

The starting point is the observation that there is no proper accounting for infrastructure. Chapter 6 recorded how we fail to account properly for natural assets. Natural capital is a form of infrastructure providing a lifeline for the preservation of our existence, but it is just one of a broader form of infrastructure for which we fail to account adequately.

National accounts are statements of current incomes and expenditures, originally designed to facilitate the management of the macro-economy. Governments record liabilities as part of public-sector deficits but only keep incomplete records of their public assets. This has several effects. First, it creates an impression of burgeoning deficits and profligacy when governments engage in investments for the benefit of future generations. Second, as in the case of natural capital, it means that there is an incomplete record of the expenditures required to maintain infrastructure assets and, as a consequence, a natural tendency, as has occurred in many developed countries, to allow them to deteriorate.

Third, since the private sector does have balance sheets, when infrastructure assets are transferred from the public to the private sector, there is a spurious increase in measured assets. The private sector pays for the assets that were not recorded on government balance sheets thereby augmenting the public-sector accounts and records the cost of purchasing the asset on its own balance sheet to offset the expenditure, thereby resulting in no deterioration in its accounts. There is therefore an apparent magical creation of economic value from the transfer of ownership, thereby providing an impetus to the programmes of privatization of utilities and infrastructure that have swept around the world.

The allocation of infrastructure between public and private sector should reflect the relative merits of the two parties in defining, implementing, and managing their assets, not arbitrary distinctions in their accounting conventions. The absence of proper public-sector accounting has created a distortion in the ownership and operation of infrastructure. But failure of accounting is just one manifestation of a much larger public-sector deficiency.

Public Commitment

The systems nature of infrastructure makes the design of infrastructure inherently a public policy matter. The size, shape, and form of a country's rail, road, electricity, water, and telecommunications systems are naturally matters of public interest. The specification of the systems is therefore the role of governments, albeit assisted and advised by private-sector parties.

Since they set plans, governments also revise and update them. This makes private-sector providers inherently exposed to changes in policies and reallocation of resources. For example, the success of a particular toll road is dependent on connecting roads and competing motorways. It is undermined by the building of neighbouring high-speed railways or improved air transport.

To the extent that the prices of the provision of infrastructure and utility services are regulated then private-sector companies are exposed to changes in the terms on which services can be offered. A tightening of the cap on the prices that can be charged diminishes the returns on the investments that have been made.

Some of these changes may be benign and undertaken for sound economic reasons but there is equally a political incentive to engage in exploitation of private-sector investments. Expenditures on infrastructure are particularly exposed because of their 'sunk' nature. They are not readily recoverable or transferable to other locations and so, once made, they are vulnerable to systematic redistribution of benefits from companies to users, and governments may feel strong political imperatives to undertake such redistributions.

Political risks are particularly great in developing-country contexts, and the prevalence of corruption makes private infrastructure providers subject to both costly and illegal activities. The consequence is under-investment and the avoidance of locations where political risks are especially significant.

Correcting these failures requires the identification of public-sector commitment devices—ways in which governments can commit to abstaining from engaging in opportunistic changes in policy and exploitation of private-sector providers. International enforcement is one such commitment mechanism through, for example, multilateral insurance agencies like the Multilateral Investment Guarantee Agency (MIGA). These agencies offer private-sector providers insurance against political risk backed up by the threat of withdrawal of support by international organizations such as the World Bank in the event of political violations. Where developing countries uphold the interests of their investors then they can obtain larger amounts of funding on more favourable terms with the insurance that MIGA offers than those countries that renege and are excluded from its assistance.

Such commitment devices can be powerful deterrents to political interference. However, there are alternatives. Where infrastructure programmes are organized by public-sector corporations then the potential exists for joint ownership and control of such organizations. Instead of granting governments exclusive control over the design and operation of infrastructure, they can be organized as collaborative arrangements between the public and private sector.

In particular, coming back to the importance of nomination committees discussed in Chapter 5, large-scale private-sector providers as well as governments can be involved in the process of selecting and removing the directors of public infrastructure companies. They can both delegate decisions regarding the nature and funding of infrastructure programmes to jointly nominated directors. Viewed from the perspective of the private sector, this provides a way of committing the public sector but equally it addresses the private-sector commitment problem that the public sector legitimately perceives.

Private-Sector Commitment

Problems of commitment are at least as pervasive in the private as the public sector. Privatization has been successful at promoting operational efficiencies but not capital expenditures. Private sector providers seek to deliver as little as possible at as low a cost as they can over as long a period as feasible. Competitive tendering is used to elicit the best value-for-money construction and delivery of infrastructure projects and services, and contracts are specified as precisely as feasible to avoid gaming. But contracts are at best incomplete and prone to abuse when they involve the provision of subjective qualities of service over long periods of time.

The problem is that the interests of government and regulators, on the one hand, and private-sector companies, on the other, are in direct conflict. Governments and regulators are (at least in principle though unfortunately not nearly always in practice) concerned with the public interest. Private companies are interested in maximizing their returns. Governments and regulators want maximum quality at lowest prices for the largest number of, in particular disadvantaged, consumers. Companies want the highest revenues from the provision of the lowest-cost projects and services. Even if competitive tendering, well-designed contracts, oversight by international agencies, and independent public bodies are put in place, they do not resolve fundamental problems of commitment between private and public sectors.

The current institutional solutions to the inherent conflict between the private and public sector in the delivery of infrastructure services are becoming increasingly fragile. And that is before we have even begun to think about our potentially most important infrastructure asset and that is our natural capital and environment. We simply cannot afford to retain a system that is degrading both our material and natural infrastructure.

There is a straightforward resolution to the governance as well as the measurement problem. Regulated utilities that provide infrastructure services operate under a licence to supply. However, those very same companies' terms of employment of the investments under the corporate laws that define their existence state something very different. The licences specify the amounts, qualities, and duration of the services they provide; corporate and company laws relate to the financial interests of their investors. The focus of infrastructure licences is on quality and value for money; the fiduciary responsibilities of directors are to maximize the returns on their companies' investments.

It is no wonder that the executives of such organizations experience a degree of schizophrenia in their professional lives. It is as if they were telling their children on the one hand to be good, honest, and upright citizens and on the other to do whatever it takes to get rich quick. It is both unsustainable and unnecessary.

This problem can be readily resolved by making the licence condition of their infrastructure operations part of the charters or articles of association of their companies, or at least the subsidiaries that provide the relevant services. That does not extinguish their obligations to their shareholders but it puts their licence conditions to their infrastructure companies on an equal footing and it aligns the private purposes of infrastructure providers with the public purposes of governments and regulators.

That is precisely how infrastructure companies were for centuries structured across the world. The railroads and canals were built by public companies under royal charters or licences issued by acts of parliament. The public obligations were a pre-requisite to the granting of licences to operate. We lost that association with freedom of incorporation in the nineteenth century, and, while liberalization may or may not have been appropriate for private companies that were not supplying public goods, it is most certainly not right for the provision of infrastructure.

Incorporation of public licences in private charters and articles of association eliminates the conflict and contractual abuse that is endemic in private–public partnerships, private finance initiatives, and privatizations. It goes beyond what was described as being needed in private companies in general, namely the incorporation of their purposes in their articles of association and a demonstration of how their corporate structures assist with the fulfilment of them, to a requirement that the stated purposes of regulated companies include their licence conditions to operate. It makes the private provision of public-sector services a natural function of the private sector and it extinguishes the divide that exists between the two sectors. It does so by converting the conflict that is intrinsic to regulated corporations into cooperation, and avoids having to trade off the inefficiencies of the public sector against the social injustices of the private sector.

Where the inclusion of such licence conditions in corporate charters and articles of association is permitted under existing corporate law then this should be a pre-requisite for the granting of an infrastructure licence. Otherwise, a legal form analogous to the Benefit Corporation in the United States, which explicitly allows companies to specify a public purpose beyond their commercial interests, should be adopted with the licence condition being the stated public purpose. In both cases, the role of the regulator then becomes essentially a governance one of ensuring that the company abides by its public duties under its charter and publishes relevant measures of performance that demonstrate this. Conversely public–private corporations can result from the injection of private capital into state-owned corporations, as occurred in China from the mid-1990s onwards, in which case their purposes should reflect the interests of private as well as public-sector investors.

Three Phases

The corporation is a powerful vehicle for binding public and private sectors together in the delivery of infrastructure programmes. The particular form that it takes depends on the nature and phase of an infrastructure programme. There are typically three phases to a programme: design, build, and operate. These have specific financing requirements and risks associated with them and consequently require different types of arrangements between private- and public-sector providers to make them viable.

In combination the three phases typically generate a long horizon. Design may take anything from two to eight years; building may take three to seven years; and the operation phase is likely to extend for at least two decades. No government or company can credibly commit for the totality of a programme; instead, they should be disaggregated into their three phases.

Phase 1: Design

The design phase sets the parameters that determine whether the subsequent stages can attract private finance. Since it sets key parameters, design is in many respects both the most critical and the most complex phase. It is critical because it defines the purposes and objectives of the project and needs to demonstrate credibly an ability to deliver in the subsequent phases. It is complex because it involves coordination with several different players and a commitment on their part to participate in the subsequent activities.

Currently insufficient resources are often attracted into the design phase, which, for a significant project, are likely to amount to tens of millions of dollars spread over several years. If this phase is to attract private finance, then from the start the prospects of commercial returns from investing in design must be sufficiently attractive. At present this is often not the case.

At the completion of the design stage, building the project needs to be a bankable proposition, recognized as advantageous by the government. Hence, the most crucial element of design is to define the governance of the programme. Investors feel exposed to risks of expropriation by governments, and governments are vulnerable to exploitation by private-sector contractors. There needs to be a common purpose and understanding from the outset, means by which the different parties can credibly commit, and ways of resolving disputes in a low-cost and effective manner.

The most effective way of achieving this is through joint ownership. The different parties—private-sector funders, contractors, and operators need to be brought together with public-sector providers (donors and government) to define the roles and responsibilities of the different parties. Projects should be ring-fenced as self-contained activities with the governance of each project delineated from that of other projects but within the context of a broader framework or architecture for the sector as a whole, set by the government after consultation with investors and other stakeholders. In other words there should be a hierarchy of collaborative arrangements between private and public parties from high-level sector-wide oversight to specific infrastructure projects.

The importance of the high-level oversight is that while the management and financing of individual infrastructure projects can be contained and ring-fenced, the impact of other activities in the sector or indeed from other sectors cannot. So for example, the success of a road-building programme might be seriously affected by the initiation of railway programmes. The potential for infrastructure assets to be stranded is therefore immense even in the absence of specific expropriation of returns from a particular project. The way to manage this is for the infrastructure programme of a country to be designed in close collaboration with investors.

Phase 2: Build

The build phase is when major finance has to be raised. It is also currently a high-risk phase. There are two critical components to effective management at the build stage. The first is commitment mechanisms and the second is collateral so there are costs and compensation for reneging on contracts. Building large infrastructure projects commonly involves substantial cost overruns and delays. There is an established psychological bias towards optimism among planners since best-case scenarios tend to become adopted as the benchmark for outcomes. At the build stage these risks can potentially inflict high costs on the private contractor, which are consequently priced into the project. Hence, these risks are borne by the private investor who undertakes upfront finance for building the project ahead of recuperating returns on the investment. To address this there need to be mechanisms for imposing penalties on defaulting governments and ways in which private-sector contractors can recover their costs.

Underwriting by international agencies is one way in which governments can commit to private-sector providers. MIGA has offered an effective method of discouraging default by acting as a collection device backed by the threat of sanctions from the World Bank. The question is whether this can be scaled to a greater level than to date. This is a matter of the amounts of capital that can be raised to provide underwriting facilities. With its strong record in enforcing contracts, MIGA has a good base on which to build its capital; however, it requires a global initiative on the scale of the European Bank for Reconstruction and Development (EBRD) for this to have real impact.

Capitalizing MIGA and similar organizations should be viewed as an effective form of aid in which, for the most part, the aid does not need to be spent because the underwriting never has to be provided. Governments should recognize their collective power to promote economic development by creating agencies such as MIGA, backed by the World Bank, that act as commitment vehicles and allow developing country governments to commit in a way in which they wish to but cannot credibly do at present. It is therefore substantially welfare-enhancing at low cost.

Phase 3: Operate

At the operate stage the risk is a government one that the private-sector operators fail to deliver their promised level of services. This requires a commitment on the part of companies to meet obligations in terms of quality and price of services and to desist from exploiting their monopoly positions to the detriment of customers. This is traditionally achieved through regulation.

The regulatory process should be seen as a commitment device on the part of companies. It forces them to avoid abusing their monopoly power in the charges that they levy on customers and the quality of services that they provide. However, regulation has to balance the benefits it confers on customers through lower charges and higher-quality services with the disincentives it imposes on providers to invest and operate in infrastructure markets. In particular, regulators can act in as arbitrary a fashion as governments in seeking to impose populist agendas. Alternatively they are subject to capture and fail to promote the interests of customers.

There is an inherent conflict between shareholder driven corporations and the public interest and in general the regulator comes off worse from the conflict. This is particularly serious in a developing-country context because of the reliance that has to be placed on overseas operators. There is, therefore, a real risk of the process of private-sector engagement in infrastructure being rapidly discredited as utility companies are perceived to be exploiting vulnerable economies.

To avoid this it will be necessary to ring-fence the utility activities of foreign operators from the rest of their activities. It is a process that has been successfully implemented in utilities in the United Kingdom where, in particular in the water industry, the regulator requires a clear delineation between the utility and the non-utility parts of businesses. Assets cannot be transferred between the two, they are incorporated as separate subsidiaries with their own boards of directors, and the payment of dividends from the subsidiary to the parent is limited. The ring-fenced activity should be structured as a benefit company with its stated public purpose being its licence condition to operate.

In sum, the three phases of an infrastructure programme are delivered by different types of corporations: publicly owned corporations with private-sector participation in the first, design phase; private corporations in the second, build phase, with public-sector engagement constrained where necessary by international organizations; and private corporations with public as well as private purposes defined by their licence conditions in the third, operate phase.

Partnership

The solution to the public-and private-sector commitment problems are mirror images of each other. In both cases, the corporate form provides a powerful vehicle for aligning interests that are currently highly divergent. Regulation does not solve the problem because conflicting interests encourage private companies to do what they can to circumvent the regulation and public organizations to renege on the terms of the regulation.

Instead we should use the corporate vehicle as a powerful instrument for promoting partnership where conflict currently exists. It does so through conferring a degree of engagement of private providers in public-service functions, such as the design and regulation of infrastructure services, and through including public licence obligations in the articles of associations of private providers of infrastructure services.

The corporate form also addresses the accounting problem of the absence of balance sheets in national accounts described above. By organizing infrastructure in public as well as private corporations, infrastructure assets are all automatically reported in corporate accounts.

A combination of proper accounting for infrastructure across the private and public sectors together with the reformulation of the purpose of private-sector providers offers the prospect of transforming infrastructure around the world. With correct measurement and diminution of the inherent conflict between public-sector purposes and private-sector interests, there is at least a chance of the world obtaining the infrastructure it needs for its future prosperity and survival; without it, there is little or none.

Closure

Infrastructure has brought us full circle back to the Roman origins of the corporation described in Chapter 3 as the provider of public works. This stands in contrast to the way in which the book opened in Chapter 1 by noting that the nature of the corporation is fundamentally altering from a tangible to an intangible entity in the guise of the mindful corporation. The most significant manifestations of this are the social networks of Facebook, LinkedIn, and Whatsapp and the Internet providers, such as Google.

By virtue of being full of minds rather than matter, the twenty-first-century infrastructure companies are low- not high-capital-intensive businesses. But far from implying the irrelevance of the principles of infrastructure described in this chapter, they magnify its significance. It is not financial capital that is ultimately the problem—it is social capital. The systems features of infrastructure with which this chapter opened are statements about the social as against the private relevance of infrastructure. It binds us as one community, society, and human race. And as such, the private provider is operating in a social space. It cannot ignore its public place or if it does then it risks the wrath of the politicians, competition authorities, and regulators bearing down upon it, as they have done increasingly over the past decade, with the ultimate threat being nationalization if it exploits its dominant market position.

This brings us back to the consciousness and values of Chapter 2. The corporation is a conscious entity that has values. But when its sphere of operation is public not private, when it interacts with others in fulfilling its functions, and when it is collectively part of a bigger whole, its consciousness has to embrace its environment, not just itself. That is the challenge of the twenty-first-century corporation, government, and world, and it is what will make the subject of the corporation one of the most fascinating for many years to come. We await the coming of the seventh age of the corporation as the trusted corporation.

Prospects

Make the private public;
The external internal;
The social commercial;
Our prospects prosper,
Our problems perish.

In his book on the clash of civilizations,[1] Samuel Huntington emphasizes the significance of race and religion, of countries and continents, of the West and the rest, but he omits consideration of one of the most important influences on civilizations in the twentieth and twenty-first centuries. Corporations are both the cause of and solution to the clash of civilizations and a breakdown of trust. They underpin the economic success and failure of civilizations and the prosperity of nations.

We have observed this on a journey that started in Babylon and Ancient Rome and took us to the Middle East, Continental Europe, back to Medici Italy, to Elizabethan England, across the Channel to Holland, India, and the Far East, to Germany, Japan, the United States, and back to the United Kingdom.

We have seen how the corporation was created to perform public functions; administered towns, religions, and universities; merged with emergent commercial, capital-raising enterprises; launched voyages of discovery and opened merchant trading around the world; undertook public work programmes of railroads, canals, water, electricity, and other forms of infrastructure; built factories, machines, and equipment in the industrial revolution; created financial and other service industries; expanded into monolithic multinational organizations; and is now spearheading the artificial intelligence, automation, communication, information, social networking revolution.

We have recorded how the conception of the corporation has developed from a body chartered by king and Parliament to small family-owned and managed businesses funded by local banks; to private enterprises that economized on the transaction costs of administering commercial activities; to businesses that raised increasingly large amounts of capital from stock markets and in the process diluted the ownership of families; to dispersed-ownership companies that were afflicted by agency problems of aligning the interests of management with shareholders; to markets in corporate control and hedge-fund activism as resolutions of the agency problem; to organizations whose sole reason for existing is to maximize shareholder value at all times.

We have witnessed the noble purposes of the founders of corporations progressively and inexorably eroded to a preoccupation with profit. It is not an edifying ultimate destination for anyone involved in it, nor is it what it can or should be. The corporation is not just a profit-generating machine. It is a living, evolving entity capable of consciousness of its living environment and its potential to contribute to it. It is not a vehicle for controlling our lives for the benefit of a small class of privileged owners. It is a body that can promote cooperation and collaboration in the realization of purposes that individually we can neither conceive nor achieve with the same degree of integrity or credibility. It does this by committing to its purposes through a combination of its values, culture, ownership, governance, leadership, and measurement. This occurred with the fusion of capital and capabilities in the guilds and the merchant trading companies laying the organizational foundations for prosperity that would have been infeasible in its absence.

At the centre of this lies the purpose of the corporation. Purpose is the reason why something is created, exists, and is done, and corporate purpose is the reason for the creation and existence of a firm and what it aspires to become. It defines the corporation and everything associated with it—its ownership, governance, leadership, finance, and performance in terms of producing profitable solutions to problems of people and planet. Its existence is dependent on the laws that enable and empower it to achieve its purpose. Its values and culture are the principles that ensure a complete and comprehensive corporate alignment with its purpose. Its strategy, goals, and targets derive from its purpose and are the basis for its implementation. Where the private purposes of companies are at variance with those of society more generally we regulate, tax, partner, and own the corporation to promote public as well as private purposes.

The book progressively describes how ownership, governance, measurement, law, regulation, taxation, and partnership can promote both private and public purposes. We have observed the remarkable diversity of form of the corporation not just across time but also across country that is used to achieve this. At one end stand the highly dispersed ownership systems of the United Kingdom and the United States. At the other are the family-owned businesses of Continental Europe and the Far East, bank and cross-company shareholdings in Japan, and state ownership, in particular in China. There are strongly shareholder-oriented systems in Sweden and employee representation systems in Austria and Germany. There are controlling dual-class shareholders and extensive protections of management against threats of takeover and removal by shareholders in the United States but not in the United Kingdom.

There are parallel forms of concentrated block holdings and widely held shares in companies listed on stock markets in many countries around the world. There are institutional investors that are increasingly accumulating significant blocks of shares in firms that they actively manage themselves over long periods of time. There are therefore diverse ways in which countries and companies have sought to manage the conflicts that arise everywhere between owner and manager, controlling and minority investor, shareholder and stakeholder, the firm, communities, and future generations. Few places have sought to resolve these conflicts simply by conferring control on minority dispersed shareholders, and where they have, the experience has not been encouraging.

There are good reasons for parallel systems of block holdings and dispersed ownership. Block holders are required to promote the creation of idiosyncratic value, and institutional and individual investors are needed to facilitate its financing and risk management. Without block holders to anchor long-term value, dispersed shareholders would extinguish its creation as well as its risk; without dispersed shareholders and liquid stock markets, it would not be funded.

While ownership is critical, it is not sufficient. The realization of idiosyncratic value in human, natural, and social as well as financial capital requires governance. So long as governance is regarded as synonymous with financial valuation in the resolution of agency problems, this will not occur. Governance is not just about aligning managerial with shareholder interests; it is about achieving the purpose of corporations where those purposes include everything from purely positive benefits for customers to the attainment of normative welfare-enhancing outcomes for society at large. Achievement of that requires innovations in management that are equivalent to those in research and development. They involve a clear identification of the purpose of businesses, the pain points in the ecosystems in which they operate, the partnerships that have to be established with other organizations, and the relationship of human, natural, and social with financial capital.

223

As capital scarcity moves from financial and material in manufacturing to human, intellectual, natural, and social in the mindful corporation, governance has to adapt accordingly. While shareholder control might once have been justified by a need to allocate scarce finance capital efficiently, it is no more. It is other capitals that now need to be enhanced and protected. More significantly, as scarcity of different types of capital intensifies, governance is increasingly seen to be more a matter of trusteeship on behalf of multiple parties rather than agency for shareholders or any particular stakeholder group. It requires commitment to the many different groups involved in realizing corporate purpose not control by any single one.

Key to this is performance measurement and in particular the correct determination of corporate profits. Once the collective nature of corporate enterprise is appreciated then the deficiencies of existing measures of profits are all too evident. Profits are reported where none exist (fake profits) and assets fail to be recorded where they have been created (human, natural, and social capital). Profits should not be reported where they have been earned at the expense of other parties to the firm, and non-financial as well as financial and material assets should be recognized where they contribute to the fulfilment of corporate purposes.

The first of these deficiencies is readily addressed through extension of the conventional accounting principle of capital maintenance to forms of capital other than financial and material capital. This is most evident in relation to natural capital but should also be considered in the context of human and social capital. The second is achieved by recognizing investment expenditures in human, natural, and social capital in addition to financial and material capital as assets of a firm.

At present, the corporation is constrained by its creator—the law. In principle, corporate law recognizes the duties of directors to the company as a whole but, in practice, this quickly morphs into the primacy of shareholders with due regard for other stakeholders and the long-term interests of the firm. This reflects the significance of notions of property and agency in the design of corporate law to preserve the rights of shareholders as owners and define the responsibilities of directors as their agents. More seriously, corporate law is viewed in a prescriptive context of defining what the corporation is or should be, as against what it could or might be. In other words it is restrictive where it should be permissive.

As a vehicle for promoting commitment to the different parties to the firm in the realization of corporate purposes, the corporation is capable of achieving outcomes that far exceed those associated with any instrument of control. It can sustain levels of trust that we as individuals can only aspire to and it can promote the contribution to a common purpose that is the essence of the corporation's success. However, to achieve this, it is necessary for corporate law to recognize its role in facilitating commitment rather than control. It should do this by requiring companies to articulate their purposes, incorporate them in their articles of association, and require them to demonstrate how their ownership, governance, values, culture, leadership, measurement, incentives, and performance uphold and promote their purposes.

In so doing, companies will be required to establish how the purposes of their owners secure the capacity of the company to deliver its purposes over the long term. This will require them to establish that voting control resides with owners who have demonstrated a length (duration), breadth (scope), and depth (scale) of commitment that is consistent with fulfilment of their purposes. This in turn will necessitate institutional investors to adopt purposes that not only reflect the interests of their beneficiaries (their investors) as at present but also the purposes of their corporate investments, which are currently regarded as no more than those of their beneficiaries.

This simple step of incorporating corporate purpose in company articles of association transforms the whole of the corporate and institutional sector and, if effectively implemented, provides the answer to the question of how we can escape from the seemingly irresolvable systemic failure we have created.

Beyond requiring companies to prioritize their purposes, corporate law should enable companies to adopt diverse forms of ownership and governance that empower different parties to the firm and give them the means to enforce their rights. It should promote diversity where the law currently imposes uniformity and encourage experimentation where at present it prefers precedent. The *quid pro quo* for precision on purpose is relaxation of regulation.

Where companies fail to respond to the permissive enabling, empowering, enforcing regime in upholding the public as well as private interest then the law reverts to its other persona as a requiring, refraining, and restoring regulator. Of late, we have come to associate this in particular with the financial sector, where the abuse of the public duty has been most in evidence. Financial regulation has intensified immeasurably in response, but it also illustrates the deficiencies of the regulatory as against the facilitating functions of corporate law.

The response of regulators to the financial crisis has been to baton down the hatches where the storms have been most intense—namely in banking. There have been a myriad of new banking regulations, in particular in countries such as the United Kingdom and United States with the worst bank failures. However, as with most regulation, there have been serious unintended consequences. In particular, the introduction of stringent bank regulation has encouraged financial resources to shift out of the banking into the nearest non-regulated sectors, resulting in an explosion of shadow banking. This is in part a consequence of the particular way in which financial regulation has been structured based on institutional form rather than functional equivalence. This is having serious consequences for the stability of the financial system as well as the efficacy of regulation. In seeking to extinguish the last financial crisis, regulation is inflaming the next.

Underlying the inadequacy of financial regulation is its failure to identify and promote the purposes of the financial sector. Where regulation is purposeful, it can be stunningly successful, as it has been in achieving an extraordinary degree of financial inclusion in Kenya in a remarkably short space of time. While the introduction of such new socially beneficial products is highly commendable, they do not capture the overall objective of a financial system to stimulate inclusive sustainable growth, development, investment, and innovation. It is against these criteria that the performance of regulation should be judged, not its success in promoting particular products or preventing the failure of others.

The financial crisis is pertinent in reminding us that its main consequences were not just the costs borne by investors and taxpayers but its enduring effects on the corporate sector. In particular, it has revealed the fragility of the dependence of corporate sectors on debt, especially long-term debt that burdens them over many years. Regulation and taxation need to be careful to avoid encouraging companies to adopt financial structures that exacerbate their fragility. Small and medium-sized companies are particularly reliant on bank finance and benefit from close enduring relationships with local banks that persist during periods of financial stringency and turbulence. Such relations are threatened by regulation that encourages banks to centralize their risk management functions and diminish the autonomy of local branches.

As companies mature, they need access to equity as well as bond markets to grow to scale. They benefit from a combination of long-term engaged block holders as well as short-term dispersed passive shareholders. Corporate tax systems encourage companies to adopt excessively high levels of leverage by subsidizing debt relative to equity finance, and regulation encourages passive dispersed shareholdings in preference to engaged block holdings by protecting minority from majority shareholders. As a result, while there has been a massive expansion of debt capital, private equity, mutual funds, and international portfolios of institutional investment, there has been a dearth of long-term engaged block ownership.

Both regulation and taxation should start from a position of neutrality in not biasing companies' preferred forms of ownership and financial structure, and only deviate from neutrality where there are compelling arguments for doing so without adverse repercussions for the functioning of the corporate sector. They should recognize the shifts in the nature of capital scarcity that are occurring away from financial to other forms of capital, such as human and intellectual capital, and take care not to discriminate against the participation and active engagement of non-financial forms of capital and their custodianship by foundations and trusts.

Underlying this is recognition of the interdependence between finance and investment that contrasts with the conventional separation between the two—an idea originally promulgated in economic theory that has permeated into regulatory policy with damaging consequences for corporate sectors. The state has a role to play not just in promoting private-sector finance but also in participating actively itself in the provision of investments where private sectors cannot be expected to undertake them on their own, namely in infrastructure, and it is not only in the realm of finance that we find extensive regulation. It is also associated with utilities and infrastructure, and quite rightly so because these provide the public goods and services on which we depend as nations and societies.

But faced with private-sector providers whose sole interest is in their financial returns, regulation is a weak instrument of protection. Equally, private-sector providers are exposed to unstable corrupt political regimes that are incapable of providing the assurances required of long-term investments in infrastructure programmes. As a consequence, there is chronic deficiency in infrastructure around the world, most prominently but by no means exclusively in developing countries.

This deficiency is a product of two-way failures of commitment—by governments to the private sector not to exploit their long-term irreversible investments and by companies to governments not to abuse customers and communities through under-provision or over-charging of goods and services. At the moment, both governments and the private sector lack effective mechanisms for committing to each other.

There are ways of resolving this through innovative legal forms and joint private and public ownership that encourage the two parties to remain true to their commitments. They encourage the development of public-sector accounts that mirror those of the private sector in recognizing the contribution that both make to the co-creation of national wealth in human, natural, social, and material assets. As we move to a world of infrastructure based on minds as well as matter, these commitment mechanisms become ever more important.

227

This book has argued that the conventional view of economic systems that sees a separation between the public role of setting the rules of the game and the private one of maximizing profits while staying within the rules of the game is at the root of the problem. It has given rise to a wholly inappropriate emphasis on privatization, regulation, competition policy, corporate governance, and investor protection as ways of solving the world's problems. It has suggested a separation between finance and investment, and the financial and real sectors of economies, when in fact they are mutual, and integration and cooperation are required.

The conventional view draws a sharp boundary round the firm, defines its assets and liabilities in terms of their legal claims, delineates rights and responsibilities accordingly, and determines that these and these alone are internal, while the rest are external, creating externalities that are the responsibility of governments not firms. It has failed to acknowledge that a primary role of business is to internalize externalities, to seek them out and manage them for the benefit of both the corporation and society. It has promoted a contrast between the commercial and social aspects of business when the two are partners in a mutual endeavour to produce profitable solutions to problems of people and planet.

Shareholders are central to our capitalist systems and it was the synthesis of capital and administration in the fourteenth century that propelled the world to the twenty-first century. But that synthesis did not involve the domination of one party over another. It was not subjugation of the world to the whims of financiers but a partnership of equals. So it should remain because it is not capitalism that is the cause of the clash of civilizations but the course that capitalism has chosen. It is the presumption that capitalism is about one class of capital that creates conflict—conflict with consumers, communities, and countries.

We should look to the democratization and diversification of corporate form and the release of corporate purposes from shareholder supremacy for the collective interest of all the members of a firm. In so doing, the development of the rights of the corporation will parallel those of the individual that occurred in the thirteenth century with the Franciscan challenge to ownership by the Church under canon law and the subsequent rejection by William of Ockham of Aristotelian rule of reason in favour of individual will constrained by obligations of equality and reciprocity.[2]

In the same way as the liberation of the purpose of individuals from autocratic rules of reason laid the foundations of scientific enquiry in the Age of Enlightenment, so too will the release of the corporation from the rule of shareholder rights presage a new age of enquiry into the role of the corporation in contemporary society that extends beyond the current confines of economics and finance to embrace all of the humanities, sciences, and social sciences. Just as the emergence of the identity of individual purpose encouraged past reasoning to be challenged in favour of future prospects, so too will corporate purpose question the relevance of the intellectual origins of the firm for societal needs of the twenty-first century.

It will lay the foundation for new forms of education that will replace the current approach of starting from the assertion that 'the purpose of business is to create shareholder value' with a question: 'what is the purpose of business?' Having identified the myriad of answers to that in the present and past, and the still more dazzling array in the future, educational programmes will then seek to identify the ownership, governance, laws, regulation, and public policies as well as the business practices that will assist with achievement of those purposes. In other words, it will lay the intellectual foundations as well as practical understanding of the role of corporations in contemporary society that will inspire our leaders and followers of the future.

All of the history and evolution of firms, their philosophical foundations, the psychology of human motivation, the biological development of organisms, accounting, and law from the around the world since the start of commerce suggest this. They all point away from the separation between public and private, finance and investment, internalities and externalities, and commercial and social towards integration and partnership to achieve private and public purposes. It is to partnerships between all of them that we need to look for both our human and commercial flourishing.

There are two worlds. There is the world of utility-seeking *homo economicus* and profit-maximizing corporations, legitimized by law, restrained by regulation, with governments internalizing the externalities they leave behind. And there is the world of this book of purpose pursuing people and companies, enabled by law, committed by regulation, partnering with government to produce a public as well as private purpose. Both are internally consistent. One persists; the other perishes.

The choice is ours not theirs, for the corporation is a creature of company and cooperation. It has emerged from the body politic, merged with an enterprise entity, and morphed into a money monster. Its proper purpose is to profit for, not from, its people and planet. Were it ever or anywhere not thus, we might conclude otherwise. But it never was and nowhere will be, and conclude we must thus for us to prosper not perish.

Postscript

Purpose first; the rest follow

Principal Propositions

- Purpose is the reason why something is created, exists, and is done, and what it aspires to become.
- Companies should articulate their purposes and demonstrate a commitment to the delivery of them.
- The significance of corporate purpose comes from the role that it plays in furthering purpose in people's lives.
- Corporations are living organisms that evolve through forming symbiotic relations with others and having a consciousness of their living environment.
- The trustworthiness of companies and other parties is central to the delivery of corporate purpose.
- It derives from the ability of corporations to commit and create commitment mechanisms.
- Through the pursuit of purposeful values, corporations can achieve greater levels of integrity than we, as individuals, are capable of realizing.
- Companies were established with public purposes that have been progressively eroded by shareholder primacy.
- Shareholders are only one of the participants in the achievement of corporate purpose.
- The paradigm shift that is required is from shareholder primacy to purpose primacy.

- In the absence of anchor shareholders, markets in corporate control militate against the pursuit of purpose by imposing continuous maximization of shareholder value.
- Companies benefit from the contemporaneous presence of anchor shareholders and liquid stock markets in the achievement of their purposes.

Practical Prescriptions

- Corporate governance should promote a company's purposes.
- The various elements of corporate governance (board composition, remuneration, performance measurement, incentives) should assist with delivery of company purposes.
- Companies should seek to internalize their externalities by recognizing the commercial as well as social benefits of so doing.
- They should be intentional in addressing pain points in their ecosystems.
- They should establish partnerships with relevant organizations.
- Companies should construct measures of human, natural, and social capital as well as financial capital and determine the relation between them.
- They should measure profits net of the cost of maintaining these capitals.
- Corporate control should reside with scarce capitals. These are no longer predominantly financial.
- Voting rights should reflect commitments to the length (duration), depth (scale), and breadth (scope) of investments.
- In the presence of multiple scarce capitals, corporate governance involves trusteeship that balances the interests of different capitals, including the abundant.
- The parallel presence of block holders and public capital markets promotes idiosyncratic value creation and innovation.
- Institutional investors should recognize their role in transforming short-term liquid safe individual liabilities into long-term illiquid risky corporate assets.
- They should hold significant long-term holdings in companies, participate in the appointment of company directors and promote corporate purposes.

Policy Proposals

- The separation between public policy in setting the rules of the game and private corporations in playing by them is invalid.
- Public policy should promote corporate purposes through law, regulation, and taxation.
- Corporate law should require companies and financial institutions to articulate their purposes, incorporate them in their articles of association, and demonstrate how their corporate structures and conduct promote their purposes.
- It should not privilege a particular party to the firm.
- It should enable companies to adopt and commit to structures and practices that further their purpose and the pursuit of idiosyncratic value.
- Regulation should be purpose driven.
- It should assist companies and institutions with committing to public as well as private purposes.
- It should target functions not institutional forms of finance and be focused on failures to promote public purposes.
- Regulation and corporate taxation should adopt policies of neutrality towards corporate structures by, for example, eliminating tax deductibility of interest payments.
- Public policy should recognize the importance of relationships between financial institutions and companies in the financing and control of firms.
- Purposeful corporations can resolve commitment problems that otherwise arise between the state and private-sector providers of infrastructure.
- Corporations should contribute to reporting public as well as corporate sector net wealth.
- Private utility and infrastructure companies should commit to their public institutions by aligning their company articles with their licence conditions.

Notes

Preamble

1. Alberto Giovannini, Colin Mayer, Stefano Micossi, Carmine Di Noia, Marco Onado, Marco Pagano, and Andrea Polo (2015), 'Restarting European long-term investment finance: A green paper discussion document', Centre for Economic Policy Research: London. Colin Mayer, Stefano Micossi, Marco Onada, Marco Pagano, and Andrea Polo (2018), *Finance and Investment: The Case of Europe*, Oxford: Oxford University Press.
2. Big Innovation Centre (2016), *Purposeful Company: Interim Report*, London: Big Innovation Centre. Big Innovation Centre (2017), *Purposeful Company: Policy Report*, London: Big Innovation Centre.
3. John Armour, Dan Awrey, Paul Davies, Luca Enriques, Jeffrey Gordon, Colin Mayer, and Jennifer Payne (2016), *Principles of Financial Regulation*, Oxford: Oxford University Press.
4. 'In pursuit of inclusive capitalism, business and approaches to systemic change', Said Business School, University of Oxford, 2016.

Preface

1. Milton Friedman (1970), 'The social responsibility of business is to increase its profits', *The New York Times Magazine*, 13 September.
2. Milton Friedman (1962), *Capitalism and Freedom*, Chicago, IL: University of Chicago Press.
3. Friedman (1970), 'The social responsibility of business is to increase its profits'.
4. ibid.
5. UNU-IHDP and UNEP (2014), *Inclusive Wealth Report 2014: Measuring Progress Towards Sustainability*, Cambridge: Cambridge University Press.
6. Victor Frankl (1959—English translation), *Man's Search for Meaning*, Boston, MA: Beacon, and (1946—original German) *Trotzdem Ja zum Leben sagen: Ein Psychologe erlebt das Konzentrationslager*, Austria: Verlag für Jugend und Volk.
7. Adrian Cadbury (1992), *Report of the Committee on the Financial Aspects of Corporate Governance*, London: Gee.
8. Colin Mayer (2015), 'Big Bang: New beginning or beginning of the end?' *Oxford Review of Economic Policy*, 31, 186–98.
9. Colin Mayer (1986), 'Financial innovation: Curse or blessing?' *Oxford Review of Economic Policy*, 2, 1–19.

Notes

Part 1

1. William Shakespeare 'All the World's a Stage', *As You Like It,* Act II, scene vii.

Chapter 1

1. This is an amended version of Colin Mayer (2016), 'Reinventing the corporation', *Journal of the British Academy,* 4, 53–72.
2. Peter Goodridge, Gavin Wallis, and Jonathan Haskel (2014), 'UK investment in intangible assets', Nesta Working Paper 14/02 and Leonard Nakamura (2009), 'Intangible assets and national income accounting: Measuring a scientific revolution', Federal Reserve Bank of Philadelphia, Working Paper No. 09–11.
3. Adam Smith (1776), *An Inquiry into the Nature and Causes of the Wealth of Nations,* London: Strahan and Cadell, Book V, Chapter 1.
4. Alfred Marshall (1892), *Elements of Economics of Industry,* London: Macmillan, Book IV, Chapter 12.
5. Ronald Coase (1937), 'The nature of the firm', *Economica,* 4, 386–405.
6. See, for example, Armen Alchian and Harold Demsetz (1972), 'Production, information costs and economic organization', *American Economic Review,* 62, 777–95, and Michael Jensen and William Meckling (1976), 'Theory of the firm: Managerial behavior, agency costs and ownership structure', *Journal of Financial Economics,* 3, 305–60.
7. Frank Easterbrook and Daniel Fischel (1981), 'The proper role of a target's management in responding to a tender offer', *Harvard Law Review,* 94, 1161–204, and Henry Hansmann and Reinier Kraakman (2001), 'The end of history for corporate law,' *Georgetown Law Journal,* 89, 439–68.
8. Eugene Fama and Michael Jensen (1983), 'Separation of ownership and control', *Journal of Law and Economics,* 26, 301–25.
9. *The Economist,* 7 February 2015.
10. Jensen and Meckling (1976), 'Theory of the firm'.
11. This quotation is often attributed to Arthur Schopenhauer, but there is no known citation to it (see Jeffrey Shallit (2005), 'Science, pseudoscience, and the three stages of truth', mimeo, Department of Computer Science, University of Waterloo, https://cs.uwaterloo.ca/~shallit/Papers/stages.pdf).
12. Christa Borsting, Johan Kuhn, Thomas Poulsen, and Steen Thomsen (2015), 'Industrial foundations as long-term owners', Center for Corporate Governance, Copenhagen Business School.
13. Adam Smith (1776), *Wealth of Nations.*
14. Adam Smith (1759), *The Theory of Moral Sentiments,* London: Andrew Millar.

Chapter 2

1. This section draws on work with Yun Hee Lee, Denis Noble, and David Vines at Balliol College, Oxford—Yun Hee Lee, Colin Mayer, Denis Noble, and David Vines (2017), 'Fusion through penetration, group sorting, and team formation: The implications of evolutionary biology for the study of cooperation in economics and management', Oxford University Working Paper.

For excellent discussions of many of the biological ideas in this chapter, see Denis Noble (2008), *The Music of Life: Biology Beyond Genes*, Oxford: Oxford University Press and Denis Noble (2016), *Dance to the Tune of Life: Biological Relativity*, Cambridge: Cambridge University Press.

2. Marilyn Roossinck (2008), 'Symbiosis, mutualism and symbiogensis' in Marilyn Roossinck (ed.), *Plant Virus Evolution*, Berlin: Springer, pp. 157–61.

3. Thomas Nagel (2012), *Mind and Cosmos: Why the Materialist Neo-Darwinian Conception of Nature Is Almost Certainly False*, Oxford: Oxford University Press.

4. This section is based on Colin Mayer (2017), 'Comment on "Putting integrity into finance: A purely positive approach (by Werner Erhard and Michael Jensen)"', *Capitalism and Society*, 12, Article 4. For a discussion of the role of identity, belonging, obligations, and responsibilities in capitalist systems, see Paul Collier (2018), *The Future of Capitalism: Facing the New Anxieties*, London and New York: Penguin and HarperCollins.

5. See, for example, Gabriele Taylor (1981), 'Integrity', *Proceedings of the Aristotelian Society*, 55, 143–59.

6. John Smart and Bernard Williams (1973), *Utilitarianism: For and Against*, Cambridge: Cambridge University Press.

7. George Akerlof and Robert Shiller (2015), *Phishing for Phools: The Economics of Manipulation and Deception*, Princeton, NJ: Princeton University Press.

8. ibid, p. 6.

9. This section is based on Colin Mayer (2018), 'Foreword' to Gay Haskins, Lalit Johri, and Michael Thomas (eds), *Kindness in Leadership*, Abingdon: Routledge.

10. https://www.youtube.com/watch?v=nwAYpLVyeFU.

Chapter 3

1. Uleikw Malmendier (2009), 'Law and finance "at the origin"', *Journal of Economic Literature*, 47, 1076–108.

2. Polybius, Historiae 6.17.3–4 cited in Malmendier (2009), 'Law and finance'.

3. William Burdick (1938), *The Principles of Roman Law and their Relation to Modern Law*, Rochester, NY: The Lawyers Cooperative Publishing Co., p. 277.

4. Frederick Pollock and Frederic Maitland (1895), *History of English Law before the Time of Edward I, Vol. 1*, Cambridge: Cambridge University Press, p. 469.

5. Jacques Cujaz (1595), *Opera Omnia: Opera Quae de Jure Facit, Vol. II*, Frankfurt: Andreas Wechel Erben, cited in Malmendier (2009), 'Law and finance'.

6. John Davis (1905), *Corporations: Study of the Origin and Development of Great Business Combinations and of Their Relation to the Authority of the State*, New York: Putnam.

7. Barbara Moe (2003), *The Charter of the Massachusetts Bay Colony*, New York: Rosen.

8. Harold Berman (1983), *Law and Revolution: The Formation of the Western Legal Tradition*, Cambridge, MA: Harvard University Press.

9. Larry Siedentop (2014), *Inventing the Individual: The Origins of Western Liberalism*, London: Allen Lane, p. 243.

10. ibid.

11. Berman (1983), *Law and Revolution*, p. 219.
12. Frederic Maitland (1900), 'The corporation sole', *Law Quarterly Review*, 16, 335–54.
13. David Runciman and Magnus Ryan (2003), *Maitland: State, Trust and Corporation*, Cambridge: Cambridge University Press.
14. The corporation sole has been discussed in other contexts, for example the monarchy, to distinguish the permanence of the office of the monarchy, from the transience of the officeholder, the monarch: 'The King is dead; long live the King.' See Frederic Maitland (1901), 'The Crown as corporation', *Law Quarterly Review*, 17, 131–46.
15. Chibili Mallat (2007), *Introduction to Middle Eastern Law*, Oxford: Oxford University Press.
16. Cornelia Wunsch (2010), 'Neo-Babylonian entrepreneurs' in David Landes, Joel Mokyr, and William Baumol (eds), *The Invention of Enterprise: Entrepreneurship from Ancient Mesopotamia to Modern Times*, Princeton, NJ: Princeton University Press, pp. 40–61.
17. Subhi Labib (1969), 'Capitalism in medieval Islam', *Journal of Economic History*, 29, 79–96.
18. Abraham Udovitch (1962), 'At the origins of the Western *Commenda*: Islam, Israel, Byzantium?' *Speculum*, 37, 198–207.
19. Timur Kuran (2011), *The Long Divergence: How Islamic Law Held Back the Middle East*, Princeton, NJ: Princeton University Press.
20. Udovitch (1962), 'At the origins of the Western *Commenda*'.
21. Angus Maddison (2001), *The World Economy: A Millennial Perspective*, Paris: OECD.
22. Alfred Lieber (1968), 'Eastern business practices and medieval European commerce', *Economic History Review*, 21, 230–43.
23. Raymond de Roover (1963), *The Rise and Decline of the Medici Bank*, Cambridge, MA: Harvard University Press, p. 372.
24. William Scott (1912), *The Constitution and Finance of English, Scottish and Irish Joint-Stock Companies to 1720, Vol. 1: The General Development of the Joint-Stock System to 1720*, Cambridge: Cambridge University Press, p. 3.
25. Clive Schmitthoff (1939), 'The origins of the joint-stock company', *University of Toronto Law Journal*, 3, 74–96.
26. Samuel Williston (1888), 'History of the law of business corporations before 1800', *Harvard Law Review*, 2, 111.
27. Philip Stern (2011), *The Company-State: Corporate Sovereignty and the Early Modern Foundations of the British Empire in India*, Oxford: Oxford University Press, pp. 25–6.
28. ibid., pp. 39–40.
29. ibid., p. 84.
30. ibid., p. 27.
31. ibid., p. 94.
32. ibid., p. 49.
33. ibid., p. 88.
34. ibid., p. 90.

35. ibid., p. 122.
36. ibid., p. 143.
37. ibid., p. 144.
38. ibid., pp. 148–9.
39. ibid., p. 152.
40. ibid., p. 152.
41. Paul Mahoney (2000), 'Contract or concession? An essay on the history of corporate law', *Georgia Law Review*, 34, 873–93.
42. Armand Dubois (1938), *The English Business Company after the Bubble Act, 1720–1800*, New York: Commonwealth Fund, 216, quoted in Mahoney (2000), 'Contract or concession?' p. 884.
43. Adam Smith (1776), *An Inquiry into the Nature and Causes of the Wealth of Nations*, Vol. I, ed. R. H. Campbell and A. S. Skinner, vol. II of the Glasgow Edition of the Works and Correspondence of Adam Smith, Indianapolis, IN: Liberty Fund, 1981, pp. 246–7.
44. Smith, (1776), *Wealth of Nations*, p. 233.
45. Scott (1912), *The Constitution and Finance of English, Scottish and Irish Joint-Stock Companies to 1720*, p. 461.
46. Pit Dehing and Marjolein't Hart (1997), 'Linking the fortunes: Currency and banking, 1550–1800', in Marjolein't Hart, Joost Jonker, and Jan van Zanden (eds), *A Financial History of the Netherlands*, Cambridge: Cambridge University Press, pp. 37–63.
47. Edwin Hunt and James Murray (1999), *A History of Business in Medieval Europe: 1200–1500*, Cambridge: Cambridge University Press.

Chapter 4

1. Cited in Deborah Cadbury (2010), *Chocolate Wars—From Cadbury to Kraft: 220 Years of Sweet Success and Bitter Rivalry*, London: Harper Collins, p. 176.
2. ibid.
3. John Ruskin first published 'Unto This' in 1860 as a series of articles in *Cornhill Magazine*. In 1908 Gandhi serialized a nine-part paraphrase of Ruskin's book in Gujarati in *Indian Opinion* and later published it as a pamphlet under the title *Sarvodaya* (The Welfare of All).
4. Cadbury (2010), *Chocolate Wars*, p. 213.
5. ibid., p. 214.
6. Julian Franks, Colin Mayer, and Paolo Volpin (2012), 'The life-cycle of family ownership', *Review of Financial Studies*, 25, 1687–712.
7. Harold Meyers (1967), 'The sweet secret world of Forrest Mars', *Fortune*, reproduced from the Fortune Archives by Fortune Editors, 31 March 2013.
8. ibid., p. 255.
9. This is extensively documented in Julian Franks, Colin Mayer, and Stefano Rossi (2009), 'Ownership, evolution and regulation', *Review of Financial Studies*, 22, 4009–56, and Julian Franks, Colin Mayer, and Stefano Rossi (2005), 'Spending less time with the family: The decline of family ownership in the United Kingdom', in Randall Morck (ed.), *A History of Corporate*

Governance Around the World: Family Business Groups to Professional Managers, Chicago, IL: Chicago University Press, pp. 581–612.

10. Zohar Goshen and Assaf Hamdani (2016), 'Corporate control and idiosyncratic vision', *Yale Law Journal*, 125, 560–617.

11. Meyers (1967), 'The sweet secret world of Forrest Mars'.

12. Cadbury (2010), *Chocolate Wars*, pp. 205–6.

13. Kee-Hong Bae, Jun-Koo Kang, and Jin-Mo Kim (2002), 'Tunneling or value added? Evidence from mergers by Korean business groups', *Journal of Finance*, 57, 2695–740; Jae-Seung Baek, Jun-Koo Kang, and Inmoo Lee (2006), 'Business groups and tunneling: Evidence from private securities offerings by Korean chaebols', *Journal of Finance*, 61, 2415–49; Marianne Bertrand, Paras Mehta, and Sendhil Mullainathan (2002), 'Ferreting out tunneling: An application to Indian business groups', *Quarterly Journal of Economics*, 117, 121–48; Yan-Leung Cheung, Raghavendra Rau, and Aris Stouraitis (2006), 'Tunneling, propping, and expropriation: Evidence from connected party transactions in Hong Kong', *Journal of Financial Economics*, 82, 343–86.

14. A more detailed description of the history of ownership discussed in the next four sections can be found in Julian Franks and Colin Mayer (2018), 'The evolution of ownership and control around the world: The changing face of capitalism', in Benjamin Hermalin and Michael Weisbach (eds), *Handbook of Corporate Governance*, Amsterdam: Elsevier. On this section, see also Franks et al. (2005), 'Spending less time with the family' and (2009), 'Ownership, evolution and regulation'.

15. Frederick Lavington (1921), *The English Capital Market*, London: Methuen, pp. 133 and 124.

16. ibid., p. 208.

17. ibid., p. 208.

18. Julian Franks, Colin Mayer, and Hannes Wagner (2006), 'The origins of the German corporation: Finance, ownership and control', *Review of Finance*, 10(4), 537–85.

19. Lavington (1921), *The English Capital Market*.

20. Julian Franks, Colin Mayer, and Hideaki Miyajima (2014), 'The ownership of Japanese corporations in the 20th century', *Review of Financial Studies*, 27, 2580–625.

21. Marco Becht and Bradford DeLong (2005). 'Why has there been so little block holding in America?' in Randell Morck (ed.), *A History of Corporate Governance around the World: Family Business Groups to Professional Managers*, Chicago, IL: University of Chicago Press; Gardiner Means (1930), 'The diffusion of stock ownership in the U.S.', *Quarterly Journal of Economics*, 44, 561–600.

22. A business group is defined as three publicly listed companies under common control through ownership; see Eugene Kandel, Konstantin Kosenko, Randall Morck, and Yishay Yafeh (2013), 'The great pyramids of America: A revised history of US business groups, corporate ownership, and regulation, 1930–1950', Working Paper, Hebrew University of Jerusalem.

23. Another important piece of legislation was the 1935 Public Utilities Holding Companies Act (PUHCA). The Act required the Securities and Exchange

Commission (SEC) to regulate the activities of utilities and in particular to restrict the use of holding-companies structures.

24. Michael Jensen (1989), 'Eclipse of the public corporation', *Harvard Business Review*, September/October, https://hbr.org/1989/09/eclipse-of-the-public-corporation.

25. Julian Franks, Colin Mayer, and Hannes Wagner (2016), 'Survival of the weakest: Flourishing family firms in Germany', *Journal of Applied Corporate Finance*, 27, 36–44.

26. See, for example, Rafael La Porta, Florencio Lopez-de-Silanes, and Andrei Shleifer (1997), 'Legal determinants of external finance', *Journal of Finance*, 52(3), 1131–50; Rafael La Porta, Florencio Lopez-de-Silanes, and Andrei Shleifer (1998), 'Law and finance', *Journal of Political Economy*, 106(6), 1113–55; Rafael La Porta, Florencio Lopez-de-Silanes, and Andrei Shleifer (1999), 'The quality of government', *Journal of Law, Economics, and Organization*, 15(1), 222–79; and Rafael La Porta, Florencio Lopez-de-Silanes, and Andrei Shleifer (2000), 'Investor protection and corporate governance', *Journal of Financial Economics*, 58(1–2), 3–27.

27. A phrase controversially ascribed to Napoleon Bonaparte.

28. 'Is this the nicest place to live in Britain?' BBC News, 9 July 2003.

29. Rick Groves, Alan Middleton, Alan Murie, and Kevin Broughton (2003), 'Neighbourhoods that work: A study of the Bournville estate, Birmingham', Bristol: The Policy Press for the Joseph Rowntree Foundation.

Chapter 5

1. Leo Strine (2017), 'Corporate power is corporate purpose: Evidence from my hometown', *Oxford Review of Economic Policy*, 33(2), 176–87.

2. ibid.

3. John Coffee (2017), 'Preserving the corporate superego in a time of stress: An essay on ethics and economics', *Oxford Review of Economic Policy*, 33(2), 221–56.

4. Strine (2017), 'Corporate power is corporate purpose'.

5. Financial Reporting Council (2016), *The UK Corporate Governance Code*, London: Financial Reporting Council, p. 3.

6. Alan Greenspan (1998), 'Testimony before the Committee on Banking and Financial Services, US House of Representatives', January; IMF (1997), *World Economic Outlook: Crisis in Asia, Regional and Global Implication—Interim Assessment*, Washington DC; and IMF (1998) 'Michel Camdessus' address to Transparency International: "Good governance has become essential in promoting growth and stability"', *IMF Survey*, p. 27.

7. A. Beltratti and R. Stulz (2012), 'The credit crisis around the globe: Why did some banks perform better?' *Journal of Financial Economics*, 105(1), 1–17; D. Erken, M. Hung, and P. Matos (2012), 'Corporate governance in the 2007–2008 financial crisis: Evidence from financial institutions worldwide', *Journal of Corporate Finance*, 18(2), 389–411; and B. Minton, J. Taillard, and R. Williamson (2014), 'Financial expertise of the board, risk taking, and

performance: Evidence from bank holding companies', *Journal of Financial and Quantitative Analysis*, 49(2), 351–80.

8. George Akerlof and Robert Shiller (2015), Phishing for Phools: The Economics of Manipulation and Deception, Princeton, NJ: Princeton University Press.

9. John Storey and Graeme Salaman (2017), 'Employee ownership and the drive to do business responsibly: A study of the John Lewis Partnership', *Oxford Review of Economic Policy*, 33(2), 339–54.

10. ibid.

11. Kate Roll (2016), 'Maua programme: Bettering lives through the micro-distribution of Wrigley products', Mutuality in Business Working Paper 4, Said Business School, University of Oxford; and Bruno Roche and Jay Jakub (2017), *Completing Capitalism: Heal Business to Heal the World*, Oakland, CA: Berrett-Koehler.

12. Dominic Barton (2017), 'Refocusing capitalism on the long term: Ownership and trust across the investment value chain', *Oxford Review of Economic Policy*, 33(2), 188–200.

13. See Sophie Nachemson-Ekwall and Colin Mayer (2017), 'Nomination committees and corporate governance: Lessons from Sweden and the UK', mimeo.

14. C. Børsting and Steen Thomsen (2017), 'Foundation ownership, reputation, and labour', *Oxford Review of Economic Policy*, 33(2), 317–38.

15. For an excellent survey of the literature see Henri Servaes and Ane Tamayo (2017), 'The role of social capital in corporations', *Oxford Review of Economic Policy*, 33(2), 201–20.

16. See, for example, Robert Eccles, Ioannis Ioannou, and George Serafeim (2014), 'The impact of corporate sustainability on organizational processes and performance', *Management Science*, 60(11), 2835–57.

17. Harrison Hong and Marcin Kacperczyk (2009), 'The price of sin: The effects of social norms on markets', *Journal of Financial Economics*, 93, 15–36.

18. S. El Ghoul, O. Guedhami, C. Kwok, and D. Mishra (2011), 'Does corporate social responsibility affect the cost of capital?' *Journal of Banking and Finance*, 35, 2388–406; Rui Albuquerque, A. Durnev, and Yrjo Koskinen (2015), 'Corporate social responsibility and firm risk: Theory and empirical evidence', European Corporate Governance Institute (ECGI) Finance Working Paper No. 359; C. Flammer (2015), 'Does corporate social responsibility lead to superior financial performance? A regression discontinuity approach', *Management Science*, 61, 2549–68; and K. Lins, H. Servaes, and A. Tamayo (2016), 'Social capital, trust, and firm performance: The value of corporate social responsibility during the financial crisis', European Corporate Governance Institute (ECGI) Finance Working Paper No. 446.

19. Eccles et al. (2014), 'The impact of corporate sustainability'.

20. C. Fornell, S. Mithas, F. Morgeson III, and M. Krishnan (2006), 'Customer satisfaction and stock prices: High returns, low risk', *Journal of Marketing*, 70, 3–14.

21. J. Derwall, N. Guenster, R. Bauer, and K. Koedijk (2005), 'The eco-efficiency premium puzzle', *Financial Analysts Journal*, 61, 51–63.

22. G. Friede, T. Busch, and A. Bassen (2015), 'ESG and financial performance: Aggregated evidence from more than 2000 empirical studies', *Journal of Sustainable Finance and Investment*, 5, 210–33.
23. M. Khan, G. Serafeim, and A. Yoon (2015), 'Corporate sustainability: First evidence on materiality', *The Accounting Review*, 91(6), 1697–724.
24. X. Deng, J. Kang, and B. Low (2013), 'Corporate social responsibility and stakeholder value maximization: Evidence from mergers', *Journal of Financial Economics*, 110, 87–109.
25. Alex Edmans (2011), 'Does the stock market fully value intangibles? Employee satisfaction and equity prices', *Journal of Financial Economics*, 101, 621–40; Alex Edmans (2012), 'The link between job satisfaction and firm value, with implications for corporate social responsibility', *Academy of Management Perspectives*, 26, 1–19.
26. L. Guiso, P. Sapienza, and L. Zingales (2015), 'The value of corporate culture', *Journal of Financial Economics*, 117, 60–76.
27. N. Bloom, R. Sadun, and J. Van Reenen (2012), 'The organization of firms across countries', *Quarterly Journal of Economics*, 127, 1663–705.
28. Matthew Baron, Jonathan Brogaard, Björn Hagströmer, and Andrei Kirilenko (forthcoming), 'Risk and return in high-frequency trading', *Journal of Financial and Quantitative Analysis*.
29. Julian Franks, Colin Mayer, and Hannes Wagner (2016), 'Survival of the weakest: Flourishing family firms in Germany', Journal of Applied Corporate Finance, 27, 36–44.

Chapter 6

1. The issues in this chapter are discussed further in Colin Mayer (2013), 'Unnatural capital accounting', Natural Capital Committee Discussion Paper; Colin Mayer (2016), 'Introduction to the Natural Capital Committee's corporate natural capital accounting project', in ICAEW, *Rethinking Capitals: Series 2—Natural Capital*, London: ICAEW; and Richard Barker and Colin Mayer (2017), 'How should a "sustainable corporation" account for natural capital?' Working Paper, Said Business School, University of Oxford.
2. Inclusive Wealth Report (2012), 'Measuring progress towards sustainability', Cambridge: Cambridge University Press.
3. Office for National Statistics (2014), 'UK natural capital: Initial and partial monetary estimates'.

Chapter 7

1. This chapter draws extensively on Colin Mayer (2015), 'Conceiving corporate commitment', in Jennifer Hill and Randall Thomas (eds), *The Research Handbook on Shareholder Power*, Cheltenham: Edward Elgar, pp. 211–30.
2. There are extensive discussions of trust in Francis Fukuyama (1995), *Trust: The Social Virtues and the Creation of Prosperity*, New York: Free Press; Russell

Hardin (2006), *Trust*, Cambridge: Polity Press. Martin Hollis (1998), *Trust within Reason*, Cambridge: Cambridge University Press; and Piotr Sztompka (1999), *Trust: A Sociological Theory*, Cambridge: Cambridge University Press. Trust in economics is discussed in the context of a number of related subjects, such as institutional economics (George Akerlof (1970), 'The market for "lemons": Qualitative uncertainty and the market mechanism', *Quarterly Journal of Economics*, 84, 488–500, and Kenneth Arrow (1974), *The Limits of Organization*, New York: W. W. Norton), game theory (Partha Dasgupta (1988), 'Trust as a commodity', in Diego Gambetta (ed.), *Trust: Making and Breaking Cooperative Relations*, Oxford: Basil Blackwell, pp. 49–72), and transaction costs (Oliver Williamson (2010), 'Transaction cost economics: The natural progression', *American Economic Review*, 100, 673–90).

3. See Stewart Macaulay (1963), 'Non-contractual relations in business: A preliminary study', *American Sociological Review*, 28, 55–67, for an early discussion of the importance of non-legally binding commitments. See also Isabelle Brocas, Juan Carrillo, and Mathias Dewatripont (2004), 'Commitment devices under self-control problems: An overview', in Isabelle Brocas and Juan Carrillo (eds), *The Psychology of Economic Decisions, Vol. 2: Reasons and Choices*, Oxford: Oxford University Press, pp. 49–66.

4. John Mill (1859), *On Liberty*, London: Longman, Roberts and Green.

5. Sandy Grossman and Oliver Hart (1986), 'The costs and benefits of ownership: A theory of vertical and lateral integration', *Journal of Political Economy*, 94, 691–719, and Oliver Hart (1995), *Firms, Contracts, and Financial Structure*, Oxford: Oxford University Press.

6. See, for example, Roger Crisp and Michael Slote (1997), *Virtue Ethics*, Oxford: Oxford University Press and Michael Slote (2000), 'Virtue ethics', in H. LaFollette (ed.), *The Blackwell Guide to Ethical Theory*, Oxford: Blackwell, pp. 325–47.

7. Margaret Blair and Lynn Stout (2001), 'Trust, trustworthiness, and the behavioural foundations of corporate law', *University of Pennsylvania Law Review*, 149, 1735–51, argue for internalized trust based on expectations of intrinsic trustworthiness. Oliver Williamson (1993), 'Calculativeness, trust, and economic organization', *Journal of Law and Economics*, 36, 454–86, suggests that trust relates to non-calculative personal relations.

8. See Edwin Hunt and James Murray (1999), *A History of Business in Medieval Europe: 1200–1500*, Cambridge: Cambridge University Press; Robert Lopez (1971), *The Commercial Revolution of the Middle Ages, 950–1350*, Englewood Cliffs, NJ: Prentice Hall; and William Scott (1912), The Constitution and Finance of English, Scottish and Irish Joint-Stock Companies to 1720, Vol. 1: The General Development of the Join-Stock System to 1720, Cambridge: Cambridge University Press.

9. Armen Alchian and Harold Demsetz (1972), 'Production, information costs, and economic organization', *American Economic Review*, 62, 777–95, and Michael Jensen and William Meckling (1976), 'Theory of the firm:

Managerial behavior, agency costs, and ownership structure', *Journal of Financial Economics*, 3, 305–60.

10. For a discussion of this see Eric Orts (2013), *Business Persons: A Legal Theory of the Firm*, Oxford: Oxford University Press.

11. Paul Davies and Sarah Worthington (2012), *Principles of Modern Company Law*, 9th edition, London: Sweet and Maxwell.

12. Felicia Resor (2012), 'Benefit corporation legislation', *Wyoming Law Review*, 12, 91–113, and Frederick Alexander (2018), *Benefit Corporation Law and Governance: Pursuing Profit with Purpose*, forthcoming.

13. Robert Hamilton (1995), 'Registered limited liability partnerships: Present at birth (nearly)', *Colorado Law Review*, 66, 1065–9.

14. See Big Innovation Centre (2017), 'Purposeful company: Policy report', London: Big Innovation Centre, Section 4.1, for further details about these alternative models.

15. Gregory Alexander (2013), 'Ownership and obligations: The human flourishing theory of property', *Hong Kong Law Journal*, 43, 451.

16. See John Coffee (1989), 'The mandatory/enabling balance in corporate law: An essay on the judicial role', *Columbia Law Review*, 89, 1618–91, and Jeffrey Gordon (1989), 'The mandatory structure of corporate law', *Columbia Law Review*, 89, 1549.

17. See Edward Rock and Michael Wachter (2001), 'Islands of conscious power: Law, norms, and the self-governing corporation', *University of Pennsylvania Law Review*, 148, 1622, for arguments for non-legally binding governance arrangements. For a discussion of commitment in investment banking in the context of a hierarchy that runs down from trust to fiduciary law and regulation, see Alan Morrison and William Wilhelm (2015), 'Trust, reputation, and law: The evolution of commitment in investment banking', *Journal of Legal Analysis*, 7, 363–420.

18. The relationship between trust and corporation has an extensive pedigree, not least Frederic Maitland (1904), 'Trust and corporation', reprinted in Frederic Maitland (1911), *Collected Papers*, Cambridge: Cambridge University Press and Frederic Maitland (1905), 'Moral personality and legal personality', *Journal of the Society of Comparative Legislation*, 6, 192–200.

19. 'Ownership conferred by the law of trusts does not seem to belong either to persons or to things . . . Yet this is precisely what allows non-persons such as "unincorporate bodies" to be the beneficiaries of trusteeship. Ownership does not belong to persons because trusteeship allows ownership in "strict law" to rest with one set of persons (the trustees) and ownership in "equity" to rest with another group entirely (the beneficiaries); it does not belong to things because trusteeship allows the things owned to vary and to be variously invested without the rights of ownership having to alter (hence the trust "fund"). Instead, the law of trust rests on the idea of "good conscience". If men can be trusted to act as owners in law for those who have an equitable claim on the thing owned, and if those with whom they deal can be trusted to see the matter in the same light, then it is possible to provide an enduring

legal identity for all manner of people and things that do not otherwise fit into the typology of *ius in personam* and *ius in rem*' (David Runciman and Magnus Ryan (2003), *State, Trust and Corporation*, Cambridge: Cambridge University Press, p. xx).

20. See Henry Hansmann and Steen Thomsen (2013), 'Managerial distance and virtual ownership: The governance of industrial foundations', ECGI Finance Working Paper No. 372.

21. See Colin Mayer (2013), *Firm Commitment: Why the Corporation Is Failing Us and How to Restore Trust in It*, Oxford: Oxford University Press, Chapter 7.

Chapter 8

1. In N. Halmi, P. Magnuson, and R. Modiano (eds), *Coleridge's Poetry and Prose*, New York: W. W. Norton, 2004, pp. 371–2.

2. This chapter is based on Colin Mayer (2017), 'Finance, wealth, technological innovation and regulation', in Kirk Hamilton and Cameron Hepburn (eds), *National Wealth: What Is Missing, Why It Matters*, Oxford: Oxford University Press, pp. 379–98. Further discussion of some of the issues considered in this chapter can be found in John Armour, Dan Awrey, Paul Davies, Luca Enriques, Jeff Gordon, Colin Mayer, and Jennifer Payne (2016), *Principles of Financial Regulation*, Oxford: Oxford University Press.

3. See, for example, the surveys by Ross Levine (1997), 'Financial development and economic growth: View and agenda', *Journal of Economic Literature*, 35(2), 688–726, and Ross Levine (2005), 'Finance and growth: Theory and evidence', in Philippe Aghion and Steven Durlauf (eds), *Handbook of Economic Growth*, Amsterdam: Elsevier, Chapter 12.

4. Raghuram G. Rajan and Luigi Zingales (1998), 'Financial dependence and growth', *American Economic Review*, 88(3), 559–86.

5. See Colin Mayer (2015), 'Economic development, financial systems, and the law', in Eilis Ferran, Naomi Moloney, and Jennifer Payne (eds), *The Oxford Handbook of Financial Regulation*, Oxford: Oxford University Press, pp. 41–67.

6. Franklin Edwards and Frederic Mishkin (1995), 'The decline of traditional banking: Implications for financial stability and regulatory policy', *Federal Reserve Board of New York Economic Policy Review*, July, 27–45.

7. Thomas Philippon (2015), 'Has the US finance industry become less efficient? On the theory and measurement of financial intermediation', *American Economic Review*, 105, 1408–38.

8. For a description of how deregulation around the time of Big Bang in the United Kingdom was predicted in the middle of the 1980s to set in train both the subsequent explosion in financial activity and instability resulting in the 2008 financial crisis, see Colin Mayer (1986), 'Financial innovation: Curse or blessing?' *Oxford Review of Economic Policy*, 2, 1–19, and Colin Mayer (2015), 'Big Bang: New beginning or beginning of the end?' *Oxford Review of Economic Policy*, 31,186–98.

9. This section is based on Ignacio Mas and Colin Mayer (2011), 'Savings as forward payments: Innovations on mobile money platforms', SSRN Working Paper No.1825122; Michael Klein and Colin Mayer 'Mobile money and financial inclusion: The regulatory lessons', World Bank Working Paper WS 5664; and Mayer (2015), 'Big Bang: New beginning or beginning of the end?' For a more detailed discussion of these issues, see Jonathan Greenacre (2016), 'The regulation of mobile money', DPhil Thesis, University of Oxford.

10. For a more extensive discussion of the issues in this section see Luis Correia da Silva, Julian Franks, and Colin Mayer (2003), *Asset Management and Investor Protection: An International Analysis*, Oxford: Oxford University Press.

Part 5

1. https://www.unilever.com/about/who-we-are/purpose-and-principles/.
2. https://www.unilever.com/Images/unilever_nv_aoa_2012_english_tcm244-417140_en.pdf.

Chapter 9

1. This section draws on the introduction to Colin Mayer, Stefano Micossi, Marco Onada, Marco Pagano, and Andrea Polo (2018), *Finance and Investment: The European Case*, Oxford: Oxford University Press.
2. Brunella Bruno, Alexandra D'Onofrio, and Immacolata Marino, 'Financial structure and corporate investment in Europe: Evidence from the crisis years', in Mayer et al. (2018), *Finance and Investment*, pp. 15–56, and Francesca Barbiero et al., 'Misallocation of investment in Europe: The role of debt overhang and credit market distress', in Mayer et al. (2018), *Finance and Investment*, pp. 57–64.
3. María Soledad Martinez Pería and Sergio Schmukler (2018), 'Understanding the use of long-term finance in developing countries', in Mayer et al. (2018), *Finance and Investment*, pp. 65–84.
4. These imbalances have recently been substantial, as the corporate sector has run small financial deficits in several countries while accumulating considerable surpluses in Germany and the United Kingdom.
5. Fabrizio Coricelli and Marco Frigerio (2018), 'Liquidity squeeze on SMEs during the Great Recession in Europe: The role of trade credit', in Mayer et al. (2018), *Finance and Investment*, pp. 85–94.
6. See N. Kroner (2009), *A Blueprint for Better Banking: Svenska Handelsbanken and a Proven Model for More Stable and Profitable Banking*, Petersfield: Harriman House.
7. See Colin Mayer (2015), 'The risk of risk committees', *SUERF Studies*, 1, 63–7.
8. A. Beltratti and R. Stulz (2012), 'The credit crisis around the globe: Why did some banks perform better?' Journal of Financial Economics, 105(1), 1–17; D. Erken, M. Hung, and P. Matos (2012), 'Corporate governance in the 2007–2008 financial crisis: Evidence from financial institutions worldwide', Journal of Corporate Finance, 18(2), 389–411; and B. Minton, J. Taillard, and

R. Williamson (2014), 'Financial expertise of the board, risk taking, and performance: Evidence from bank holding companies', Journal of Financial and Quantitative Analysis, 49(2), 351–80.

9. A. Ellul and V. Yerramilli (2013), 'Stronger risk controls, lower risk: Evidence from U.S. bank holding companies', *Journal of Finance*, 68(5), 1757–803.

10. A. Morrison and L. White (2013), 'Reputational contagion and optimal regulatory forbearance', *Journal of Financial Economics*, 110(3), 642–58.

11. Gilles Duruflé, Thomas Hellmann, and Karen Wilson (2018), 'From start-up to scale-up: Examining public policies for the financing of high-growth ventures', in Mayer et al. (2018), *Finance and Investment*, pp. 179–220.

12. Alvin Warren (1974), 'The corporate interest deduction: A policy evaluation', *Yale Law Journal*, 83, 1585–619.

13. Vasso Ioannidou, José Liberti, Thomas Mosk, and Jason Sturgess (2018), 'Intended and unintended consequences of government credit guarantee programmes', in Mayer et al. (2018), *Finance and Investment*, pp. 317–26.

14. Claire Célérier, Thomas Kick, and Steven Ongena (2018), 'Changes in the cost of bank equity and the supply of bank credit', in Mayer et al. (2018), *Finance and Investment*, pp. 169–78.

15. The United States has recently made a move in this direction through the US Tax Cuts and Jobs Act (2017), which limits the deductibility of net interest payments in US corporate income tax to 30% of earnings before interest, taxes, depreciation, and amortization for four years and 30% before interest and taxes thereafter.

16. Dionysia Katelouzou and Mathias Siems (2015), 'Disappearing paradigms in shareholder protection: Leximetric evidence for 30 Countries, 1990–2013', *Journal of Corporate Law Studies*, 15, 127–34.

17. Ross Levine (2004), 'Finance and growth: Theory and evidence', National Bureau of Economic Research, Working Paper No. 10766; Asli Demirguc-Kunt and Vojislav Maksimovic (2002), 'Funding growth in bank-based and market-based financial systems: Evidence from firm-level data', *Journal of Financial Economics*, 65, 337–41; James Brown, Gustav Martinsson, and Bruce Petersen (2013), 'Law, stock markets, and innovation', *Journal of Finance*, 68, 1517–31.

18. Colin Mayer (1988), 'New issues in corporate finance', *European Economic Review*, 32, 1167–83.

19. The theorem establishes the conditions under which the valuation of firms is invariant to their financial structure (for example, leverage and dividend policy).

Chapter 10

1. This chapter draws on Dieter Helm and Colin Mayer (2016), 'Infrastructure: Why it is under provided and badly managed', *Oxford Review of Economic Policy*, 32(3), 343–59, and on work with Paul Collier on infrastructure investment in developing countries.

2. Atif Ansar, Bent Flyvbjerg, Alexannder Budzier, and Daniel Lunn (2016), 'Does infrastructure investment lead to economic growth or economic fragility? Evidence from China', *Oxford Review of Economic Policy*, 32(3), 360–90.

Prospects

1. Samuel Huntington (1996), *The Clash of Civilizations and the Remaking of World Order*, New York: Simon and Schuster.
2. Larry Siedentop (2014), *Inventing the Individual: The Origins of Western Liberalism*, p. 243.

Index

Index